MW00453094

Axure RP 6 Prototyping Essentials

Creating highly compelling, interactive prototypes with Axure that will impress and excite decision makers

Ezra Schwartz

BIRMINGHAM - MUMBAI

Axure RP 6 Prototyping Essentials

Copyright © 2012 Packt Publishing

All rights reserved. No part of this book may be reproduced, stored in a retrieval system, or transmitted in any form or by any means, without the prior written permission of the publisher, except in the case of brief quotations embedded in critical articles or reviews.

Every effort has been made in the preparation of this book to ensure the accuracy of the information presented. However, the information contained in this book is sold without warranty, either express or implied. Neither the author, nor Packt Publishing, and its dealers and distributors will be held liable for any damages caused or alleged to be caused directly or indirectly by this book.

Packt Publishing has endeavored to provide trademark information about all of the companies and products mentioned in this book by the appropriate use of capitals. However, Packt Publishing cannot guarantee the accuracy of this information.

First published: January 2012

Production Reference: 1170112

Published by Packt Publishing Ltd.
Livery Place
35 Livery Street
Birmingham B3 2PB, UK.

ISBN 978-1-84969-164-2

www.packtpub.com

Cover Image by AnnaMarie White (anna-mariewhite@sbcglobal.net)

Credits

Author
Ezra Schwartz

Reviewers
Michael Blakely

Jeff Harrison

Mark Johnston

Elizabeth Srail

Acquisition Editor
Wilson D'souza

Lead Technical Editor
Susmita Panda

Technical Editor
Azharuddin Sheikh

Copy Editors
Neha Shetty

Brandt D'Mello

Project Coordinator
Jovita Pinto

Proofreader
Linda Morris

Indexers
Hemangini Bari

Monica Ajmera Mehta

Graphics
Conidon Miranda

Production Coordinator
Alwin Roy

Cover Work
Alwin Roy

Foreword

Axure is a powerful tool to transform abstract requirements into a working detailed visualization to support implementation and reduce project risks. We have experienced these benefits with many of our clients, allowing us to successfully lead enterprise design efforts with the world's largest corporations. The lessons Ezra shares with you in this book—planning what your specification will look like, and structuring masters to substantially reduce redundancy and rework, to name a few— will help you unlock Axure's full potential and will save you significant amounts of work later in your project.

Here is a brief story about how Axure and the techniques in this book were used successfully on a recent enterprise project: We were engaged with a large Silicon Valley client to lead the User Experience effort for an enterprise Oracle implementation billed to "transform" the company's Quote to Cash internal systems. The big IT consulting players were on board with teams of business analysts, Oracle experts, and project managers. We began our efforts by heading out to the clients to conduct field research with the company's business partners and internal users. We followed this with a "Baseline" usability test of the existing system and concluded that an entirely new user interface was needed to truly transform the business. While conducting our research, the initial business requirements were starting to unfold, and we were sketching out user stories and task flows to understand the current business processes and areas for optimization. We then used Axure to visualize what the new system could look like.

Things were going along smoothly when an e-mail came in at 5 pm on Friday, requesting my presence at a brief executive meeting that same day. The execs were very happy with all the research we had accomplished and excited about seeing the future. In fact, we were informed that the executive sponsor would be having an annual meeting with the top 170 company leaders at an offsite resort in Carmel in 2 weeks and wanted to present a vision of what the transformation would look like. This was great—true executive sponsorship—however it did not match with our project plan. The requirements were just being defined and we had barely cracked open Axure to begin wireframes. The executives asked me to show what we had designed so far. I summarily showed them a left sidebar menu and a blank screen.

They looked at me perplexed and said, "We don't see anything." "I know," I replied. "We have been completing our user research and are just finishing early sketches of potential designs. The vision you want to see was scheduled for six weeks from now."

That obviously was not going to meet the needs of our executive sponsor, so we quickly began creating a vision of the future in Axure. Loren Baxter (a contributor to this book) was evolving the prototype as fast as we could think of new ideas. He truly played Axure like a pianist at Carnegie Hall. Mastery of the tool (in this case, Axure) was critical to our ability to start from an empty slate and define a vision in days versus weeks or months. We met daily with execs and showed our builds as they evolved. This in turn accelerated the refinement of the requirements since the visualization clearly communicated the requirements as they were being discussed. The executive presentation was a resounding success and the entire company leadership became aligned with the new vision we created.

Moving from vision to a detailed set of wireframes and specifications was our next challenge. Ezra was brought on board to lead this effort and he applied the principles and strategies presented in this book. Our team of UX designers worked tirelessly during the next several months visualizing over 90 Business Requirements Documents, totaling over 1.5 million words. Many of the features in Axure 6 are a direct result of feedback we provided to the Axure team as we built our wireframes and detailed specifications. We used the naming strategies outlined in this book to keep us organized and to communicate to the larger project team as we ensured that our wireframes and specifications were in sync with the business requirements.

Once our UX wireframes and specifications were complete, we handed off our UX deliverables to the developers for implementation. By this time, the project team had grown to nearly 200 people working globally towards a very aggressive implementation date. All the work we had put into using Axure for detailed annotated wireframes, interaction models, and detailed specifications was leveraged to keep the project on track despite the usual changes in scope, IT implementation challenges, and changes in requirements.

The QA team used our wireframes to build test cases long before the development code was available. We continuously updated wireframes and specifications as changes to the requirements occurred and the naming conventions provided critical traceability between our wireframes and the business requirements. At the same time, we continuously used Axure prototypes to perform usability tests on areas of known concern to validate our design decisions as the project evolved.

Whether your project is a small effort for your department or a larger enterprise effort like the one I have described, the techniques and strategies in this book will help you successfully bridge the gap between abstract business requirements and what ultimately gets implemented by your development team. Axure can provide significant value to your organization while dramatically reducing project risks. I suggest you read this book in layers. First, master the great new techniques available in Axure 6 for creating rich visualizations. Then, apply the naming and architecture strategies and adapt them to your project needs.

Good luck with your prototypes!

James Hobart
President, Classic System Solutions, Inc.

About the Author

Ezra Schwartz is an Information and User Experience Architect, who specializes in logistics of complex user interface frameworks. He focuses on device and locale agnostic global enterprise applications, team collaboration strategies, and UX requirements traceability and specification documentation for phased, multi-release projects.

Ezra helps clients to integrate successfully rapid UX prototyping, validation, and testing with their development culture. He assists clients with adoption of user-centered-design methodologies, compliance, and best practices. He has lead mission-critical user experience projects in the finance, aviation, healthcare, mobile, publishing, media research, manufacturing, academic research, and software development industries. Ezra also provides his services pro-bono to select not-for-profit organizations.

Ezra is the founder and organizer of **AxureWorld.org**, a free community-driven international conference, dedicated to rapid UX prototyping. He talks regularly about user experience topics at conferences and on his blog www.artandtech.com.

Acknowledgement

Many colleagues and friends have contributed directly, or indirectly, to the writing of this book. I would like to extend special thanks to Oren Beit-Arie, Udi Arad, Carl Grant, Dino Eliopulos, Frank Torbey, Robert Albrecht-Mallinger, Dennis Connolly, Jirka Kende, Helena Porczak, Loren Baxter, Jerry Smith, Tim Robb, Marco Mastrapasqua, Vince Torres, Jim Hobart, and Victor Hsu, for their support and encouragement over the years.

I am tremendously grateful to my colleagues Elizabeth Srail, Michael Blakely, Jeff Harrison, and Mark Johnston for their work on my drafts and their detailed, honest, knowledgeable, thoughtful, and generous comments.

My sincere gratitude to the editors and staff at Packt Publishing, Susmita Panda, Jovita Pinto, Azharuddin Sheikh, and Wilson D'souza for their guidance, patience, and continuous encouragement throughout this project.

To my family and friends, Julia, Hillel and Eitan Gauchman, Eda and Hedva Schwartz, Ruth and Doron Blatt, Christine and Scott Marriott, Ayelet and Alon Fishbach, Galila Spharim and Yigal Bronner, thanks for cheerleading, and a special thanks to Lisa Comforty for her counsel, and to Barbara Drapchow whose clarinet lessons provided much-needed creative breaks.

Finally, a big hug to Orit, Ben, and Yoav, who waited patiently for me to resurface and resume normal family life.

About the Reviewers

Michael Blakely is a leading expert in User Experience Architecture, specializing in excellent design solutions. He works as a freelance contractor, creating everything from large-scale website redesigns to enterprise-level web applications. During his 15 years of experience in the industry, he has worked with many noteworthy clients, some of which are Disney, Cisco Systems, Bloomberg, Ernst & Young, and Walgreens. His current work involves designing mobile apps using Axure RP to communicate solutions and the user experience to clients and stakeholders.

Educated at Utah State University, Michael Blakely holds an MSc in Instructional Technology. Mike is an Axure Master and Trainer. A devoted power-user, he is active in the Axure community, contributing as a Beta-Tester and a Technical Reviewer for Axure RP 6 Prototyping Essentials.

He maintains his portfolio at www.behance.net/michaelblakely. You can know more about him at www.blakelyinteractive.net. He is also available on Linkedin at http://www.linkedin.com/pub/michael-blakely/1/67b/5a0.

Jeff Harrison is a senior User Experience Consultant at Evantage Consulting in Minneapolis, where he specializes in interaction design, information architecture, and data visualization. In addition to his client work, Jeff is an Axure trainer and frequent contributor to the Axure forums, where he is unhealthily motivated by the impossible.

Jeff lives in the Twin Cities with his wife, Jenna, and two kids, Evelyn and Eli.

Mark Johnston has lived and breathed design and its application to software and the Internet for over a decade and a half. He has been on an evolutionary journey through the print and Web to his current passion of user experience design. During this time, he has pursued the development of many skills and techniques, including visual design, HTML, CSS, Javascript, accessibility, interaction design, and information architecture and usability.

He has applied the knowledge he has gained while learning his craft to websites ranging from the small and static through to large dynamic media rich sites, as well as B2B solutions and line of business applications.

He enjoys getting his hands dirty, forging better experiences for the people that are sometimes forgotten in large companies; people who deal direct with the customers, to make their life a little easier and in turn help provide better support to its customers. He aims to create solutions that work well for the customers without sacrificing the needs of the company.

Mark settled at Austar, Australia's leading regional subscription TV provider and ASX200 company, a little over 7 years ago, where he has been honing his skills as a practitioner in the user experience field, while at the same time helping to further develop programs within Austar to drive user centered thinking, design, and processes.

Mark believes that in every worker's toolbox, there are a handful of great tools to help in order to get the job done. For Mark, Axure is a very important tool to build rich prototypes to gain direct feedback.

I want to thank Ezra for the opportunity to work with him and Packt on this book. I also want to thank Victor and the team at Axure for being one of the most supportive and responsive software companies I have dealt with, putting up with all my e-mails. Last but not least, I would like to thank my great team and the people at Austar that I work with, who have allowed us to effect real change for our customers through our work.

Elizabeth Srail has been interested in learning about people her entire life. Drawn to this field because the idea of helping business executives understand that they should learn how the company's customers behave and think before making strategic decisions was reason enough.

Elizabeth's philosophy of a good user experience is a thoughtful, scalable architecture, an amazing visual design that does not become quickly outdated, and a smart and flexible technical architecture. Elizabeth was the UX designer on a website that incorporated each of these elements, earning a Webby Honorable mention in the Parenting/Family category.

Since 1999, Elizabeth has worked at large financial institutions, marketing/branding agencies, and for UX specific services companies. Therefore, she has done UX work in many industries: financial, retail, education, spirits, and health and wellness. This diverse experience has helped aide her success in the UX field. She has been using Axure continuously for three years, and is convinced; she is a proficient user of Axure, because Mr. Schwartz taught her many tricks that are too, in the book.

Elizabeth graduated Summa Cum Laude from Ohio University with a BA in Finance and a BA in Management Information Systems. She also accidentally earned a minor in Spanish because she enjoyed speaking the language so much.

On a personal note, Elizabeth is a devoted yoga student of the Ashtanga yoga system and believes that an expansive body leads to an expansive mind.

www.PacktPub.com

Support files, eBooks, discount offers and more

You might want to visit www.PacktPub.com for support files and downloads related to your book.

Did you know that Packt offers eBook versions of every book published, with PDF and ePub files available? You can upgrade to the eBook version at www.PacktPub.com and as a print book customer, you are entitled to a discount on the eBook copy. Get in touch with us at service@packtpub.com for more details.

At www.PacktPub.com, you can also read a collection of free technical articles, sign up for a range of free newsletters and receive exclusive discounts and offers on Packt books and eBooks.

http://PacktLib.PacktPub.com

Do you need instant solutions to your IT questions? PacktLib is Packt's online digital book library. Here, you can access, read and search across Packt's entire library of books.

Why Subscribe?

- Fully searchable across every book published by Packt
- Copy and paste, print and bookmark content
- On demand and accessible via web browser

Free Access for Packt account holders

If you have an account with Packt at www.PacktPub.com, you can use this to access PacktLib today and view nine entirely free books. Simply use your login credentials for immediate access.

Instant Updates on New Packt Books

Get notified! Find out when new books are published by following @PacktEnterprise on Twitter, or the *Packt Enterprise* Facebook page.

To my parents, Eda and Zeev Schwartz

Table of Contents

Preface

User experience (UX) has gone mainstream. It is finally recognized by business and software development stakeholders as a critical pillar of social acceptance and commercial success. The timing coincides with an explosion in expressive means to create new and highly compelling user interfaces that operate on a wide range of powerful devices, such as smartphones and tablets. UX encompasses a wide range of disciplines including cognitive psychology, user research, and visual design, and it all comes together in the prototype—an interactive simulation that excites decision makers and validates the design approach before it is coded.

Boxes and arrows just don't cut it anymore. Axure, the leading UX tool for wireframing, rapid prototyping, and specifications has quickly become the UX tool of choice for thousands of practitioners worldwide. The UX community is fortunate to have a growing number of dedicated simulation tools, but currently few are getting close to striking Axure's balance of maturity, features, and cost.

This book offers a holistic overview of Axure and its use throughout the interface development life cycle. The intent is to help you construct wireframes and prototypes with your 'headlights on', taking into consideration the inherent iterative nature of the UX process. A sample project is weaved into the chapters. It provides an opportunity to discuss, in context and in sequence, practical topics such as addressing business and technical requirements, handling use cases and flow diagrams, low and high-fidelity wireframe construction, naming conventions, creating interactions, writing annotations, generating detailed UX specifications, and requirements traceability.

You may not be in a position to change how projects are scheduled, budgeted, and managed, but hopefully, by the time you finish this book you will feel confident about adding Axure to your set of trusted UX tools. Based on my personal experience, I can promise you that it will enhance your ability to deliver top-quality deliverables and tackle the demands for rapid iterative UX projects of any complexity and size, for any platform and device.

What this book covers

Chapter 1, Prototyping Fundamentals, offers a checklist of considerations for using Axure in various project types, and introduces the perspectives of various stakeholders who collaborate with UX in a typical project.

Chapter 2, Axure Basics – the User Interface, introduces Axure basics: file formats, the workspace, wireframe pane, sitemap pane, masters pane, widgets pane, widget properties pane, page properties pane, dynamic panel manager, toolbar and menu bar.

Chapter 3, Prototype Construction Basics, covers various aspects of requirements and use cases, flow diagrams, navigation, masters, dynamic panels, and prototyping for mobile apps.

Chapter 4, Interactivity 101, details various Axure interactions, events, cases, actions, and naming conventions.

Chapter 5, Advanced Interactions, covers some advanced topics such as raised events, variables, conditions, drag and drop, and animation.

Chapter 6, Widget Libraries, introduces masters and widget libraries, built-in libraries, and community libraries. Using the information given in this chapter, you can create your own widget libraries, manage libraries, manage visual design patterns, and device specific libraries.

Chapter 7, Managing Prototype Change, helps manage widget style editor, style painter, and iteration management. It also covers topics such as prototyping for multiple delivery formats and devices, strategic annotation, manage phased and multi-release projects.

Chapter 8, Functional Specifications, provides information that lets us manage elements such as page notes and annotation fields, annotation strategy, requirement management and configuring specifications generators.

Chapter 9, Collaboration, provides useful information about shared repository, naming conventions for teams, responsibilities, workflow, training, troubleshooting.

What you need for this book

In order to follow the demo project in this book, and to experiment on your own, you will need the following:

- Axure 6 for Windows or Mac, you can download a free, 30-day evaluation copy from `http://www.axure.com/`, and the company is very generous in extending the trial period. To get the most current list of system requirements to run Axure on either Windows or Mac visit the Axure's website.

- For specifications, you need Word 2000 and a newer version for Windows and Word 2004 and newer for Mac.

- Firefox, in both platforms is the recommended browser.

Who this book is for

This book is intended for:

- UX practitioners, business analysts, product managers, and others involved in UX projects

- Consultants or in-house staff working for agencies and corporations

- Individual practitioners or UX team members

- UX practitioners who seek to deliver higher value in a fraction of the time involved in wireframing and annotating with traditional, drawing tools-based techniques

- UX practitioners who want to dramatically improve their productivity and skills with expertise in delivering rich interactive prototypes and extensive specifications instead of static documents

The book assumes either no or a little familiarity with Axure. Perhaps, you are evaluating the tool for an upcoming project or are required to quickly get up to speed on a project you just joined.

The book assumes some familiarity with the principals of the User-Centered Design methodology.

Conventions

In this book, you will find a number of styles of text that distinguish between different kinds of information. Here are some examples of these styles, and an explanation of their meaning.

Code words in text are shown as follows: "One or more actions are organized in a unit named **case** and a case is associated with a specific event, such as OnClick".

New terms and **important words** are shown in bold. Words that you see on the screen, in menus or dialog boxes for example, appear in the text like this: "The **Subscribe** and **Log In** buttons (A) in the dynamic panel **DP Subscribe Actions Bar** (B) fit the width of the dynamic panel".

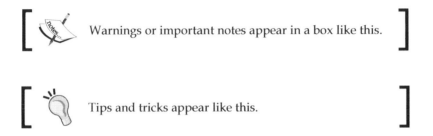

Warnings or important notes appear in a box like this.

Tips and tricks appear like this.

Reader feedback

Feedback from our readers is always welcome. Let us know what you think about this book—what you liked or may have disliked. Reader feedback is important for us to develop titles that you really get the most out of.

To send us general feedback, simply send an e-mail to feedback@packtpub.com, and mention the book title through the subject of your message.

If there is a topic that you have expertise in and you are interested in either writing or contributing to a book, see our author guide on www.packtpub.com/authors.

Customer support

Now that you are the proud owner of a Packt book, we have a number of things to help you to get the most from your purchase.

Downloading the example code

You can download the example code files for all Packt books you have purchased from your account at http://www.packtpub.com. If you purchased this book elsewhere, you can visit http://www.packtpub.com/support and register to have the files e-mailed directly to you.

Errata

Although we have taken every care to ensure the accuracy of our content, mistakes do happen. If you find a mistake in one of our books—maybe a mistake in the text or the code—we would be grateful if you would report this to us. By doing so, you can save other readers from frustration and help us improve subsequent versions of this book. If you find any errata, please report them by visiting http://www.packtpub.com/support, selecting your book, clicking on the **errata submission form** link, and entering the details of your errata. Once your errata are verified, your submission will be accepted and the errata will be uploaded to our website, or added to any list of existing errata, under the Errata section of that title.

Piracy

Piracy of copyright material on the Internet is an ongoing problem across all media. At Packt, we take the protection of our copyright and licenses very seriously. If you come across any illegal copies of our works, in any form, on the Internet, please provide us with the location address or website name immediately so that we can pursue a remedy.

Please contact us at copyright@packtpub.com with a link to the suspected pirated material.

We appreciate your help in protecting our authors, and our ability to bring you valuable content.

Questions

You can contact us at questions@packtpub.com if you are having a problem with any aspect of the book, and we will do our best to address it.

1
Prototyping Fundamentals

"We shape our tools, and thereafter our tools shape us." — Marshal McLuhan

I find Marshal McLuhan's insight to be especially intriguing in the context of tools that help us conceptualize and express user experience. In fact, my motivation to write this book has been shaped by my personal experience with Axure, since I started using it back in 2007.

What struck me then, and continues to excite me today, was the freedom to design, test, iterate, and present fully-clickable interactive prototypes. I did not need a developer. I did not need to spend months to learn a programming or authoring language. It was easy, fast, and fun. As someone who does user experience for a living, Axure afforded me my own user experience.

Within a few hours, I had my first prototype running, and since that day, I never looked back, and have since rarely used Visio, my previous wireframing tool. I also realized that, in addition to being able to create interactive prototypes, Axure helped me deal with a major chore—creating and updating the user interface functional specifications document.

If you ever created a specifications document the traditional way by using Visio, Word, and a screen capture utility, you know the drill—a tedious process that involves adding footnote tags to Visio wireframes, taking screenshots of these wireframes, saving them, importing them to Word, and finally, writing the relevant annotations. If you update the wireframe, you have to retake the screen capture, save, replace its version in Word, and update the annotations. Multiply this process by the number of wireframes in your project, and the magnitude of the effort becomes clear and daunting.

As the UX design is inherently an iterative process, the specifications update process is a real drain of time, money, and energy, which is bad for everyone involved in the project. With Axure's integrated specifications, I found an innovative approach that reduces, greatly, the manual process. Axure numbers the annotations on the wireframes, takes the screenshots, and organizes the entire content in a customizable layout. While configuring the specifications document takes some experimentation, the effort pales in comparison to the manual process. Moreover, once you are happy with the way the specifications generator works, you no longer need to deal with it.

Axure's support for team collaboration was an important enhancement that helped cement its adaptation among UX professionals, because it underscored the dramatic shift in the perception of UX among business stakeholders, as critical to the success of software projects. As any sizable project requires multiple UX resources, collaboration has become a prerequisite that Axure addresses with its **Shared Projects** feature.

As I started to use Axure, I occasionally stumbled on technical issues or had questions I could not figure out. Responses were prompt and detailed, files I sent for checkups were reviewed and issues explained, and occasionally, immediate follow-up of software updates that fixed bugs I mentioned. This dedication to customer support has been, and continues to be, by far, the deepest I have ever encountered.

I also discovered an incredibly helpful and responsive community of fellow users worldwide, on Axure's Discussion Forum. Typically, you can get a helpful response to your query within hours and people are generous with their expertise. Over the years, as I gained some expertise with the tool, it has been nice to be able to help others in the forum. I will admit that this level of support is very important to me. When a tool becomes critical to my work, it has a direct impact on my livelihood. Support feels like a lifeline in times of crisis, and knowing that such a level of support exists, plays a major role in my loyalty and tolerance.

Axure's value was so compelling that I was able to convince clients and team members to approve the use of the tool, back when it was far less known among UX practitioners. This UX-centric integrated environment for wireframing, specifications, and collaboration also carried a price tag that was a small fraction of the cost and implementation complexities of enterprise tools. Occasionally, clients would raise a concern about the ability to find UX resources who know how to use Axure. UX designers would raise a concern about switching from tools they were very familiar with to a new tool. These two perspectives can potentially feed each other in a loop, which makes it difficult to effect change. It really takes external pressures to drive change.

Indeed, the growth of Axure's popularity among UX designers paralleled two important trends: The solidification of UX as an integrated part of the overall software development process, and technological advances that afforded the creation of rich user experiences. As more companies recognized the business value of modern user experience, budgets opened up, and with them, the demand for UX professionals.

With increased demand came also the pressures to deliver on time and within budget, both often aggressive to absurdity. At a certain point, too-ambitious schedules create serious friction with core principles of user-centered design, an inherently time consuming methodology that calls for contextual research, iterative design, and user validation. I realized, as many others did, that on top of helping me produce excellent deliverables on a tight schedule, Axure is helping me stay profitable, because I can deliver a lot more value to my clients, in less time and less sweat.

This is an important point. At the end of the day, design agencies and independent consultants need to turn a profit in order to stay viable. It is impossible to stay viable for long, if you have to double and triple your working hours just to keep up with the pressure of constant updates to a prototype and specifications. In-house UX teams must also control their cost and increase their productivity. Axure helps maintain profitability, because it is relatively easy to master, and it affords substantial efficiencies through clever use of customizable patterns, templates, and automation.

In conclusion, and reflecting back on McLuhan's observation earlier in this chapter, Axure is a tool that has been shaped by UX designers over the course of nearly a decade. At the time of writing this book, it is widely used, with over 30,000 licensed copies world wide, running on Mac and Windows. Axure is probably the de facto UX design tool in our industry. To what degree does it shape its users? It is for each of us to discover.

In this chapter, we introduce a prototyping checklist that covers the diverse set of variables that are involved in user experience projects, and how your approach to constructing an Axure project file might be affected by the specifics of your own project. Also, in the spirit of **User Centered Design**, and because UX projects are a collaborative effort, I thought it will be valuable to include the insights and expectations of real people who've experienced work on UX projects in various roles ranging from business, project management, visual design and development, as well as other user experience practitioners.

The art of UX prototyping

Prototyping is an ancient practice. Back in the fifteenth century, Leon Battista Alberti described an event that took place in the First century BC. In his classic text named *On the Art of Building in Ten Books*, Alberti mentions that Julius Caesar "completely demolished a house on his estate in Nemi, because it did not totally meet with his approval". He continues to recommend "the time-honored custom, practiced by the best builders, of preparing not only drawings and sketches but also models of wood or any other material…".

One might think that, given his authority as the ruler of the Roman Empire, Julius Caesar was perhaps abusing his powers by acting in a capricious, short-tempered manner. We can also think about Caesar as a typical client, reacting somewhat badly to a design that did not meet his requirements and specifications.

Another way to think about the event has an immediate relevance to us, two millennia later. The core of the problem is how to figure out what the client wants and deliver a product that meets those expectations. This is a problem of communication, and UX designers face the challenge of resolving it satisfactorily on every project they work on. Often, the client might have a clear idea in their head of the exact way the building—and for that matter, the software—should look and function. Sometimes, the client has no idea about the structure or the function of the software but has a pressing need to have such a structure in place, in order to fulfill a business or some other pressing need.

From the early days of computer science, people found the obvious parallels to physical architecture and borrowed from it liberally, terms and titles such as architect, build, configuration, and so on. Indeed, like architects and builders of physical structures, we too need to create a functional product, face the challenges of tracking against tight budgets and schedules, and keep our clients happy.

However, beyond borrowing the terminology from architecture, aspects that relate to engineering and process rigor take much longer to implement. For example, the use of modeling in user interface and user experience design, as we see it today, came in quite late in the software development life cycle. This perhaps explains why a very high number of software projects fair badly, but our cities are not littered by the ruins of collapsed buildings. Compare a large architecture project to build a 100-story skyscraper, with a large enterprise software project. What are the odds that both will be fully up and running within years? They are very high for the skyscraper, and far less for the software.

In other words, if we compare the rigor, efficiencies, and processes that translate a cardboard model and blueprints into a skyscraper to the typical chaos of software projects (perhaps with the exception of software for airplanes and such no-failure use), we probably have some ways to go. It is an evolutionary process.

The truth is that, of the billions of private residents, public buildings, and industrial structures that humans constructed on earth, since moving out of caves, relatively few ever benefited from the design of an architect. Not that these are necessarily bad, in fact, many of the structures we see today evolved successfully over millennia. People build their own homes, individually or as a communal effort. You can read Donald Harington's *The Architecture of the Arkansas Ozarks*, for a wonderful account of such an evolutionary process.

Alberti further writes that "Having constructed those models, it will be possible to examine clearly and consider thoroughly the relationship between the site and the surrounding district, the shape of the area, the number and order of parts of a building. It will also allow one to increase or decrease the size of those elements freely, to exchange them, and make new proposals and alterations until everything fits together well and meets with approval. Furthermore, it will provide a surer indication of the likely costs, which is not unimportant, by allowing one to calculate costs".

It is fascinating to 'translate' Alberti's writings about modeling for buildings, to UX prototyping for software. He is talking about the ability to articulate the layout, hierarchy, organization, order of entities, and also the ability to use the prototype for cost and effort estimation.

Another example of providing a client with 'wireframes' and ensuring alignment with their needs is mentioned in the book *Painting and Experience in 15th-Century Italy* by *Michael Baxandall*, who writes about the fifteenth century painter Filippo Lippi. Back in 1457, Lippi was commissioned to paint a triptych for Giovanni di Cosimo de' Medici, the Italian banker and Patron of the Arts. In a letter to Giovanni, Filippo writes "...And to keep you informed, I send a drawing of how the triptych is made of wood, and with its height and breadth...".

Prototyping interaction

Therefore, it turns out that we did not quite invent the prototyping wheel after all. The value, ROI calculations, and fancy technical terminology of prototyping have been around for a couple of millennia, if not more. There are, however, several important differences that make prototyping a rich user experience that is particularly challenging for UX practitioners.

Most structures don't involve dynamic interaction with the user. Buildings stand there, whether there is an occupant or not. Moreover, when you enter a building, rooms do not contextualize themselves instantly to reflect your identity. When it comes to software and prototyping a rich user experience, the complications come from the need to demonstrate the following:

- **Action and response**: The prototype needs to simulate possible paths that a user would have on any given screen and the system's appropriate responses to actions the user is taking. Often, the path could be conditional and take several steps to complete in a coherent and satisfactory way. The arsenal of interaction patterns that is available to UX designers today is significantly richer than what was available a decade ago.

  For example, the prevalent navigation model back in the client-server model of the '80s involved moving from one window to another, as part of a workflow involved in completing a task. In the '90s, common web navigation was hyperlinking from one page to another, facilitating a similar goal. These days, with asynchronous in-page data updates, the need to negotiate multiple windows has been greatly diminished, but the complexities of prototyping in-page data refreshes have increased.

- **Personalized experience based on login**: The prototype needs to simulate how the system will render for different users, based on the entitlements. In the case of non-registered users, the site might display special offers to entice the user to register. A registered user may get information based on preferences they have set in an earlier session, and a paying user needs access to additional content, based on past activity on the site. Increasingly, we are asked to model all of these permutations.

- **Scalability and future scope**: Many applications are deployed in phases, making it possible for the business to prioritize their investment in the project, based on strategic goals, practical budgetary, and technical constraints. The prototype, which often begins as a fully-fledged visionary concept, needs to be able to support 'graceful degradation', or fallback to less-ambitious capabilities of the present, and scale in the future.

- **Adaptability to localize**: In a global economy, a common requirement is to develop an application that can easily be localized to reflect the language and cultural preferences of the locale or demographics of its users. The prototype needs to demonstrate the ability to render in multiple languages.

- **Exception handling**: One of the toughest requirements is to demonstrate the way an application will respond to the rules for moving through an interaction path; this can be subject to either user or system override.

Like architecture and construction, software is an evolving art and science, but unlike construction, many of the tools and methodologies are evolving at such a rapid pace that it is very difficult to establish solid patterns of development. While physical architecture and construction have evolved over centuries and stay relevant for a long time, in technology, what worked ten years ago is practically ancient and moot by now.

The prototyping checklist

Before you embark on an Axure prototyping project, you should carefully consider several variables that will affect your approach to the prototype's construction and logistics. The following checklist is probably relevant to any type of prototyping software you may use, and not just to Axure. However, as you will see, neglecting to think in advance about these issues can cause serious roadblocks at various points in the project. The checklist is driven by the deliverables you are contracted to, or are expected to, deliver. This, in my opinion, is the most practical and beneficial angle with which to approach the work ahead.

The project

In the case of UX projects, size and scope matters, the type of application, and the purpose for which you are going to prototype can have a significant impact on the time, budget, and number of UX resources needed to get the job done on time. Surprisingly, it is not uncommon for projects that begin as small-scale efforts, to mushroom into increasingly complex and expensive ones.

UX resources, including internal teams, often do not have good visibility into the real drivers that move the project within the company. As a result, you may not always have the benefit of knowing in advance about what is going on, and changes to the scope and direction may come as a disappointing and frustrating surprise. There is little that can be done about such situations, but you can take a proactive approach to the way you construct your prototype, such that you have the ability to handle change, with reduced impacts to your own workload.

Simple websites

I am not sure what a simple website is, but we know one when we use one. I am using the word "simple" on purpose, because often, initial conversations around a project begin with "we need a simple website, something very basic...", which later turns out to be not that simple or trivial at all. A common understanding of 'simple' tends to focus instinctively on the number of pages involved. However, this can be a gravely misleading measure.

- Modern web applications have a small number of page templates (for example, an overview page, a list page, and a details page), but within each, the level of transformation and complexity can be significant.

- Another measure could be how many audiences the application will serve. Does it need to dynamically change the content and functionality based on login? Are any types of registrations involved? Are there any transactions? If the answers to all of these are no, and what you are looking at is stringing a number of pages together with some global navigation, then you are most likely looking at a simple project.

Is using Axure a good option for such simple tasks? Most likely not, especially if this is a one-time project, and you don't build user interfaces quite often. One could easily argue, and quite successfully, that in order to concentrate on the creation of content for a simple site, a common tool such as PowerPoint, will be more productive, because you can concentrate on the content and not lose energies on learning the prototyping tool. Additionally, the deployment of simple websites today is most successful when people use existing platforms, such as, **WordPress** or **Squarespace**. These enable a non-technical person to experiment and create highly sophisticated websites using prebuilt and easily-customizable templates.

Web applications and portals

This class of prototypes is probably the 'meat and potatoes' for Axure use. While there are many portal platforms, corporations often require custom developments and enhancements that feed their business needs. For many organizations, such projects are viewed as transformative and strategic, and are a significant financial investment. The following list shows some attributes such projects have in common:

- In order to secure approval and a go-ahead from corporate leaders, the initial UX involvement may be limited to the creation of a highly polished vision prototype. The UX footprint may be small, in terms of actual resources involved, but is significant in terms of the impact on moving forward.

- The application involves multiple modules that often represent discrete organizational business units. It is not uncommon for these business units to be spread across the country or the world. Each business unit may have its own rules, requirements, and supporting technologies, which need to be streamlined and unified to make the integrated application work as envisioned.

- If you are tasked with creating a high-fidelity prototype, keep the organizational complexity in mind. As much as possible, document your working assumptions, the guidance, and feedback of various stakeholders, their priorities, and potential areas of friction.

- Forward and backward vision. On one hand, a UX often enjoys a mandate to come up with an all-new, efficient, and great design. Then, there comes push back, and sometimes blame; the UX is too ambitious and too risky, and at times the UX team is ignorant of the constraints of legacy and business rules. The ability to maintain the fine balance between pragmatic and innovative is important, especially because a UX rarely gets enough time to gain deep knowledge of the business.

- Don't assume anything. Ask as many questions as you need to clarify the terminology and processes that you don't understand.

- Point out, early on, the potential gaps and implementation risks. In Axure, annotate the risk field for relevant widgets and layout regions you are concerned about, and go over those items during review sessions.

- To handle the complexity and specific needs of each module, developing such an application requires a large team for business and technology stakeholders, and to work with everyone, a big UX team.

- Start using a shared project early on, and communicate a lot with the team about establishing design patterns and other common elements. There is a need to maintain the balance between providing each workstream with the flexibility to address the unique needs of the part it is tasked with, but also, to keep in mind the overall consistency and integrity of the application.

Mobile apps

Apple continues its long tradition of affecting the user experience in profound ways. As it narrows the gap between mobile devices and the traditional computer experience, new interaction patterns, such as figure gestures, have been introduced in the lexicon of direct manipulation methods. With Axure's shared libraries, you can easily create prototypes that simulate the appearance of most popular mobile devices, from iPhones and iPads to Android.

Increasingly, organizations seek to extend their web applications from the Web to the mobile space, and you can prototype such apps in Axure, demonstrating their use on the targeted device.

Heuristic evaluation

One of the initial steps that UX designers are often asked to perform, at the inception of a redesign project, is a heuristic analysis of the existing user interface. The outcome can help decision makers to determine the scope, budget, and timelines for the project, with an opportunity to get the UX designer familiar with the application and its user experience issues.

You can, very rapidly, create a mini replica of the actual application by placing and linking screen captures in Axure pages. Add more details, such as droplists, form fields, and action buttons, at the appropriate places in the screen captures, to create a hybrid of images with a widget-based prototype. Add your comments in relevant annotation fields and generate an HTML prototype and a Word document, which you will use as you guide stakeholders through the findings.

User validation

A by-product of creating an interactive prototype in Axure is, of course, the fact that you have a tremendous instrument to use in various user validation activities, such as, focus groups and **usability tests** (**UT**). This is a no brainer. However, it is important to include, in the project's budget and timeline, the refactoring work necessary to use the prototype for such activities. This is especially important for complex applications that adjust the user interface based on the user login.

- Make sure that the scenarios planned for UT are actually built into the prototype. If not, adding those may involve considerable work and modifications to the construction of the file.

- If the file is also intended to be used to create specifications, how will the tweaks and added interactions, needed to make the prototype work for UT, affect the generated specs?

- Does it make sense to duplicate the current file and have a dedicated file just for the purpose of UT? It really depends on where you are, in terms of construction. The benefit of developing the file separately is that you can work quickly and tweak the construction without having to worry about the specifications or impacting other sections of the project. On the other hand, it means that any updates made to the production file will have to be updated in the UT file.

Deliverables: Prototype and specifications

Are you contracted, or expected, to deliver only an interactive prototype or also annotated specifications? The following list takes you through some important pointers to consider. Don't worry about Axure terms and functionalities you are not familiar with, as we cover those later in the book:

- If specifications are in play, what are the expectations for the format and delivery of those specifications? Is it, for example, an exhaustive Word document, or a light HTML-based annotated version of the prototype?

- Did you have an opportunity to discuss these flavors of documentation with the relevant stakeholders (typically, the development team), or are specifications mentioned casually, with their scope only implied? If the latter is the case, you should get explicit clarifications as early as possible.

- Ask for an example of a previous specifications document used by the development team, to get a sense of what is acceptable.

- If you are contracted to deliver an interactive prototype, what level of fidelity is expected? Interactivity means different things to different stakeholders. Their expectations are often shaped by past experiences, if any, with user experience projects.

- If the application needs to support different types of user roles based on login, are you expected to simulate the entire user experience for each of these roles, or just a primary role? This point alone can make or break a project, because stakeholders may demand to see the differences for each role, while you have budgeted and scheduled the work for simulating only one.

- Wireframe planning and construction: Knowing in advance that various sections have to reflect different types of users or states, should mean use of masters and dynamic panels. This will reduce redundancy of wireframes and rework, as the use of masters will require the use of raised events.

- Axure skills and techniques: Demonstrating how the interface renders for different users or different workflow paths, is likely to involve use of variables and functions, and as mentioned, use of masters, dynamic panels, and raised events. Knowing what is expected will help you acquire the Axure skills you need, in advance.

- Are you expected to simulate features such as type-ahead, or is it enough to call out such behaviors in the annotations? It is not that difficult to build the simulation in Axure, but, is there value, and more importantly, is time and budget allocated for constructing such common interactions?

- How much of the interface is expected to be prototyped, and how much can be just defined by static wireframes?

- Often, the conversation around the scope of work occurs before the beginning of the actual work. It is a good idea to agree with stakeholders on the set number of high-priority screens and flows that will be simulated in detail, with the rest to be addressed as static wireframes.

- Is the plan to quickly deliver a high-fidelity vision prototype first, and once the project gets the green light, use it for detailed design and specifications? If this is the case, keep in mind that refactoring the need to rebuild sections of your Axure file is likely to be required. There are several reasons for this:

  ○ To begin with, the work on a vision prototype tends to be very high-level show off, with "best-of-all-possible-worlds" functionalities and features. Often, there may be enough time or details to validate that the proposed user experience can actually be supported by the underlying business processes or technology. When the work on the detailed design moves forward, many of the assumptions that were made for the vision need to be scaled back in order to meet actual business requirements and technical constraints.

  ○ One particular pitfall to watch for has to do with administration screens. Most applications have some sort of administrative functionalities that range in capability, for example, allowing a superuser to assign access permissions to other users for setting the values of a wide range of defaults and other parameters. As very few users will actually interact with this part of the application, it is often dismissed casually in early conversations, only to resurface once deep into the project.

  ○ Create an inventory of all the application's modules and key screens. With the relevant stakeholders, agree which screens are in scope for what treatment. This will be the blueprint for working on the prototype, and for change management, as a result of scope realignment.

Balancing act: What stakeholders have to say

In his classic movie *Rashomon*, *Akira Kurosawa* unfolds the details of an event, by telling the story from the perspectives of multiple characters, including a dead person. Each character, who was also a direct witness to the event, recounts the story by telling the narrative from their point of view. That some form of the event actually happened, is undisputed, but as it happens, the stories, while similar in structure, end up contradicting each other.

User experience practitioners often find themselves in a Rashomon situation because of UX's unique position at the intersection of business, technology, people, and systems. The success of the UX project rests on our ability to fuse the various entities in a coherent and elegant way.

Understanding the perspectives of the stakeholders we work with is important, not only to arriving at a good solution, but also for a strong collaborative environment capable of handling the stress of constant change and fleeting schedules. The coming pages provide the insights of real people: business process architects, product managers, project managers, visual designers, development managers, and developers. I had the pleasure and benefit of working closely with many of these people over the years, and their insights are provided below, as they correlate to various chapters in this book.

Business stakeholders

You are likely to interact regularly with several types of business people: top executives, business process architects, product managers, and others. In many projects, the entire effort is driven by the business, and the success or failure of UX initiatives indeed rests on the informed support of top executives, who firmly understand the benefits of investing in user experience. UX practitioners often do not get much visibility into the tactical or strategic goals that the top management has for the project, which may lead to frustration and misaligned expectations on both sides.

Management

I have asked Oren Beit-Arie, Chief Strategy Officer at Ex Libris, a leading global provider of library automation solutions, to share his thoughts about management and UX. This is what he has to say:

Organizationally, a company may not be built around UX core competencies, and outsource it. Consequently, UX may be the first to be cut because it is not clear to management that UX contributes enough value, and there is suspicion that the consultants are just exaggerating up the value of their work. The recognition of the importance of UX for our company and products has evolved over the past decade, as we gradually learned to integrate UX with the development process.

When you are designing a customer facing application, it is easy for stakeholders to form their own personal opinion on how compelling a proposed UX is. That's because we can see ourselves in the role of the user, compare the experience with the competition, and with other applications we are familiar with.

But when you develop expert systems, and administration tools, Management and other stakeholders face a true challenge with the UX because it is difficult to figure out the best user experience. Managers have less intuition about how expert users do their work, how to improve and innovate something you are not fully know in great detail?

As a result of the evolutionarily path we took, we have a lot more confidence in dealing with this situation, and the impact of UX on our products. Today, we can also invasion how to use patterns we experienced on our iPhone and other mobile devices, might work on a particular product, because such patterns are so ubiquitous.

Generally, we find that, as Management, we think about UX as an investment effort that has two aspects to it:

The first deals with relatively straight-forward questions that are easy for management to drive towards and benchmark against: How to facilitate tasks and workflow via the UX? How to improve the productivity and efficiency of an application? How to satisfy the need to demonstrate lower cost of ownership? How to get a smart UX especially for complex tasks, How to make a product accessible, and so on. This is a very important aspect, but perhaps more tactical, as it is a solution-based approach.

The second aspect is less clear but more strategic and far-reaching; where Management, often struggles to determine the appropriate answer and make the proper investment: It involve aesthetics, design language, high production values, and our product, even corporate identity: How to balance between sleek, supper commercial design, and a more appropriate, practical design?

Increasingly, the standards and expectations our customers have, are not related to the specific class of applications we are dealing with. Rather, they form their experiences based on their experiences with applications from totally different domains. The issues become - are user expectation set too high due to these other apps? Think about Pixar producing eBooks…How to balance between making you product unique - and yet not so different - How to preserve your identity?

New realities force management to think about the competitive landscape, and new customer demands such as dealing with multi-device delivery: Mobile, tablets, desktops - which translate to the cost and complexities of multiple technologies, and on top of these - creating the UX for these. Another example for a challenging dilemma was, should we wait to HTML5 or do something now with existing technologies? Other questions related to this aspect involve localization, personalization and customization - How much to spend on these features and capabilities?

It is a process, and working closely, and iteratively with UX helps resolve many of those questions and concerns.

Business process architects

Tim Robb is a senior manager at NetApp, with whom I had the pleasure of collaborating some time ago. I have to admit that I am still under the spell of his leadership style and the way he worked to get the team through challenges that, at the time, seemed insurmountable. Here are Tim's thoughts on collaboration with UX, in this case, a team of UX designers.

Q: What are your expectations from the UX team?

I'm looking for the UX team to understand the context in which our users will interact with an application and what the users value above all else… That is, I expect the UX team to go beyond time-on-task analyses and develop a full understanding of why the users would want to use an application AND then how the application will impact user productivity, how it will hold their interest, how it will pique their curiosity, how it will help them understand and hopefully encourage them to return and view the application as an enabler rather than a "burden"…

The UX team should apply its expertise to help the business/functional/technical teams from "getting in their own way". We can all fall in love with automation, technology, the latest-and-greatest, "process simplification", our pet features, etc. However, the UX team should be speaking as the surrogate voice of the user. They should keep the business teams honest in representing and protecting the users' best interests. They should help the project team approach "stretch goals" in fostering end user satisfaction. Don't lull us into adopting "best practices" at the expense of delivering something remarkable, something that could deliver a competitive advantage.

In some respects I expect the UX team to serve as a kind of safety net that drives the business to deliver a harmonized blend of critical functionality and usability. The UX team should play a key role in leaving users with the impression that application delivery is not something we did TO THEM, rather something we did FOR THEM.

Q: What are some challenges in reviewing UX?

Protecting the time to do it… the business is trying to balance requirements-gathering, BRD (Business Requirements Document) development, conversion to functional/technical documentation, etc. and bringing UX team up to speed on all the nuances within and across workstreams.

Given challenge above, we had to 'divide and conquer' to review and advise… I think preferences for UI elements tend to be very personal which can result in different opinions when different parties review at different points in development lifecycle (and I would assume, frustration on the side of the UX team when the feedback changes depending on who is weighing in and when)

Trying to understand how to wade thru a wide variety of options… Looking at Wireframes, mockups or some other graphic representation is very helpful – critical for me (and also I think for sales and marketing users, who I think tend to be more "visual")… but then it can be a challenge to keep up with the changes and proposed changes and user-reaction/feedback to those over time.

Q: Do interactive prototypes help clarify the UX, or do they make things more complicated, slowing down the project?

I think the answer is "Both". Prototypes definitely help clarify the UX and in many respects "bring it to life"… but they do take time to develop, review, refine, review, assess, refine, etc.

I think an equally impactful issue for consideration is how close can/will the final product be to the prototype?... Project capacity/timeline, technical limits or performance considerations (for instance if application is integrated to or embedded in another application framework) can all impact the ability to match a prototype to the final deliverable. Users who see a prototype seem to magically develop a "photographic memory" of that cool new UI or UX treatment of something they've labored with in the legacy system for years... If the end product can't or doesn't deliver those one or two favored aspects, you can run the risk of not meeting up to the expectations the prototype set in their mind. I don't think this is a reason to shy away from prototypes, just a cautionary note to be careful how you position prototypes/wireframes.

That being said, we don't subscribe to the "under-promise, over-deliver" strategy. Despite good intentions, that can easily turn into a "under-promise, under-deliver" situation and worse, can actually prevent the team from reaching stretch goals or creating differentiating outcomes.

Q: What can UX teams do to improve the communication with business people?

Simply be honest with the users and the project team... don't tell either of them what you think they want to hear, tell/show them what is realistically possible within the constraints of the technology and the project scope. At the same time, convey the UX team's excitement and energy to those possibilities.

Communicate visually, communicate visually, communicate visually – whether with mockups, wireframes, prototypes or by showing other websites for comparisons or just to trigger thoughts/ideas.

Don't dwell on the legacy system, but understand it well enough to understand what users think are the top detractors/barriers to productive use AND what they think are top 5 positive aspects. Keep in mind that when you do deliver the new system, regardless of current "shortcomings" the legacy system will instantly become "the best thing we ever had". So help protect the project team by understanding not to "miss what's not broken".

Don't underestimate or under-invest in the value of the end-user feedback as part of the review process. And if you are developing an application that is utilized both internally and externally be certain to capture both perspectives... walk thru "a day in the life" of both parties and then frame that in the perspective of the end user values (not what the project team values, not what project management values).

M is a director-level business process architect at a global consulting firm, who has years of experience leading the development of business requirements effort for highly complex software development projects:

During the requirement gathering and high-level design phases of a complex implementation project partnership between the Business Architecture and the UX team can greatly enhance the final product.

By using a prototype-driven approach, the business is able to grasp possible options and make better informed decisions. At the same time, the risk is that what is presented is assumed to be "set in stone" by the executive team therefore creating an expectation that cannot be maintained due to budget constraints or availability of functionalities.

The Business Architecture team can and should leverage ideas generated by the UX team and evaluate the business requirements accordingly. In multiple occasions, we found our requirements to be lacking the users' perspective. By communicating with the team and by evaluating its reaction, we were able to adjust the requirements to achieve an enhanced user experience.

Of particular help was the use of wireframes. One of the most effective interactions I have experienced with the UX team was the creation of wireframes making the requirements come to life.

The back-and-forth between the teams and the ability to see a draft of the final product while finalizing the requirements was instrumental in the achievement of a successful product. For example, one of the requirements called for the ability to indicate that one account can be indicated as "Same As" any other account on the object being developed. After reviewing the wireframe and going through the steps a user would have had to take to comply with the requirement, the Business Architecture team realized how cumbersome the interaction was and modified the requirement accordingly.

Although the use of wireframes and prototypes greatly enhances the ability to deliver a good final product from a user experience standpoint, some considerations need to be taken into account.

The UX team has generally limited knowledge of the processes being enabled; this requires the Process Architecture team to spend a considerable amount of time, at least in the beginning, transferring knowledge. This is especially daunting when the UI being designed is completely knew. In projects with limited time and budget this can cause friction between the teams and poor cooperation.

The Process Architecture team's expectations need to be managed when interacting with the UX team. In the early stages of a project, there should be a clear understanding of the rules of engagement between the two teams and the expected deliverables the UX team will produce. In my experience, teams that did not work on projects with heavy involvement from the UX team had difficulty understanding the benefits and the deliverables the UX team can provide. One of the major points of contention has been, in my experience, the demarcation between BRDs and UX specs. It has been challenging to identify which document should contain what requirements and to what extent to the point that, at times, there were conflicting directions for the functional teams to follow.

The UX team should use tools capable of producing an output that speaks not only to functional teams but to Business Architects as well. While reviewing UX specs I frequently found the documents to be very technical and not immediately understandable. This slowed down the process of creating a cohesive output and, in time-sensitive situations, has created friction between teams.

We live in a world where most of us spend a considerable amount of time each day on the Internet or using products from well known software providers such as Microsoft Office and Adobe Creative Suite. This provides all of us with access to well thought out user interfaces that have been refined over the course of several years and have been widely accepted as standard. When interacting with the UX team, Process Architects tend to apply their experience with such software packages and websites sometime overstepping their area of expertise. Interaction with the UX team, in such circumstances, has resulted less than fruitful. The Business Architecture team should clearly understand and recognize the UX team's expertise and rely on its inputs to craft a good user interface.

In my opinion, the inclusion of the UX team on complex system implementations is fundamental for being able to provide the best product. Although the interaction with the other teams involved in the development is not always easy, the benefits far outweigh the challenges.

Project management

Project managers are tasked with tracking the progress of projects and facilitating solutions that help resolve roadblocks along the way. In many projects, UX professionals do not have the benefit of a dedicated project manager, which can be a problem for medium and large projects. If a project manager is not budgeted to the project, it is a good idea to raise that as a flag and take extra effort in developing a comprehensive, mid-level plan, by yourself. If there is a project manager, make sure to review the entire project plan and flag dependencies where the UX effort has not been considered.

For example, many plans do not account for the time it takes to refactor the Axure file from vision prototype to detailed design prototype. Others don't take into account the time it takes to iterate and revise the prototype. Sometimes, the time it takes to arrange the logistics of usability tests such as recruiting, is not considered. The more time spent early on with the project manager, as the plan is being developed and revised, the better off the project will track later on.

Tom Hackett is a project manager with a background in web development. He has worked with UX designers as a front-end web developer and a project manager:

Q: What are your expectations from the UX team?

As a project manager my expectation from a UX team is that they are able to identify user issues, and suggest design solutions that solve customer problems. I would expect that a UX Engineer can identify issues through both interviews and observation. A UX Engineer who can create clickable mockups and walk users through a prototype helps clarify if suggested changes will have the desired effect. It's also important that the final designs incorporate functionality and workflow notes for the development teams, clarifying expected behavior that isn't implemented in the interactive prototypes. It's a huge benefit if the wireframes are written in such a way that the development team can leverage the HTML/CSS in implementation.

Q: Do interactive prototypes help clarify the UX or make things more complicated, slowing down the project?

My experience has been that UX prototyping seems on paper to increase project timelines, but in practice can reduce development cycles since users can give feedback on an interactive UX design much sooner than waiting for the first generation system. This reduces the amount of feedback necessary in the development cycle itself and allows developers to focus on functionality rather than incorporating design or layout feedback during the build phase. An interactive UX often clarifies whether implied or assumed functionality that isn't documented formally exists, both for end users and development teams.

Q: What can UX teams do, to improve the communication with business people?

UX Engineers can improve overall team communication by ensuring development teams are behind suggested solutions and feel confident in implementation. An interactive prototype that pleases the business but cannot be implemented due to performance constraints or ties to legacy system workflows, etc... can cause problems with scope management.

Visual design

The Medium is the Message—Marshal McLuhan

Visual design introduces some of the most daunting challenges for rapid prototyping projects and a hidden iceberg for Axure prototypes. Why? Because of a gap, sometimes a serious one, that grows between the wireframes in the prototype and the visual design. This poses both UX and development risks because of the need to reconcile between two representations of the same screen. Eventually, a refactoring of the Axure prototype will be needed, especially if the intent is to keep using the file throughout the entire life cycle of the product.

The two sets of wireframes are developed asynchronously. Normally, we start with Axure wireframing as rough conceptual sketches that evolve through rapid iterations. These wireframes address information architecture and actionable tasks, and the layouts are often tentative. With Axure, we can enhance those estimates and evolve the concept as an interactive prototype that demonstrates the vision for navigation and interaction patterns.

All this work, however compelling, tends to be in grayscale, without visual design. As user experience architects and designers, we want to isolate the feedback we obtain from stakeholders and potential users. The conventional wisdom is that adding visual design cues at such an early point is adding unnecessary 'noise' to the feedback. That is because people's response to colors and layouts is both extremely subjective and strong, and the concern is that such feedback tends to push to the background more substantive issues.

However, referencing McLuhan's point that the medium is the message, is the argument that it is not possible to separate visual design from user experience. This argument sounds especially compelling when it comes to the design of mobile apps. This is a case where beauty is inherent to the design of the user experience.

What often happens is that, at some point in the UX process, visual design gets involved, and the ugly duckling emerges as a beautiful swan. Now, everyone needs to start looking at the two sets of wireframes. Often, the two sets will continue to evolve on separate tracks because, while the work with the visual designer takes place, work on finalizing Axure wireframes for specifications continues. It is easier to manage the situation if it is taken into consideration early on. Resolution is still going to be an effort, but at least it will be accounted for in the project plan.

I have found that UX designers, myself included, sometimes do not completely appreciate the complexities and challenges that the visual designers on the project face. Busy and stressed by our own issues, it is tempting to dump on the visual designer a great deal of information, often not fully baked, and expect that somehow the designer will 'get it'.

Therefore, I have asked Yael Alpert and Colin Ochel, two exceptionally talented principal visual designers, to share their perspective. Here are Yael's thoughts:

Q: What are your expectations from your UX partner (team or individual) on the project?

Get informed about the client's business and UI requirements as much as possible and get the full understanding of any background research for the project done by the UX team.

Be involved the UX's process of creating personas and users' and stakeholders' interviews, when such process exists, and understand the audience for the project.

Get involved in the UX process as to why they made certain decisions in design and interaction; this can help the visual designer better make their decisions in visualizing the wires and see what limitations, if any, the specific project has.

Meet the UX designer to go through the wires; this is very important, so the visual designer can fully understand every intention of the UX in the project.

Have meetings critiquing the visual designs; it is important to have these meetings so the visuals are viewed from a UI perspective before being presented to the client.

Q: What are some challenges of integrating the visual design with a conceptual wireframe?

Keeping true to the UI while creating an engaging braded experience. Many times it is tempting to design interactions that are 'more fun or unique' but are less 'user friendly'; the challenge is to find the balance between the two.

Come up with appropriate solutions - many time the wireframes will not be obvious in what's the best solution for a certain interaction or page; the visual designer will than need to communicate the UI intention in a way that makes sense to the user. It's the visual design that the user sees in the end and these do not come with an explanation, so the visual design needs to be very clear to the user.

Be creative: a good visual designer will try and see the wire frame page in a few different ways and explore a few ways of visualizing the same thing. This is a challenging practice but a very good one especially if user testing of the UI are conduced.

Q: What should UX designers keep in mind when communicating with visual designers?

Everything happens for a reason: Have every element in the wire thought about (even if they are made just for the purpose of visual design), even elements such as color; if you color a certain item in the wires, the visual designer will see it as a meaningful thing, if there's no reason for the color / differentiation – do not use color.

Be consistent: Describe or visually represent specific elements in a similar way and keep to it throughout the wireframes. Elements such as icons representation, navigation items, buttons etc.

Be clear: The visual designer in a way is like the client to some extent; s/he needs to understand the wires as much as anyone else to achieve the best outcome; to save a lot of back and forth clarity is important.

Be open: Many times, inspired by the wires and the project in general, the visual designer might come up with a different layout and or interactions than the UI that still serve the project well. Be open to discuss updates if they make sense; visuals designers in the interactive area understand interactions and have an opinion; they are not just 'coloring' the wireframes; a good visual designer brings his or hers experience to the table that can work well together with UX.

Here are Colin's insights:

Q: What are your expectations from the UX team?

To be the voice of the client. I expect that the wire frame are the translation of the client's needs and if I have any questions or suggestions, the UEA can answer me as if they are the client.

I also expect the UEA team to be open to change. Because the UEA gathers the requirements from the client, they are led down the client's vision of the product/ site/widget and it very difficult to view it from another direction. I get to see the requirements from a bird's eye view through the raw wire frames so I can view the content/flow from a non-influential eye. This allows me to make suggestions the UEA might not have considered.

Q: What are some challenges of integrating the visual design with a conceptual wireframe?

Space. Often wireframes pack in a lot of information in a small space. It looks fine when it's small text in a bounding box but not when it is in a designed layout.

Less is usually more when it comes to design. Just because something is content rich does not mean that it needs to be cluttered. Do not be afraid to brake down a page into parts that are shown only when needed. Finding a clever yet clear, intuitive way to display the content is always a challenge though. The more you hide, the more risk you run into bad usability.

Q: What should UX designers keep in mind when communicating with visual designers?

Most designers do not think like architects so it is a good test to see if your wireframes are clear. If the designer gets hung up on any part of your wireframe then you need to revise that interaction to make it more clear because if they do not get it, the end user will not get it.

Development stakeholders

One would not be blamed for thinking that developing the user experience and software development are complementary processes. However, as we often find, there is a gap between UX and development. There are many reasons for friction, but a fundamental means to resolve these is communication.

It is surprising to hear stories about large projects where the interaction designer and developers only got together well after a spanking, high-fidelity vision prototype, commissioned by the business side of the organization, had been used to drive top management to move forward with the project.

The problem, from the perspective of the development team, is that the expectation now is that the amazing application will be developed and will work just like the prototype, and will be in production in no time…as if life was so simple! Development leaders often express concerns that UX does not always take into account the constraints of available technology, impact of the new UX on performance, scarceness of development resources available to the organization, or the complexities involved in implementation of the new UX.

These concerns are often valid and true. With Axure, however, UX has a tool that helps improve communications through visualization of interactivity and integrated annotations. Conversations, analysis, estimation, and adjustments can start early on in the development life cycle and reduce the stress on the development team.

The following are the thoughts of Mark Roeser, a senior technology executive with extensive experience and focus on large-scale data systems:

Q: What are your expectations from the UX team?

At the core of course the UX team builds out the interface design, looking for the most effective way to bridge the user's wants with the application. What I like to see most are openness and curiosity. UX needs to navigate around shifting product goals, technical constraints, a variety of user personas, and other unique challenges that have the potential to lead to an unsatisfying compromise. Having the freedom and curiosity to explore a number of possibilities is the best path toward inspired solutions.

Q: What are some challenges in reviewing UX?

Removing ourselves and our assumptions when reviewing UX, and imagining new contexts and situations in which to review a design. Also, focusing on the right elements at the right stage of the project: don't review or discuss art when things should still be handled at the wireframe stage.

Q: Do interactive prototypes help clarify the UX or make things more complicated, slowing down the project?

Prototypes should be carefully considered with specific goals in mind and not always be included. Prototypes that are easy to produce but too simplistic can lead to false validations. For example, a hardcoded workflow reviewed with an end user can seem easy and clear to understand, whereas a final working product might reveal excessive clicks, repetitive tasks, etc. when they use it for real w/out the idealized storyline.

Q: What can UX teams do, to improve the communication with business people?

As much as possible, share share the methods and teach the language of UX. Give them a language to effectively communicate their ideas and concerns, and draw them into the process. Be a guide and partner with them to discover solutions together, rather than asserting authority or attempting to dazzle with cleverness.

I'm also very much interested in finding ways to improve how UX works in an iterative development process, particularly in the context of the "minimal shippable functionality" aspect of agile/scrum. Here the goal is to learn early from a simple product in the field, rather than concentrating all UX work at the start. For this to be effective, the UX team needs to work closely with the development team to plan meaningful iterations and build in the feedback/measurements necessary to drive the process forward. Easier said than done!

The UX perspective

User interface/experience practitioners come in many flavors. There is no standard certification or professional accreditation that can help a client determine who is a truley qualified UX resource. While you will not take on an uncertified architect to design a skyscraper or your home, the evolution of user experience as a discipline matches other segments in software design, where a degree is not the only measure of expertise and skill.

However, there is also an aspect that relates to the technical skills we bring to the table. For someone who is only versed and comfortable with wireframing in Visio, developing an interactive prototype in Visio, will be a challenge.

Of course, it is a lot easier to create such a prototype in Axure. However, should you embrace this tool? It is best to avoid heated tool-camp loyalty arguments, as the answer typically boils down to a strategic business and professional decision:

- Are you a single user? Perhaps an independent consultant, or the single UX practitioner in an organization? In this case, you need to consider the cost of investing in the tool, and the return on your investment.

- Think about the projects you have created so far with the tool(s) you have. Is there a gap that you need to fill?

- Axure is becoming a good skill to master. Will learning the tool open up new opportunities?

- What about the cloud-based services for which you pay a subscription? Certainly, it is a good idea to review the option. However, the thing to consider here is that many corporations may frown upon having their strategic plans placed on some cloud. Moreover, firewalls and other security barriers may make it difficult for stakeholders to access the work.

- Are you a member of an interface design agency, or in an in-house design team?

- What are the challenges of running a shared Axure project?

- What kind of training is needed to level the team's prototyping skills?

- What are the project opportunities that open up with using shared project and the efficiencies, savings, and increased profits in terms of re-use of widget libraries, masters and generators?

The UX practitioner

I have asked a few colleagues to share their honest perspectives on the use of Axure. I think you might find Katrina's and Saikat's account very relevant to your experience. Here are Katrina Benco's thoughts:

I used Visio for a long time before using Axure. The thought of switching tools was a daunting, but enticing proposition. I started using Axure with an open mind and haven't looked back. It has a small learning curve and is continually proving itself as a clever and useful tool.

One way Axure has supported my design process is its flexibility for documenting highly complex or configurable systems with a rich, interactive UI and layers of business rules. The mechanisms to prototype also allow me to document and annotate the different states of the wireframes in an object-oriented manner. I can use dynamic panels and masters to show different states in the UI not only based on interaction, but also business rules, roles, configurations, etc.

My primary use of Axure has been to design and specify wireframes and generate printed wireframe specification documents for the developers, not to do prototyping. However, Axure's prototyping features have reshaped my design process in two ways:

I can quickly prototype an interaction and test it out myself. There is nothing like trying on your own design for size. I prototype my design concepts to pitch them to the business and tech folks. Seeing concepts in action is a powerful way to show design concepts and gain buy-in, or to sell one design over another.

My suggestions for successful adoption by a large UX team are to:

First, have best practices for using the tool in place to ensure everyone documents their wireframes in the same way. Second, take advantage of the masters to globally spec as much of your UI as you can and to share design patterns.

And here are Saikat Mandal's thoughts:

Axure is an amazing prototyping tool. It can be all-inclusive tool for a UX designer. It helps you ideate; create bubble diagrams, flow diagrams, sketchy-low fidelity prototypes. Where it is hugely helpful is its capability to make high fidelity prototypes, which can mimic the actual system at quarter of its cost and time. This is not just a tool for the designers but also for the whole team, which includes Project Managers, Business Analysts, developers and even the Quality Analysts. Rapid visualization gets all these team going. They now don't have to wait for the other team to pass the ball.

The beauty of all complex things is its simple structure (I am reminded of Clarke's Law: Any sufficiently advanced technology is indistinguishable from magic.) Your work just gets done like magic and you don't even have to think of the mechanism behind it. (Disclaimer: Sometime this can set wrong expectations at workplace). The Layout is similar to a website. A simple structure which tells you that there is a website with simple three pages. A common man can make a website and have a web presence. It does not need any prior knowledge of website building. Simple knowledge of hyper linking will get a person going. You can then make it more complex based on your need.

There are some challenges to Axure's adoption. Most of the design fraternity has grown up using Adobe suit and Dreamweaver as prototyping tool. Thus adapting to a new product that does things differently can be a challenge in the beginning. The other disadvantage is that Axure does not have the capability of layers . Layers in Axure can add whole new meaning. This will make it closer to Photoshop and can have the versatility of Auto Cad.

However, there are ways to customize the dynamic panels to behave as layers. So an advanced user, familiar with layers can modify dynamic panels and get it to perform the functions of layers.

'Nomenclature' is another problem. Naming widgets and panels correctly and reusing them as masters is the crux of Axure. Unique Ids can be separated from a class of object by naming objects properly. A new user without guidance will not get to know the pattern and thus there needs to be some scaffolding to help them. The good news is that a user has complete ability to customize the system. Thus giving tremendous power to the user.

Overall one tool doing so much is in itself a marvel. It has its shortcomings but the team behind it is doing a tremendous job of mitigating the problems. Axure is a powerful tool, which can make wonders when used correctly.

The UX team lead

I asked Alfred Kahn to share with us his insights, based on his experiences with the previous version of Axure, while leading a large UX team on a complex project:

The challenge

Create a new, consistent, unified design for the J.P. Morgan Treasury Services portal, using a large team spread across three locations.

Team structure

My team consisted of 12 designers divided into four workstreams, each responsible for a different part of the design: Portal, Payments, Information Management and Standards. Each workstream had a lead responsible for overseeing the design work and ensuring that the workstream's designs complied with the standards that were developed over the course of the project. The Standards team was responsible for maintaining the User Experience standards and reviewing each team's designs for compliance.

Process

Based on prior experiences working with standards that were developed in the abstract, I established an iterative process that would enable us to evolve standards organically. Our standards were derived from solving real-world design problems specific to the context and the domain in which we were working. Each workstream had an ownership of the wireframes for the screen designs in its area of the portal and published its own specifications. The specifications were consumed by the product and tech teams (BSAs, architects, and developers) for that area, but starting with the initial designs, we identified common functionality and created a set of standard patterns that were then used in all wireframes.

Each of the three specifications included a "Globals" section, maintained by the Portal and Standards workstreams, containing specifications for widgets used for common functionality. As a result of this approach, the Client Experience team became the central point for maintaining consistency across the entire portal project in terms of both design and requirements.

Axure was the easy choice as the primary design tool, to a large extent based on its shared project, masters, and UI specification generation features. Had we used any other tool, the project would likely have required at least 2-3 additional designers to just support distribution and integration of common design elements.

Extending the process

After the design of the first release was done, we explored ways to integrate the functional specification content into Axure, in order to provide a single point of reference for the developers building the application. We piloted and then rolled out a process whereby the Business Systems Analysts (BSAs) would enter their content into the shared Axure file in a separate set of annotations through a customized view. The BSA annotations were published in the UI specification in a separate table following the annotations entered by the Client Experience designers.

This approach was limited to those parts of the functional specification that related to the UI, but provided a single point of reference for the developers building the user interface. It had the added benefit of lowering the overhead around maintaining consistency between the functional specification and the UI specification; prior to establishing this process, the Client Experience and the BSA teams spent a significant amount of time reviewing each other's documentation to make sure that they were in alignment and that there were no conflicts.

Axure: The Good

There were two main features in Axure that helped ensure consistency of the design across the three workstreams: the **shared project** and **custom widget library** features.

The shared project feature enabled the team to use the same set of masters, which meant that we could centrally update designs common to all workstreams. The custom widget library provided designers with an easy option to use widgets that complied with the standards. We regularly re-factored the custom widget library to reflect modifications made to the user experience and the visual design standards, so that they always had an up-to-date version available to them. Other Axure features that helped streamline the design process were:

- **Access to wireframes across workstreams**: As every designer had access to every wireframe, they could easily refer to another team's design to prevent duplication of functionality and drive consistency across the application.

- **Wireframe categorization and navigation**: We used the tree in Axure's left navigation to categorize our many wireframes. Each team had a node, and as we had established a numbering and naming convention for wireframes, masters and dynamic panel states, it was easy for us to find each other's wireframes.

- **Page Notes**: These enabled us to provide a categorized overview of each screen, and the sections we established within Page Notes served as a template to prompt designers to enter critical information.

- **Integrated specification generation**: It drastically reduced the overhead related to maintaining the UI specification, especially as we ended up with multiple versions of each specification related to point releases. Had we been forced to use a separate tool for managing and generating the UI specifications, it would have doubled the level of effort for the project, at the very least.

- **Restore feature**: On a number of occasions, Axure's restore feature saved us many days of rebuilding screens. Coupled with the fact that the subversion instance was backed up centrally, we were able to reduce our file management overhead as well.

Axure: The Bad

The single biggest downside to using Axure (Version 5.6 and earlier) on a project of this size is that the project file got extremely large, creating significant latency in checking files in and out. It was not unusual for it to take up to 5 minutes to check a screen in or out. This was a source of frustration for the team and became a drag on productivity.

An easy way to mitigate the check in/out latency would have been to break the file up into separate projects for each workstream. Unfortunately, Axure does not have an "include" feature; there was no way to store, maintain, and share common elements outside of the main project file. For this reason, we maintained a single project file and lived with the frustration.

While we loved the custom widgets library feature, it didn't update when the library modified; each time we updated the library, it had to be published and imported manually. It would have been much better to be able to push custom widget library updates out to all designers automatically, through the project file.

The functionality associated with the **Specification Generator** not as robust as other features, however, Axure was very responsive to our feedback. We sent the company a list of new features and upgrades that we thought would significantly improve the utility of Axure for us. When we met to review the list, we indicated that the Specification Generator feature upgrades were of the highest priority for us (Axure 6 addresses many of those requests).

Despite all of these issues, Axure was a huge boon to the project. Given the scale of the effort, if we had not selected Axure as our design tool, each workstream would have required an additional designer just to manage the distribution and integration of the common design elements, significantly adding to the overhead of the project. After leading a team through the design of four releases using Axure as our design tool, I think we made the right choice, and would do so again without hesitation.

Tips for using Axure on large design projects

The following are some tips that should help you get the most out of using Axure on a large project:

- Axure can promote, but not enforce, consistent design; ensuring a consistent design still requires a governance process

- It is critical to construct wireframes properly and consistently across all teams

- Create a naming convention for wireframes and dynamic panels; validate proper naming during governance reviews

- Agree on a common structure/organization of wireframes and enforce that organization across all teams

- Allow time to train new users in the finer points of using Axure

- At the beginning of the project, pilot a number of ways of using masters and dynamic panels, and then settle on a common approach; validate the implementation during governance reviews

- Be sure to bake time into your project plan for maintenance of the Axure file:

  ○ Refactor the project file at strategic points in time—between completion of wireframes and writing the spec, and after the completion of a release

- Plan to have one wireframe structure for prototypes and another for specifications

Axure around the world

The world is getting smaller, and I think that UX plays a small role in getting people from all over the world closer, by propagating good user-centered design patterns. I am curious about the practice of UX, and the use of Axure, as a design tool around the world. I have posted the question to the **AxureWorld** group on **LinkedIn** (see here: `http://lnkd.in/52g3h8`). You can read the responses from practitioners in Brazil, the Netherlands, India, Israel, the UK, and many other countries...and please add your comments as well!

As a more in-depth response, I have asked Richard Tsai, Chief Information Architect at UserXper Digital Consulting Co., to share with us the perspective on Axure's use in China and Taiwan, and this is what he has to say:

My first experience with Axure RP happened in 2006. This all started from a colleague who observed that lots of prototyping tools, which I had never heard before, were introduced by the Western UX bloggers. After downloading and using Axure RP v4.0, I immediately realized that this is exactly what I want. It is highly valuable in managing large-scale website projects.

In 2007, I left from my ex-company and setup UserXper Digital Consulting Corporation. Our major business is focusing on providing the service of information architect and website planning, including prototyping. At the same time, UseXper became the Sales & Training Partner with Axure Company and stared to promote Axure RP in the Greater China Area.

The obvious advantages of Axure RP itself and word-of-mouth advertising by users took effect better than our promote activities; therefore, many famous and top-class enterprises such as Internet company (Yahoo! Taiwan, Alibaba, Baidu,...), software companies (Trend Micro,..) , even hardware companies have used the Axure RP and taken it as the first choice of UI prototype tool.

How the users in Great China area apply the Axure RP to their job? There are three different usages from beginners to fabulous users.

First are beginners using Axure RP, nonracially identity as freelancers or small teams. They would simply use basic function such as wireframing and lo-fi prototype to concretize their ideas. These users may not employ themselves in Axure RP's complicated interactive design; however, they still make a good thing of communicating accurately to reach the requirements.

Secondly, advanced experienced design team design the ui & interaction via Axure RP which tends to mockup the system flow to verify the interface usability as soon as possible.

Last one would be fabulous team. These people would process the "Design Management plan" by using Axure RP. For instance, team members can coordinate UI design pattern through the Widget Libraries function. More important thing is to create excellent user experience by using the linked-up company standard with design guideline.

Except dot-coms, there are more and more MIS departments of traditional industries and hardware manufacturers start to using Axure RP to design the interface of Mobile App or Tablet PC UI.

Furthermore, there are some interesting and creative examples about using Axure RP. For example, a IT team in Beijing use Axure RP to control SA(System Analysis) and Specification approval. Another example is a company in Taipei generates the system operation handbook by Spec generation function. Moreover, one of my colleagues loves Axure RP so much that he uses Axure RP for making training contact to replace traditional PowerPoint.

More and more industries pay attention to User experience in Great China area. Famous UX events in Taipei such as HPX party & UiGathering used to taking Axure RP prototyping as the main lecture. There was about 700-800 persons attending the User Friendly Conference, the biggest user-experienced conference and held in SuZhou, China. One of workshops in User Friendly 2011 was Axure RP Prototyping this year.

The Axure perspective

As this is a book on prototyping with Axure, it made a lot of sense to approach the company about the vision for the future. There are several considerable challenges that the company has to deal with:

- The more Axure can do (logic, variables, functions, and so on), the more complex the tool becomes. In fact, we already find a demand in the market for specialized Axure 'prototypes': people who can take Axure to the max and create really powerful vision prototypes. Ironically, however, freeing ourselves from the dependency on developers, and the ability to quickly and easily create interactive prototypes, is exactly the goal Axure set out to achieve, being a tool for non-developers. So, here's how the company can balance these two extremes:

  - Prototype versus specifications: The demand for high-fidelity vision prototypes is on the rise and is becoming a norm. The turnaround on such prototypes is fast, and they are extremely influential in getting decision makers to give the green light to ambitious development projects. However, turning a vision prototype into a specification—a deliverable that is often contracted for—is most likely to require refactoring. The refactoring effort can be substantial, and yet— often not planned for—budget or schedule wise. Clearly, there are some challenges around reducing the gap between the prototype construction and specification generation. How would Axure try to address this in the future?

○ The rapidly changing landscape of UX: Apple, for example, with its iPhones and iPads and its integration of the mobile operating system iOS with the desktop operating system OS-X, has changed the user experience in profound ways. As a result, the syntax of interaction patterns is evolving. New multi-finger gestures are a good example. How will Axure support the creation of prototypes for the next generation of devices?

I have asked Victor Hsu, who, together with Martin Smith, started Axure back in 2002, to share some of his thoughts:

When we started Axure, we set out to build a tool that would reduce project costs and timelines by introducing interactive prototyping into the process. Axure RP 1.0 was built, and it was a flop. It was difficult to use and had a lot of features that overlapped with existing tools that did a better job. Looking back, it just wasn't a tool many people would want to spend their day using. Luckily, the user experience profession was about to take off. And we discovered a new approach to designing Axure RP.

Instead of thinking about the project, we started focusing on you, the people actually using Axure RP. We prioritized features that made it faster and easier to use and gave you the prototyping capabilities other tools did not. We trusted you to take advantage of those capabilities to reach better designs and to communicate with your teams. It worked. You delivered cost savings to the projects and helped build better software. Axure RP is now the standard for software prototyping tools.

Time and time again, we've seen your successes lead to recognition, and recognition lead to more responsibility. This is a great thing. The Axure RP roadmap is evidence of the increasing demands on UX professionals and your increasing influence. Turnaround times need to be faster. The prototypes are getting richer as user testing becomes more prevalent. They need to be presented on the target devices like iPhones and iPads. And your prototypes are replacing requirements lists and documents as the reference for visual design, copywriting, development and testing.

We will continue to help you take advantage of these opportunities and at the same time make Axure RP more enjoyable for you to learn and use. You will find excellent resources from prototyping and Axure RP experts like Ezra to help you along the way. And all we ask of you is to produce great work and accept the credit and influence you've earned.

Summary

Our success as UX designers rests on our ability to synthesize and express the many diverse, often conflicting, inputs we gather from sources, such as business and development stakeholders, user research, business requirements, and various constraints. At the end of the day, our goal is to find the pragmatic balance, opportunities, and innovation for the best user experience possible. In order to visualize and document our vision, a specialized UX tool is invaluable, and in recent years, Axure has become the tool of choice for many UX designers who feel it has the right balance of features, complexity, and cost, and is the right tool to demonstrate their vision.

The coming chapters will introduce you to the wealth of features Axure offers, in the context of real-life circumstances. As you read the book and get a better sense of how Axure might fit your needs, keep in mind the various perspectives of the stakeholders and partners you are collaborating with. At the end of the day, Axure is just a tool, and it is through true collaboration that we can develop a successful and hopefully innovative prototype.

2
Axure Basics—the User Interface

Like all creative professionals, that rely on tools to express their ideas and deliver their work, we must understand the possibilities and limitations of the tools we use. There is no substitute for diving into Axure and discovering its features through first-hand exploration. However, investing some time early on, to familiarize yourself with the nuances and capabilities of its user interface, will help you approach Axure prototype construction in a more skilful, robust, and timesaving way.

This chapter is designed to help you establish a solid familiarity with Axure's concepts and rich capabilities. The topics include:

- Getting started
- The Workspace (Mac and PC version)
- The Wireframes pane
- The Sitemap pane
- The Masters pane
- The Widget pane
- The Widget properties pane
- The Page properties pane
- The Dynamic Panel Manager
- The Toolbar and Menu bar
- Axure file formats

Getting started

When you launch Axure, you are presented with the Welcome Screen and Licensing window, as shown in the following screenshot:

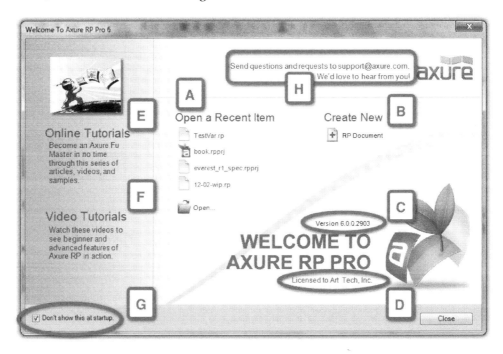

This window allows you to:

- Open recent files (A).
- Create new RP files (B).
- See which version of Axure you are running (C). Typically, Axure releases several updates during a version's life cycle; currently, there is no automatic update feature, so it is a good idea to check the **Downloads** section on the Axure's website, and update to the latest point release. If you are part of a team, it is recommended that all team members use the same version and point release. If you are upgrading from an earlier version of Axure, then keep a backup copy of your files. Once you save a version 5 file in version 6, you will not be able to open it in version 5 again.

- Check whether the software is licensed to you or your organization (D). This information should reflect the information you provided when you purchased the software.

- Access online tutorials (E) and video tutorials (F).

You have the option of preventing the **Welcome screen** from appearing when Axure starts up (G), and if you do, the window can be accessed it at any time by selecting the **Welcome Screen** and **Licensing** option, from the **Help** menu.

Finally, there is an invitation to contact Axure with questions and requests at support@axure.com (H). My personal experience with Axure's support has been consistently great since the first time I contacted the company, several years ago.

Working with multiple project files

What if you want to have two or more Axure files open at the same time? No problem, but the Mac and Windows versions are slightly different: The Mac version supports the launching of multiple files. Use the Windows menu to navigate between your open files.

On Axure for Windows, only one file can be open at any given time. For example, if you have one project file open and you choose the **Open** command from the **File** menu (as you want to review another project), the current file will close and will be replaced by the newly opened project file. In order to work with multiple files, launch another instance of Axure from your program menu.

The Axure workspace

Axure's workspace is straightforward, as seen in the following screenshot:

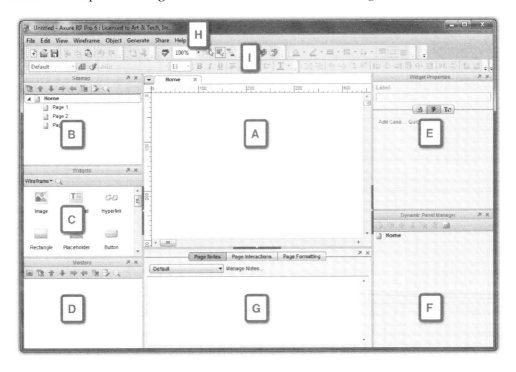

Your main wireframing construction space is the Wireframe pane (A), which is at the center of the screen, flanked by supporting panes on the left, right, and bottom:

Left panes:

- The **Sitemap** pane (B)
- The **Widgets** Pane (C)
- The **Masters** pane (D)

Right panes:

- The **Widget Properties** pane (E)
- The **Dynamic Panel Manager** (F)

Bottom pane:

- The **Page Properties** pane (G)

The menu bar (H) and toolbar (I) complete the composition on the top.

The preceding screenshot is a Windows version. The Mac version of Axure (see the following screenshot) is nearly identical; except the menu bar (A) and the appearance of the toolbar (B), variations that stem from the difference in how toolbars are implemented on Windows versus OS-X:

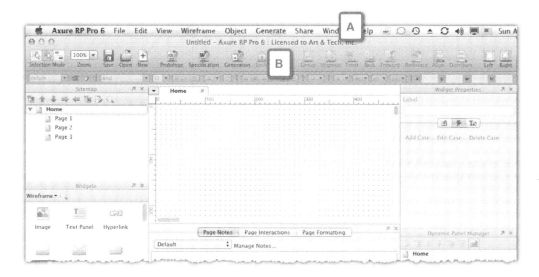

Think of the various panes as lenses that allows you to switch your view from a macro perspective of the project to a micro perspective of a widget.

- **Project level perspective**: The top-most level is that of the Sitemap and Masters panes. These panes provide a view of all the pages and masters in your project, and the ability to add, delete, re-order, and apply other actions to those assets.

- **Wireframe level perspective**: When you open a page, a master, or a dynamic panel state for editing in the Wireframe pane, two panes are relevant:

  ○ The Page Properties pane is where you annotate, style, and attach interactions to the page or the master wireframes (but all these options are disabled for the dynamic panel state).

  ○ The Widgets pane is where you access your collection of built-in or custom widgets, from which you will construct your wireframes and diagrams.

    °   If you include dynamic panels and masters on your page, then they will be listed in the Dynamic Panel Manager pane. It is possible to nest dynamic panels within other dynamic panels, masters within masters, dynamic panels within masters, masters within dynamic panels, and so on. The ability to view, at a high-level, the construction of a wireframe is tremendously important, especially if you did not create the wireframe, a situation that is common in team projects.

- **Widget level perspective**: Wireframes are composed of widgets. Use the Widget Properties pane to annotate, style, and attach interactions to widgets.

The following table shows a summary of how Axure's workspace corresponds to the main entities of project, wireframe, and widget:

Prototype perspective	Wireframe perspective	Widget perspective
Sitemap pane	Wireframes pane	Widget properties
Masters pane	Page properties	
	Dynamic Panel Manager	
	Widget pane	
All levels		
The Toolbar and Menu bar		

Customizing the workspace

You have some control over the arrangement of the workspace (as shown in the following screenshot), which includes:

- The ability to hide or show all the panes with the exception of the Wireframe pane (A).

- The ability to detach the panes and move them around. This feature is very useful if you work with two monitors. A convenient way to organize your space is moving all the side and bottom panes to one monitor, while keeping the Wireframe pane on the other monitor:

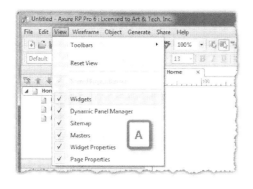

Note, that you cannot change the default location of panes when they are in their docked state. For example, the **Sitemap** pane is always parked on the upper-left and cannot be placed in any other location.

The Sitemap pane

In the **Sitemap** pane (shown in the preceding screenshot), you create and organize Pages. Pages are the highest-level elements in Axure. When you launch Axure, it opens a new, untitled document. The **Sitemap** pane of this new project has a default structure that includes a home page, and three nested pages. This will be the foundation of your own project.

The name of this pane may suggest an antiquated web-centric approach that is restricted to websites. However, don't let the label mislead you, because it is possible to create high-fidelity prototypes of highly complex, enterprise-grade web or desktop applications with Axure.

If you are migrating from Visio, an Axure page is similar to a tab in a .vsd file. Although it is technically possible to create an entire prototype using only page level wireframes, this approach, like traditional methods of creating wireframes in Visio or a drawing program, is limiting and may be sufficient only for simple, fairly static, and small applications. However, as you start exploring Axure, building static pages will be a logical place to start.

In the **Sitemap** pane, you can:

- Create new pages (A).
- Change the order of pages (B) by moving them up and down the sitemap.
- Organize pages to reflect a page hierarchy by changing their nesting level (C). Note, that by nesting one page under another, you are only creating a visual representation of the sitemap structure. The pages themselves are not associated to each other programmatically as a result of the nesting. You create the navigation interactivity yourself, a topic we will discuss shortly.
- Delete pages (D).
- Edit pages (E).
- Search pages (F). For very large prototype projects with many nested pages, the search capability is a tremendous time saver. Click on the magnifying glass icon (F) to toggle the visibility of the search field, which appears below the pane's row of icons.

Finally, you can hide the Sitemap pane or toggle its docking state by using the controls on the upper-right corner of the pane (H). These options are depicted in the following screenshot:

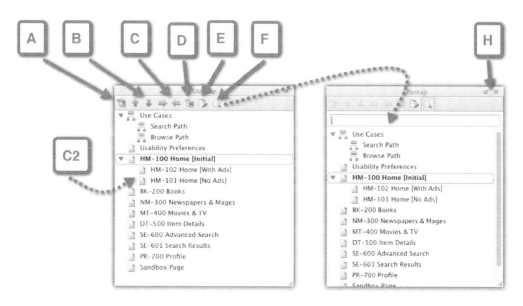

Also, note that by placing your mouse over a page and right-clicking, a context menu (A) will pop up, as shown in the following screenshot. Some of the items there are redundant to those offered by the icons bar:

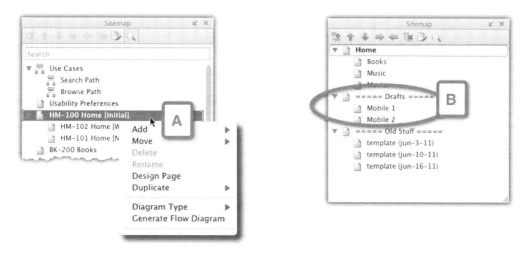

Finally, a word about organizing the Sitemap. The number of pages in your project are likely to mushroom. Many of them will be pages that are not used in the prototype or specification. Rather, they will be ideas for new pages, old drafts, various approaches you had in mind, and so on. There is a natural tendency to try to keep all of this work, because, who knows, you might need it at some point. You cannot create actual folders in the Sitemap pane, so a work-around method for keeping your work tidy is to create blank "category" pages, and label them in a visual way that communicates they are actually dividers (B). Then, nest the related pages under those blank pages. For example, create a blank page, label it "old work" or "Archive", and then move down and nest all the related pages that you no longer use and which currently clutter your working section.

There are two types of pages in Axure:

Wireframe pages

A wireframe page, in the Sitemap pane, corresponds to a discrete application screen. Only wireframes that appear in the Sitemap pane are generated in the HTML prototype. It is an important fact to remember because master wireframes, which when being edited in the Wireframe pane look much like page wireframes, cannot be directly accessed in the prototype.

Flow pages

Flow diagrams are essential for developing a comprehensive understanding of the application before we begin prototyping. Diagrams are abstractions of knowledge and, when done right, are a great communication aid that facilitate shared understanding between the project's stakeholders. We use them extensively to illustrate the various dimensions involved in a UX project. The typical diagram types include:

- Site maps
- Business process diagrams
- UML diagrams
- Flow charts
- Org charts
- Venn diagrams
- Task flows

Axure includes built-in diagramming capabilities, which are not as robust as dedicated diagramming tools, but offer a significant benefit: Your project flows and wireframes can be created, edited, reviewed, and stored in a single tool. Moreover, the output of these diagrams is generated automatically in the HTML prototype or Word specification document.

Consider a review meeting with stakeholders. As you walk the audience through a task in the clickable HTML prototype, you can switch from a diagram that illustrates the pages that are part of the flow, to the wireframes of the pages, and back. No need to switch between tools, export Visio files to pdf, and so on. It is efficient.

See the following screenshot for an example of an automatically generated Sitemap diagram:

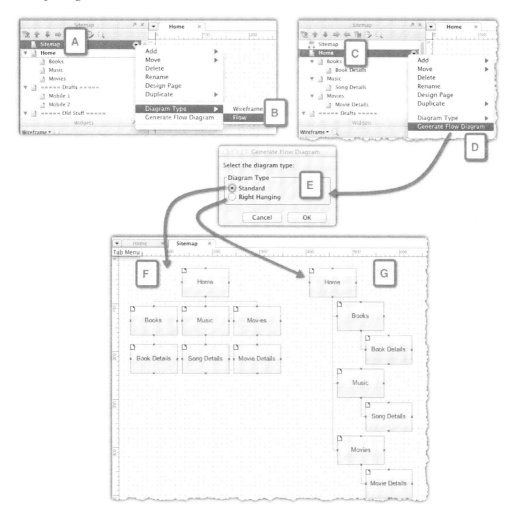

- Start by creating a new page above the Home page or whatever is the topmost page in your project. Rename it **Sitemap** (A), and right-click on it. In the contextual menu, select the **Flow** (B) option from the **Diagram Type** menu. Notice that the icon of the page changes to reflect that the page is now a flow page.

- With the Sitemap page open and active in the **Wireframes** pane, right-click on the Home page or equivalent and select **Generate Flow Diagram** (D) from the contextual menu.

- The **Generate Flow Diagram** pop up (E) will appear and you can choose between a **Standard** (F) or **Right Hanging** (G) diagram.

- The resulting diagram will appear on the Sitemap page. Note that once you generate the HTML prototype and select the sitemap page, clicking on any of the pages' rectangles will link the user to the corresponding page.

The Page Properties pane

This pane is divided into three sections:

- **Page Notes** (A): For annotating pages and masters
- **Page Interactions** (B): For creating **OnPageLoad** interactions for pages and masters
- **Page Formatting** (C): For applying formatting properties to pages

These sections are shown in the following screenshot:

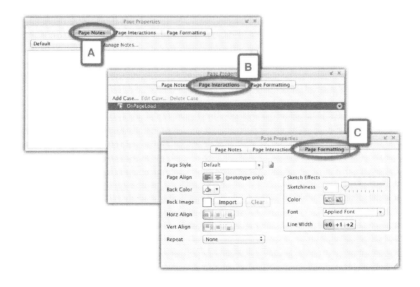

Page notes

As mentioned earlier, Axure provides an integrated wireframing and annotation environment. The page notes tab is where you enter page level information, such as description, entry and exit points, restrictions, and so on. Obviously, this feature is relevant mostly for those who need to generate a specification document or HTML annotations. However, even if you are not on the hook for that deliverable, it is still an extremely useful spot to capture questions, feedback from stakeholders, and so on. Instead of managing such information in notebooks, e-mails, and other documents, why not just store it all within the wireframe?

As illustrated in the following screenshot, page notes text can be formatted. Highlight any section of the text and change font family, color, bold, italic, and underline properties (A):

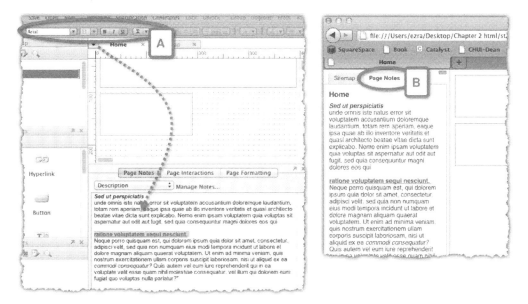

However, you cannot change the font size, create bullets, or change paragraph alignment. Once you generate the HTML prototype, your notes, including their formatting, will appear in the notes tab (B)

Managing notes

In the Page notes section, you describe an entire page or master, and there are basically two approaches to creating and managing your notes:

1. A single notes "bucket" in which you type all relevant information.
2. Multiple note sections, each dedicated to a specific audience or UX aspect.

Which approach to adopt for your project depends on the complexity of the project, and stakeholder expectations. It is a good idea to discuss expectations early on, to make sure that your documentation is satisfactory.

The benefits of using just a single notes field is obviously simplicity, at least for you. The drawback is that stakeholders might find it difficult to consume the information. In most projects, you are addressing an audience that has specific interest in only part of your description. For example, developers might be interested in behavior patterns of the screen and other technical information, while the business team is looking for the fulfillment of the business requirements. If all your information is packed in a single field, then readers will have to weed through information that is irrelevant to them.

As Axure lets you segment page level notes into several note sections, it is highly recommended to take advantage of this feature. Examples of such sections include:

- BRD references
- Accessibility (WAI/Section 508) Notes
- UX description
- Exceptions, personalization, or localization notes
- Review notes, follow-up questions and internal notes to self or team

Axure lets you control:

- The titles of notes sections
- Inclusion of the notes in the HTML prototype
- Inclusion of the notes in the Word specification documents
- Which notes section to include in the output

Creating additional note sections should also be used in shared projects, if several teams contribute content to the same wireframe pages. For example, the UX team provides UX related notes, business analysts add business requirements notes, and system analysts add functional notes. Keep in mind, however, that Axure is NOT a business requirements system.

Page interactions

This tab allows the UX designer to define how the page will render in the HTML prototype. This is an awesome feature because it affords an economy of construction. For example, instead of creating a unique page that visualizes how the page looks when a first time visitor accesses it, and another unique wireframe to show the page after the user logged-in, you can use a single page with dynamic panels. Each state in the dynamic panels will correspond to a visitor view and a registered user view.

You specify an `OnPageLoad` event that fires when the page is being loaded by the browser. The browser will then execute the actions that you specified for the event and will render either the visitor page or the registered user page. We cover this technique in detail later in *Chapters 4* and *5*.

Page formatting

As mentioned earlier, page formatting can be applied only to pages, and not to masters or dynamic panel states. You can define the following attributes:

- Page alignment (left or centered)
- Background color
- Background image, including horizontal and vertical alignment and repetition
- Sketch effects (which are described in the following section)
- You can save a combination of these attributes as a custom style and apply this custom style to other pages—a great time saver for ensuring consistency across pages

Sketch effects

Remember the good old days when we used to sketch lions on the walls of caves and later, wireframes on napkins? There is an amazingly compelling quality to the human touch and in the context of prototyping Axure lets you apply a sketchy effect to your wireframe that lends them a 'handmade' feel.

Using this style during early conceptualization can help you communicate implicitly to stakeholders and reviewers the fact that they are looking at a draft. See the following screenshot for a standard styled wireframe (A) and the same wireframe at 100% Sketchiness(B):

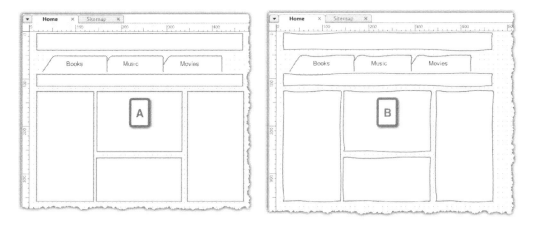

The Widgets pane

For a Visio user, and for any user of a painting tool, the widgets pane should be all too familiar. It is a collection of shapes that you can drag over to the **Wireframes** pane and use to construct a wireframe.

The Widgets pane allows you to access Axure's built-in widgets collections, manage, and organize imported third party widget libraries, or your own custom widgets collection, and to search for widgets, in your building and loaded widget libraries.

- By default, the pane shows Axure's built-in Wireframe widgets (See the following screenshot, A). This is a collection of geometric and basic user interface components such as radio buttons, fields, drop-lists, and so on.

- Use the drop-list menu (B) to switch between the built-in or loaded libraries and to manage your own or third-party libraries.

- To switch to another library, select it from the menu (C).

- The built-in Flow widget library (D) is a collection of diagram related shapes that can be used to create flow charts and other diagrams.

- To search for a widget, click the magnifying glass icon (E) and the search field will be displayed.

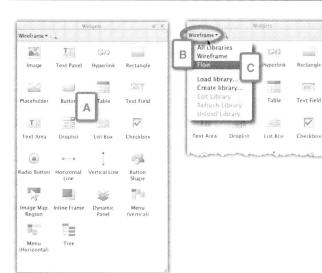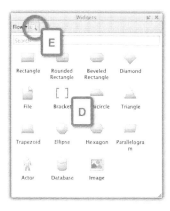

Wireframe Widgets

Axure's drawing capabilities are somewhat limited when compared to full-fledged drawing or diagramming programs such as Visio or Fireworks. For example, you cannot rotate, skew, or distort a rectangular widget, which also means that you cannot create diagonal lines. Also missing are free-hand drawing tools and shapes such as polygons and arrows. A work-around to consider is to create the shape you need in a drawing tool, such as Fireworks, and use the Image widget to import it to your wireframe.

Axure widgets are not just simple shapes. It is possible to associate most of the widgets to an interaction and make it do things. The text label of some widgets can be set by variables and the visual styling can change in response to mouse events. Finally, you can annotate each widget.

Axure offers all the necessary visual vocabulary needed to create fully robust prototypes. Mastering the capabilities of each widget will help you construct better wireframes.

Flow widgets

Flow diagrams are interesting because they are an abstraction of a flow, an algorithm expressed not as a mathematical formula, but rather in concrete shapes, arrows, and text. A flow diagram is an image. In addition, here is a situation where the phrase "A picture is worth a thousand words" underscores a general problem with flow diagrams. Flow diagrams are often not very easy to understand and you actually need a thousand words to explain exactly what is going on.

There are several methodologies to create flows: eXtreme Programming (XP), the Microsoft Solutions Framework (MSF) for Agile, the Rational Unified Process (RUP), the OpenUp (Eclipse), the Agile Unified Process (AUP), the Enterprise Unified Process (EUP), and there are still more.

You may also need to use several types of flow diagrams such as Affinity process, sequence, sitemap, interaction model, hierarchy, and so on.

Whatever choices you make for creating flow diagrams for your project, Axure 6 can help you put them together in a compelling way, as shown in the following screenshot:

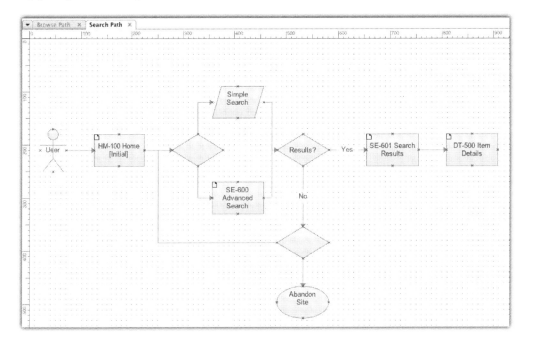

In addition to the geometric shapes commonly used for diagramming, such as the Diamond for decision points, there are specialized shapes such as Database and Bracket, and most importantly, the Actor shape.

Creating your own widget library

Widgets are like Lego blocks—they are the simple raw materials with which you have the potential to construct and express complex designs. Widgets are generic templates from which you can quickly assemble less generic structures or patterns. Most importantly, widgets are used to apply consistent design patterns throughout the entire prototype.

In order to extend Axure's built-in widget libraries, you can create your own collections. These collections can be project-specific pattern libraries or patterns that you find yourself using repeatedly on various projects.

In order to create your own library, you select the **Create library** option from the droplist in the **Widgets** pane. You will be prompted to name the library and point to a location where you want to save the file.

Axure widget libraries are independent files that have the suffix `rplib`. In other words, the custom library can be edited and managed independently of your current project file. The `rplib` files open in an instance of Axure that has a **Widget Library** pane (see the following screenshot, A) instead of the **Sitemap** pane. This is good, because the idea is to be able to use and reuse the libraries across projects. We will discuss this topic extensively in *Chapter 6, Managing Patterns with Widget Libraries*:

Third party widget libraries

Before you embark on creating your own custom library, it is worth doing a little research to check out the growing collection of free and commercial widget libraries that are listed on the Axure's website at `http://axure.com/widgetlibraries` (see the following screenshot). At the time of writing, there are collections for iPad, iPhone, Android, OS-X, touch screen hand gestures, social media, icons, and various useful patterns. There is a high probability that someone, somewhere, has already done the work and saved you the time and effort:

Ultimately, you need to use widgets and patterns that best match the needs of your project. The nice thing about Axure's custom libraries is that you can tweak and extend a library that someone else has created.

The Widget Properties pane

This pane is similar to the Page Properties pane, in that it facilitates the three major aspects of a high-fidelity prototype: Interactivity, visualization, and documentation. The pane is contextual to a widget selection: It becomes active only when you have a single widget selected. Once a widget is selected, the widget properties pane allows you to define its behavior and attributes in the following three tabs:

- Annotations
- Interactions
- Formatting

Annotation tab

In order to appreciate this simple yet profound tab, one needs to compare Axure's annotation workflow with one involving **Visio** and **Word** (**VW**). While light annotations can be placed within a Visio wireframe, Word must be used in order to create comprehensive UI documentation. Therefore, this is the VW workflow:

1. Create the wireframe in Visio.
2. Add numbered markers where needed. Add light annotations, as space allows.
3. Take a screen capture of the wireframe.
4. Name and save the screen capture.
5. Paste the screen capture into Word.
6. Create an attributes table for each of the numbered markers.
7. Write the extended annotations and details that could not fit into the Visio file.

This process has to be repeated for each wireframe and the inherent ongoing iteration requires constant tweaking of the Visio wireframe, cascading a repeat of the preceding process. I listed this workflow in such detail because each step translates to time: A few seconds perhaps, but per wireframe, this workflow adds tremendous overhead when schedules are tight—significant pressure on the UX designer or team.

To summarize, The VW workflow for UX documentation can be painful and expensive. It is also prone to errors, especially in large projects, where keeping the Visio and Word documents in sync is complicated; often requiring an Excel spreadsheet to track updates and changes. Finally, both Visio and Word are single-user applications, simultaneous use of the same document by team members is impossible.

The Axure workflow for documentation, on the other hand, involves selecting the widget you want to annotate (see the following screenshot, A), and typing your annotations in the customizable annotation fields (B). A numbered annotation footnote is added automatically (C). With one click you can generate a specifications document in Word, whenever new updates to wireframes requires a fresh version of the specs. The screenshots are always up-to-date, and they are generated automatically. The numbered footnotes on the screenshot correspond to annotation tables:

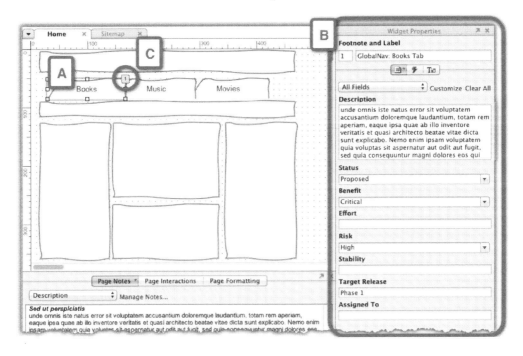

Axure's integrated environment means that wireframes and annotations are tightly coupled. Whether you generate an HTML prototype or a Word interaction, the most updated screenshots are created along with numbered footnotes. In Word, the annotation tables are listing the attributed widgets referenced in the screenshots. The timesaving is significant. This means that you can spend less time on the tedious mechanics of prototype documentation and more time on refining the design.

Annotation fields

Annotation fields capture attributes associated with the widget. Axure comes with a default set of annotation fields, but most likely, you will end up with your own set—those that best fit the needs of your project. The fields come in four data type flavors:

1. **Text fields**: Use these to capture attributes such as description, default value, and so on. You can type as much text as needed.

2. **Select list fields**: Use these for as many attributes as possible, to enforce consistency of values, and to save time while annotating. For example, status, release versions, and so on.

3. **Number fields**: Use these when you want to enforce a numeric attribute. However, I have to admit that I have not found a good use for it. For normal attributes such as release or phase number, the Select list is probably more appropriate because you have set values. However, it is there in case you do need it.

4. **Date fields**: Use for date-specific attributes. For example, you can create a field called last updated and update the value after each edit to the widget. This sounds like good and useful information to track, but remember that the update is manual. You will have to remember to make those updates for all widgets, as you update them.

To customize the default annotation fields, click on the **Customize** link on the **Widget Properties** pane (A) to launch the **Customize Fields and Views** dialog (B), as shown in the following screenshot (the process is discussed in detail in *Chapter 8, Functional Specifications*):

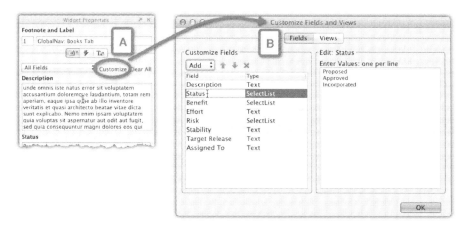

Very early in the project, discuss the optimal field set with business and development stakeholders. They are typically the primary consumers of the annotations. Work collaboratively with these groups to agree on the attributes that provide them with the most value.

> Agree on annotation fields with the primary consumers of the UX spec.
>
> Be practical about the number of annotation fields — less is more.

Although you can have as many annotation fields as you want, be practical. Remember that these fields are widget level fields and you will have tens, if not hundreds, of widgets in your project that require some annotation. The more fields, the more effort to create and update the attribute data, especially as requirements keep changing up to the last moment.

Don't be shy about educating your partners about the effort involved in wireframing and annotation. I recommend this approach especially for Agile projects, where requirements are developed on the go and it can be a real challenge to write specifications for an evolving product.

Annotation views

Axure provides a useful feature to help organize annotation fields in smaller subsets named **Views** that make the input of content more convenient. As you may have noticed, the **Widget Properties** pane and the **Dynamic Panel Manager** pane share the right-hand side of the Axure's workspace. As you add your annotations, they take more vertical space. As each view has few fields, fewer vertical scrollings will be needed as you create your annotations. Some of the uses of Views are as follows:

- You want to organize business-related fields in one group and development-related fields in another. Normally, you annotate the business attributes earlier in the project, as requirements are being discussed with business stakeholders. As the project moves from vision to detailed design, the more technical annotation fields become the focus of annotation.

- Views are useful in a shared Axure project files, where multiple UX designers collaborate on the project file. Some of the annotation fields might be specific for a module or a work stream, and each team can have its own view.

- Another use is in projects where a team of business analysts (BA) populate functional annotations in dedicated annotation fields. Adding a dedicated BA view shields them and the entire team from accessing UX specific fields.

Annotation views help plan the sequence in which the annotations are written to balance the load and to avoid a last minute crunch. Configuring views is easy: Switch to the **Views** tab in the **Customize Fields and Views** dialog (as shown in the following screenshot, A). Views are listed in the left-hand column (B), where you can add, reorder, and delete views. In order to associate views with specific annotation fields, select the view, and use the **Add** drop-list (C) on the right-hand column.

In the **Widget Properties** pane (D), you switch between views by selecting the view you want from the drop-list (E). The selected view appears in the drop-list and below the associated annotation fields (F). The one issue to keep in mind is to be careful to enter annotations in the right view and field. The views are not contextual to the widget and view-switching is a manual task:

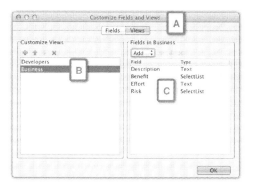

Interactions tab

With Axure, UX designers, with limited or no programming skills, can rapidly simulate an interactive user experience and communicate the proposed interaction design to stakeholders in a compelling and convincing way. The learning curve to creating more advanced, high-fidelity prototypes in Axure is not steep, especially when compared to authoring environments such as Flash ActionScript. UX practitioners, in general, have a good understanding of logic, process, and flow. Therefore, they are well-positioned to master interactions with Axure. UX designers with experience and background in scripting and programming can advance further into the realm of hyper-fidelity prototypes. In short, Axure affords all UX designers the ability to create interactive simulations at their level of comfort.

The effectiveness of simulating interactivity in UX projects cannot be exaggerated. The reality is that most stakeholders have a hard time imagining how something might work, even when they are presented with a sequence of static wireframes.

Less than a decade ago, desktop and web software landed themselves easily into a page-to-page sequencing because most actions were followed by refreshing of the entire page. It was easy to model flows with static wireframes. Modern interfaces, on the other hand, are dynamic and increasingly beautiful. They respond to a growing array of user actions and gestures, with smooth, engaging visual effects. Data on various sections of the screen is seamlessly and fluidly updated in the background, independent of other sections, and without page refresh.

That is perhaps why the slowly emerging expertise that was known years ago as User Interface Design has transformed itself to what we refer to today as User Experience Design. You cannot communicate the intended experience with static wireframes.

For example, think about communicating a simple "mouse over" interaction where the user's mouse is hovering over a text. The styling changes from normal to bold and underlined. Its color changes from black to orange, the background color changes too. After two milliseconds, a small pop up appears on the upper-right corner of the link. This is what you will have to SAY, if you are using a static wireframe.

Imagine a stakeholders' meeting with high-level executives to whom you want to communicate your vision of the design. The most trivial of interaction patterns requires so much explanation that it inevitably slows down the overall delivery of the application-flow. Alternatively, you can use an Axure prototype to demonstrate the interaction by moving the mouse over the text. The experience is communicated instantly.

Interactions

Interactions are the things that makes an Axure prototype interactive. You can create page and master level interactions in the **Page Properties** pane and widget level interactions in the **Widgets Properties** pane.

In a nutshell, there are two things you have to remember about widget interactions:

- They are contextual to the widget you select
- Each interaction is a self-contained unit, which is made of three components:
    - **Event**: Each interaction is tied to a single event, for example, `OnClick`
    - **Case**: Each event can have one or more cases
    - **Action**: Each case can have one or more actions

The following screenshot illustrates the structure of a simple interaction:

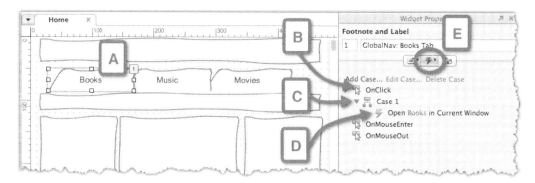

In our case, this is what should happen when the user clicks on a navigation tab:

- A widget (A) is selected in the **Wireframes** pane. This widget happens to be a **Left Tab** widget, which is based on the **Rectangle** widget. This type of widget can respond to three possible events: **OnClick**, **OnMouseEnter**, and **OnMouseOut**.

- In order to make this widget respond to a click, we are going to choose the **OnClick** (B) event, and add a **Case** to it (C).

- This is a simple interaction that involves just a single case, but you can interact with multiple cases. We will discuss all of that in *Chapter 4*, but for now, all that needs to happen when the user clicks on the widget is that he or she should be linked to another page.

- Nested below the case is the action; in this case, open a page in the current window (D).

- Finally, note the asterisk on the **Interactions** tab (E). If you are on any of the other tabs of the **Widget Properties** pane, this visual indicator is a useful reminder that an interaction is associated with the widget. Additionally, when you create an interaction for a widget, a footnote is automatically added to the Widget (A). A footnote is also added to the widget when you annotate it, so the asterisk, which appears on any, or both, of the tabs, indicates whether the footnote is related to an annotation, interaction, or both.

As you can see, an Axure interaction is constructed of simple, natural language phrases. The example above shows that:

- Onclick, opens a link in the current window

Therefore, while behind the scenes Axure will generate some code that will run the interaction in the browser, you do not need to write or interpret a single line of code. Axure uses Pseudo-code, which is the enabler that helps non-programmers to create interactive prototypes.

Events

Most of Axure's built-in widgets support some sort of event. As mentioned earlier, events are contextual to the widget. Click on the widget in the **Wireframes** pane and the available events will be listed in the **Widget Properties**' pane **Interactions** tab. The following screenshot illustrates the difference between the events that are available for a drop-list widget, and the single event that is available for a **Button** widget:

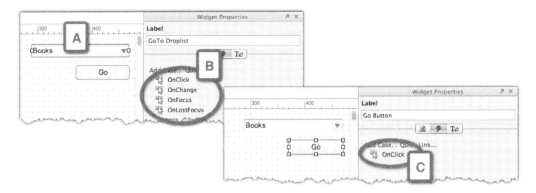

Cases

Context is among the important attributes of a good user experience. Given a user, the interface renders the relevant content and functionality in a way that informs, and guides, the user to a successful, positive, and even enjoyable completion of their interaction with the application or the site.

Context is determined by certain conditions and parameters. The system needs to evaluate those conditions in order to apply the appropriate business rules and render the appropriate experience as we designed. For example, a website that offers subscriptions services to content will provide access to this content to users who signed into their account. For visitors, the site will offer functionality that is meant to entice them to subscribe. This is the kind of situation that we can model in Axure and demonstrate in the prototype.

A widget event with a single case associated to it means that whenever the event is triggered, the case will fire the action or actions that are tied to it. Basically, the widget will have just one behavior whenever that event happens. However, of course, we normally need to simulate a lot more complex situations, based on the context of the event. The following screenshot illustrates a simple example of two possible outcomes, for the same **OnClick** event (A):

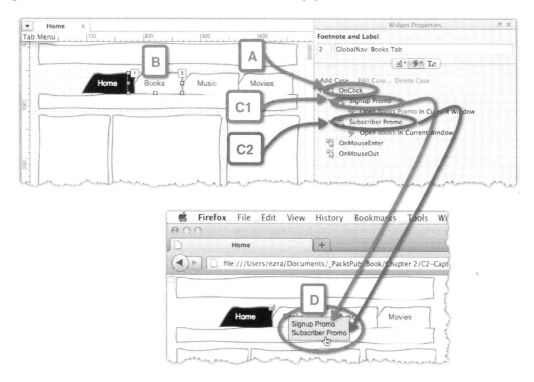

The business rules require that, from the Home page:

1. When a visitor on the site clicks on the **Books** tab (B), a special promotional page of a book will be presented that may influence the user to subscribe.

2. When a subscriber to the site, who has signed in, clicks on the **Books** tab, the standard template for the books page should be presented with some promotional materials.

As you can see in the **Widget Properties** pane, two cases are nested under the **OnClick** event: The **Signup Promo** case (C1) and the **Subscriber Promo** case (C2). When you generate the prototype and click the **Books** tab on the home page, a menu listing the two cases appear and depending on your selection, an appropriate page will be loaded.

As you notice, Axure provides the ability to create interactions on the **Page Interactions** tab, and here, in the **Widget Properties** tab. While the manner of composing the interaction is identical, there is some difference in the way multiple cases are executed.

A case associated with an OnPageLoad event is executed automatically by the browser, when the page or master associated with the interaction loads. When there are multiple cases tied to a single OnPageLoad event, how can the browser figure out what do do? In software, when a single path splits into two or more branches, the automatic determination of which of those to follow is based on the evaluation of some conditions. In *Chapter 5, Advanced Interactions*, you will learn how to create conditional logic that will determine how the page should render.

By comparison, when you attach multiple cases to a user-triggered event on a widget, the determination of which case to execute is manual, as was described earlier. We will see this in more detail in *Chapters 4* and *5*.

Actions

An Axure action is a discrete, specific instruction, such as to open a link in a pop-up window. One or more actions are organized in a unit named **case** and a case is associated with a specific event, such as OnClick. The event will execute when its case is triggered by the event.

At the time of writing, Axure provides 24 actions, organized in four categories:

- Links: It is a group of seven actions that handle the hyperlinking navigation from one page to another using windows or iFrames.
- Dynamic panels: Seven actions that control dynamic panels widgets.
- Widgets and variables: A set of eight actions that help control the behavior of widgets.
- Miscellaneous: Only two actions here, one that enables timing and the other which provides a text field where you can describe, in detail, some action that you don't want to, or can't simulate in Axure. (You can also use the other action to document a complex interaction for later reference.)

In order to manage and configure the actions in a case, you use the **Case Editor** (see the following screenshot, A), which is structured to guide you through a multistep process. You can rename the case in **Step 1** and add conditions, if needed. The main body of the dialog is divided into three columns:

- **Step 2**, add actions to the case (B): Actions that you select in this column are added to the columns for Step 3 and Step 4, where you will configure and order them.

- **Step 3**, where you organize multiple actions (C): When you have multiple actions in a case, the order of actions is important due to the way they are processed by Axure and the browser.

- Finally, you configure the actions in **Step 4** (D).

All Axure actions are structured similarly as a sentence which includes a configurable action (the one exception is other). The color of the configurable part is green. For example, the action sentence is **Open Link in Current Window** (E), and the word **Link** (F) is the configurable part:

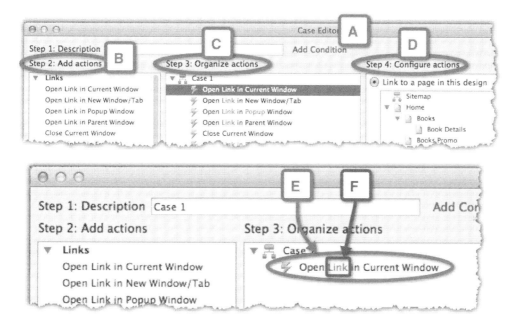

Formatting tab

At its core, a wireframe is nothing but a framed rectangle with some boxes, interface controls, and text. It can work perfectly when sketched on a napkin or an index card, but this technique can get you only that far. With the evolution of user experience as an established discipline, there has been a shift towards higher fidelity. We are rapidly moving away from static, low fidelity wireframes, where explication of the user experience relies on supporting text and the audience's imagination, to sleek, high fidelity interactive HTML prototypes that get very close in approximating the software to be delivered.

We are in the user experience business and the "experience" is determined as much by how the interface looks as by how it behaves. The tension between form and function is exceptionally strong. On one end, user experience designers want to keep the discussion subjective, focused on structure, and flow. "Sketchy" styling can help enforce the tentative aspect of an emerging design, which is important during early phases of a project. On the other hand, companies spend considerable effort on creating "Vision" prototypes to entice top management to invest in expensive new applications. Such prototypes are often executed in hyper-fidelity, including refined visual design and features that often would never make it to production. Nonetheless, such prototypes play a critical role in galvanizing support for the new project.

Whatever are the stylistic expressions appropriate for your project and design philosophy, you can define the visual properties of widgets by using the **Widget Properties Formatting** tab.

Like the **Annotations** and **Interaction** panes, the **Formatting** pane (see the following screenshot, A) is contextual to the selected widget (B). As opposed to other tabs, however, you can also use the **Formatting** tab to style multiple selected widgets. The tab is divided into six collapsible sections (C):

1. **Location + Size**
2. **Font**
3. **Alignment + Padding**
4. **Style**
5. **Ordering**
6. **Fills, Lines, + Borders**

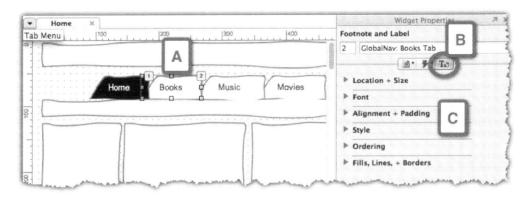

Most of the formatting attributes that appear in this tab are also available through the **Format** Bar, and the **Format** menu, but here you get a one-stop access to all of the formatting under a single tab.

Location and size

With a single widget selected (see the following screenshot, A), you can:

- Set the **Left** and **Top** position, and **Width** and **Height** of the widget (B)
- Lock or unlock a single selected widget (C). The selection border of locked widgets changes from blue to red (D)

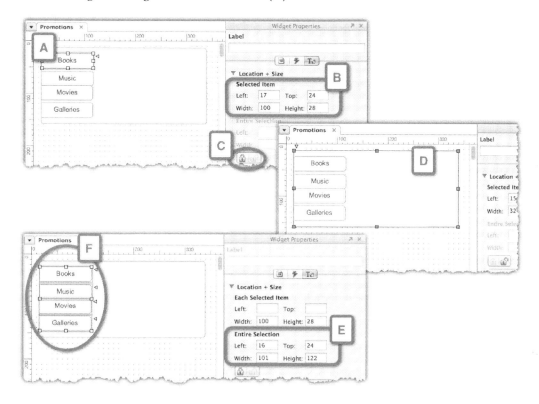

In addition to the attributes of a single selected widget, you can also apply size and location attributes (E), and lock or unlock a group of selected widgets (F). This is useful when you are arranging a group of like-widgets.

Benjamin Franklin was perhaps the person who coined the phrase "A place for everything and everything in its place". While he was probably not talking about wireframes, I like to mention the phrase in the context of wireframe construction and the placement of widgets on a page.

In this section, you can enter the exact height and width of widgets, which is faster than manually reviewing and resizing using the mouse. Additionally, resizing a group of selected widgets "by the numbers" is convenient on various occasions; for example, when you want to uniform a few input form fields.

Finally, knowing the exact position and size of widgets helps when you add interactions that involve moving a widget to a different position.

Font

In this section (see the following screenshot, A), you can modify the font attributes of a single (B), or multiple selected widgets:

- Font family
- Font size
- Font styling, bold, italic and underline
- Font color
- Toggle bullet list styling

The role of typography in your prototype cannot be underestimated. The typeface, its size, styling, color, and spacing can make a sea of difference in how your work will be perceived by stakeholders and end users:

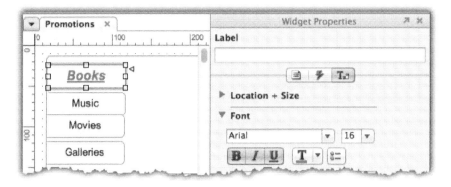

Alignment + Padding

This section is closely associated to the *Font* section, in that it affords control over text attributes in widgets. You can control:

- The horizontal and vertical alignment of text in relation to the widget:
  - ○ Left, center, and right
  - ○ Top, center, and bottom
- The left, top, right, and bottom padding of the text from the edge of a widget
- The line spacing of text lines in the widget

The following screenshot illustrates an example of changing the default settings (A) of a widget (B), and the outcome (C):

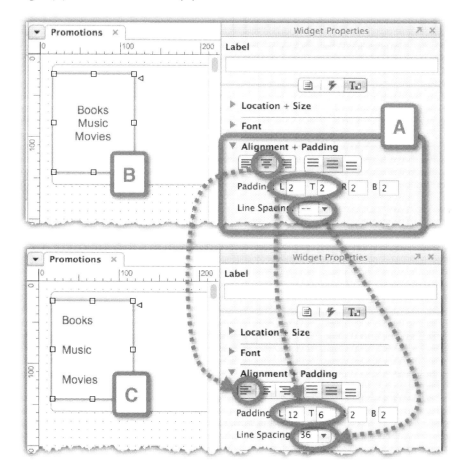

Style

An Axure style is a collection of formatting attributes that can be applied to the shape and text components of a widget. Each widget type in Axure has a default style, which determines how it appears when added to a wireframe and when it is generated in the prototype. Also, note that Axure's concept of style is closely related to CSS. While currently, you cannot associate a CSS file created for your application with your Axure file, it is not difficult to apply the style manually.

There are a few methods to modify the style of a widget, which are illustrated in the following screenshot:

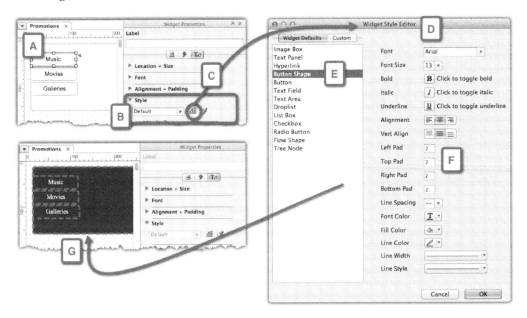

- Manually change various attributes of a selected widget (A) using the Formatting tab, Format bar, or Format menu. This can become slow and repetitive when you want to apply a consistent look across a group of widgets.

- Change the default style of a widget. In the **Style** section (B), click on the **Widget Style Editor** icon (C) to bring the **Widget Style Editor** dialog (D).

- Widget types are listed on the left column. Note that the list is not contextual to the selected image, which means that you have to remember to click on the right item in the list. In addition, the labels are not consistent with those in the **Widget** panel. For example, you will not find the **Rectangle** widget on this list, but its equivalent is labeled **Button Shape** (E).

- Make changes to the various attributes as needed (F) and close the dialog.
- Note, that at this point, as you have modified the default style of the widget, *all* the instances of this widget across all the wireframes in your file will change to reflect the new style (G).

Modifying the default style of widgets can be useful, for example, when you want to change the default font family from Ariel, or font color, from the Hex value of #333333. However, as a widget can be used to create any number of elements across a prototype, modifying the default style is limited. This is where the Axure **Custom Style** feature comes in. The following screenshot illustrates how you can create and apply a custom style:

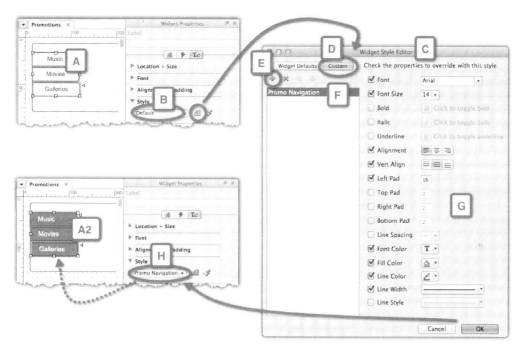

- The selected widgets (A), which are based on the **Rectangle** widget type, have the Default style (B).
- Under the **Widget Style Editor** (C), switch to the **Custom** tab (D), and click on the **Add** icon (E) to create and rename a new style (F). Note, that by default, the custom styles list is empty.
- Configure the new style as needed (G) and close the editor. The new style will be listed in the **Style** drop-list (H) and the style will be applied to all the selected widgets (A2).

- From this point on, you can apply the custom style, and others that you add, to your widgets. By changing the custom style, all the widgets that were assigned this style will be updated instantly — a considerable time saver.

Ordering

The ordering section is straightforward and self-explanatory. When multiple widgets are selected, you can:

- Vertically align widgets to left, right, and center and horizontally align top, middle, and bottom widgets
- Distribute widgets horizontally and vertically
- Group and ungroup widgets
- For a single widget, control it's depth placement relative to other widgets, by placing it in front or back, of all other widgets, or use the a more granular control of pushing it forward and backward so that it is behind some widgets, but in front of others

The following screenshot illustrates the use of the **Ordering** section (A) to left-align and vertically distribute a group of widgets (B) and the end result (B2):

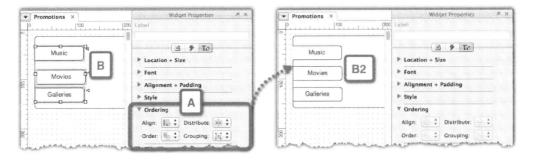

Fills, Lines, + Borders

This section too is straightforward and self-explanatory. You can apply the following attributes to a single or multiple selected widgets:

- Set Fill color
- Set Line color
- Set Line width
- Set Line pattern, otherwise referred to as borders (solid, dotted, and so on)

The following screenshot illustrates the use of the the the **Fills, Lines, + Borders** section (A) to set the line color and border pattern, of a group of widgets (B), and the end result (B2):

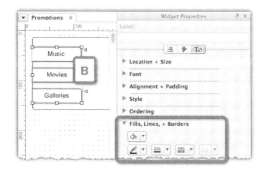 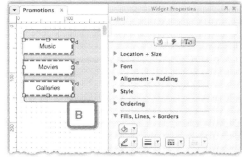

The Wireframe pane

Simply put, in this pane you build your wireframes. You can have multiple wireframes open, each in its own tab. There are three types of wireframes in Axure:

1. **Page wireframes**: You manage and organize these in the **Sitemap** pane.

2. **Master wireframes**: You manage and organize these in the **Masters** pane.

3. **Dynamic Panel States wireframes**: You manage and organize these in the **Dynamic Panel Manager** pane.

Tabs display the name of the wireframe (see the following screenshot, A). You can change the order in which the tabs appear by clicking on a tab and dragging it to the left or right. You can scroll to the left and right using the directional arrows (B), which is useful when there are more open tabs, than can fit into the width of the **Wireframes** pane. The **Tabs** menu (C) lists all the open wireframes (D), and affords quick navigation between tabs when many are open.

Finally, you can close an individual tab by clicking on the close icon (E):

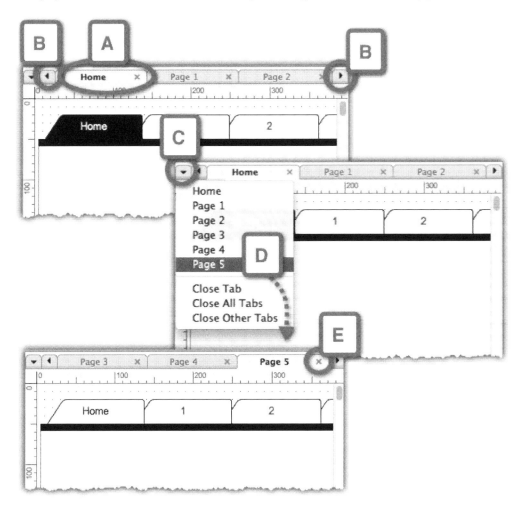

It is common to work with multiple open wireframes. Pretty quickly, you find yourself flipping through the tabs in search of the wireframe you want to focus on next. To quickly clean up a clattered Wireframes pane and isolate only the wireframe you want, use the **Close All Tabs**, and especially, **Close Other Tabs**.

Grid and Guides

Grid and Guides are standard features we come to expect in any graphic software as they provide a visual aid for alignment and composition. In order to access these features, right-click anywhere in the wireframe area, for the **Grid and Guides** context menu (see the following screenshot, A), or, from the **Wireframes** menu. The menu is divided into grid-related options (B) and guide-related options (C):

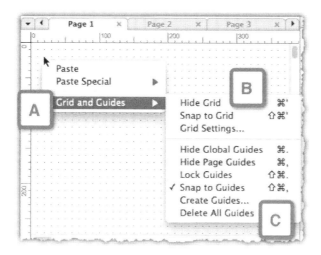

You can control the display of the grid and change its settings from the **Grid Dialog** (see the following screenshot, A), where you select from two types of grids, **Intersection**, (B) or **Line** (C) to set the grid's spacing. Note that the grid is not visible in the HTML prototype or in the screen captures that will be generated in the Word specification document:

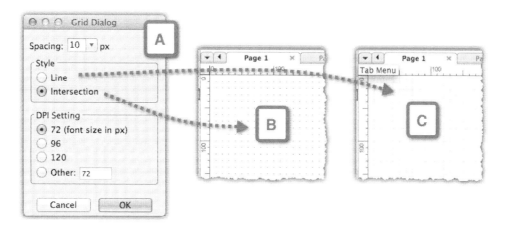

The grid provides a uniform visual backdrop to all wireframes, if you choose to show it. Guides, on the other hand, can be used in a number of ways, depending on your personal method of constructing wireframes, and Axure offers two types of guides that are suitable for a wide range of construction circumstances.

Local guides work well with a more tentative construction mode, which is probably the common approach for rapid, conceptual exploration: You begin by dragging widgets over and placing them as needed. Not much attention is placed on the exact positioning or alignment (see the following screenshot, A). Once the structure is set, guides can help align and space the widget to create a professional and visually pleasing composition (B). As you add other widgets, they can be easily snapped to the appropriate guide for fast alignment and consistent sizing with the existing widgets:

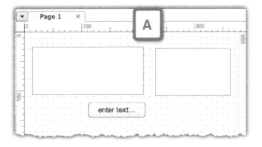 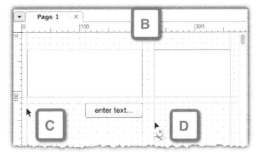

You add new local guides to the wireframes by dragging them from the vertical and horizontal rulers, which is the standard method for guides across graphics software. Selected guides are green and once placed, they are blue. You can lock the guides to prevent unintentional change of their position. Local guides appear only on the wireframe on which they were placed.

Axure's Global guides are meant for a more structured, layout-driven construction. This approach is common in the world of print, such as magazines and books, where guides provide the organizational skeleton for placing content on a page. The idea is to divide the width of the page into a set number of columns. The width of widgets placed on the page, is based on the width of one column. The following screenshot illustrates the concept:

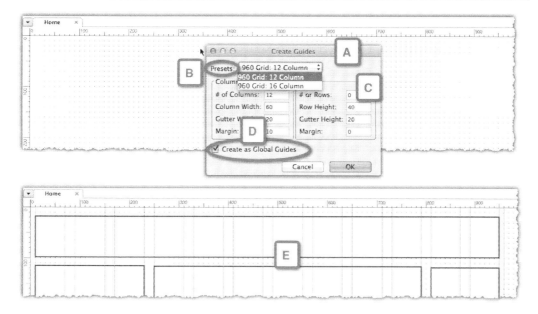

From the **Create Guides** dialog (A), you choose a 12 or 16 column preset from the **Presets** drop-list (B). You can tweak the guides and add rows (C). Finally, you can check the **Create as Global Guides** checkbox (D), so that the guides will appear on all your wireframes.

As you create your wireframe, you set the width of widgets according to the guide. Some widgets can span the width of all columns, others have a one-column width, and so on. You can start thinking about widgets as one column, two columns, and so on. This 'Lego'-like approach helps communications with the development team and as a side benefit, contributes to a visual harmony of the screens, as all elements there are proportionally related.

The current implementation of Axure's Global Guides ties the persistence of the guides across all pages with two specific presets based on the 960 grid system from 960.gs (check out `http://960.gs/` for more information on standardized grid systems). You can change the settings of the presets, but you cannot save your modified guides. This is a new feature in Axure 6, and we are likely to see enhancements to the guides' features in the coming releases.

The Masters pane

As the name suggests, a master is a single wireframe that can be reused on other wireframes. When you change the master wireframe, the change will instantly be applied to all the instances of this master, effectively updating all the wireframes where the master has been placed. There are several good reasons to incorporate masters into your prototype construction as much as possible:

- You can manage consistency of design patterns across the user interface
- You can save yourself an enormous amount of time: Make the update to the master wireframe and Axure will reflect the change on all other relevant wireframes
- You can save more time: Write your annotation once, in the master wireframe, and avoid extra work, redundancy, and errors in the UI Specifications document
- You can reduce the size of your Axure file, because masters reduce the redundancy of duplicated widgets

Use the Masters pane to:

- Manage and organize the project's masters, including the option to add, delete, rename, group in folders, change order, and so on
- Select a master for editing
- Set the behavior of masters on the pages they are placed on
- Add or remove masters from pages
- View usage report: See if a master is actually used in your prototype, or not
- Search masters, a useful feature when you have many masters

The following screenshot illustrates the contextual menu (A), which you get on right-clicking a master or a folder in the Masters pane:

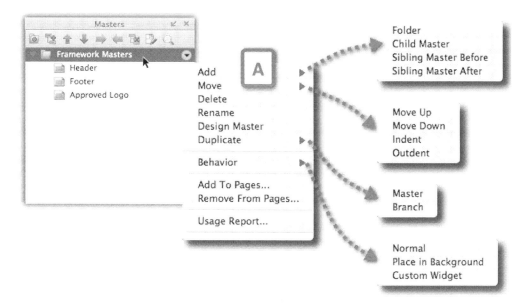

When you are prototyping, you do not always know in advance whether or not a particular element in a wireframe is a repeating element and thus, a good candidate to becoming a master. How do you tell if a widget should be a master? When you copy it from one wireframe and paste it into another. In order to support this type of on-the-go construction, Axure's **Convert To Master** feature provides a really productive method for creating masters out of any widget or collection of widgets on the screen:

1. Select the widgets that make up the reusable object you want to convert to a master (see the following screenshot, A).

2. Right-click and select the **Convert To Master** option (B) from the contextual menu.

3. The **Convert To Master** dialog (C) appears. The verbiage explains that the selected widgets will be replaced by a master containing copies of those widgets. It sounds more complicated than it is.

4. More importantly, replace the default name of the master, from `New Master 1` to some meaningful name. It helps to add the prefix `M-` to a master's name, to help distinguish masters from other wireframes.

Naming conventions are discussed throughout the book, but I cannot stress enough on how important it is to label widgets.

5. Presto! your widgets will be converted to a master. How can you tell? Masters have a red mask which helps identify them on a wireframe.

6. The new master will now be listed in the Masters pane (E):

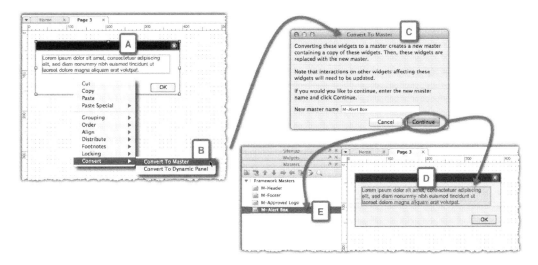

Master behavior

This feature allows you to determine how to apply a master instance to a wireframe. The term behavior is somewhat confusing, but the actual options are straightforward and useful. There are three options:

1. Normal

2. Place in Background

3. Custom Widget

The three options are explained in detail in the following sections:

Normal

This is what Normal master behavior means: Place the master anywhere on a wireframe, update the master, and the changes will be reflected in all the wireframes that have an instance of this master. The only attribute that the master and its instances don't share is the location. The following screenshot illustrates the feature:

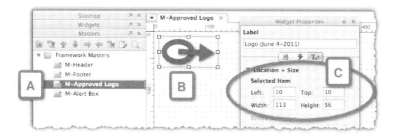

As you begin work on the header part of an application, one of the first elements you might need is the logo. Logos are great candidates for use as masters because they are often placed on multiple pages and you want to make sure that only one approved version of the logo is used across the prototype.

- Create a new master and label it `M-Approved Logo`. The prefix `M` will help you distinguish between master and page wireframes when they are open in the Wireframes pane.

- Use the **Image** widget to import the logo image file into the master page (B). Where you place the logo in the Wireframe pane, does not really matter. I like the upper-left position of a wireframe to always be 10px from the left and top (C).

- In the Home page wireframe (D), place the logo master (E) as needed. In this example, the upper-left corner of the master is at 330px from the left, and 20px from the top (F).

- Over the course of developing the prototype, you might change the logo image, if a new version becomes available. You will make the update only on the M-Approved Logo master wireframe and the Home page wireframe will be updated. However, the placement of the logo on the Home page, or any other wireframe, will never change.

Place in Background

This is what **Place in Background** master behavior means: Place the master on a wireframe, and its location on the wireframe, the left-top position of its left-top corner, will automatically inherit the location of the master. You will not be able to change the location of the master on the wireframes you place it on. All other changes you make to the master will be immediately applied to its instances, just like the **Normal** master behavior. The following screenshot illustrates the feature:

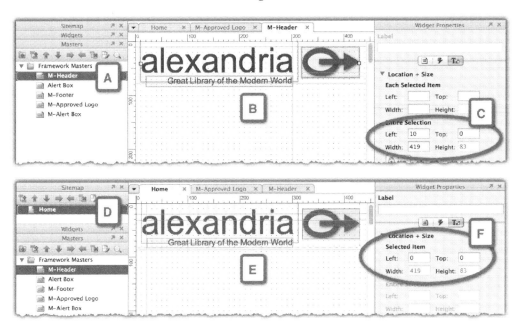

The header part of an application is another example for an element that should be constructed as a master, because it is likely to be used on many wireframes.

- As we want the header to have the same location across all wireframes, let's change its default behavior to Place in Background. Note that the icon of such masters is gray (A), while the icon of masters with Normal behavior, is pink.

- In our example, the header master (B) includes the application name and tag line, and the logo, which is constructed as a master. As you can see, it is possible to include masters in other masters.

- It is important to position the widgets at the location where you want them to appear in wireframes (C).

- On the home page (D), make sure to delete header widgets that you created in earlier iterations. Drag over the header master. The instance of the master will automatically snap to position zero from the left and top of the page (E), and all the widgets of the header master will show a red border when selected, indicating they are locked. You will not be able to change the position in the wireframe. The master will have a gray mask when not selected, as opposed to the pink mask of a master with Normal behavior.

Custom Widget

This is what Custom Widget master behavior means: Place the master anywhere on a wireframe, and that instance loses its tie to its master. Changes that you make to the master wireframe will NOT be applied to its instances. This is the opposite of the **Normal** master behavior.

A master with a **Custom Widget** behavior functions just like a custom widget created in the Widgets pane as part of a custom widget library. Both are instances of templates, which lose their link to the parent master, once they are dragged-over from their respective panes into the wireframe canvas. Changes to a master with a custom widget behavior will not cascade down to its instances.

The main difference between a master with Custom Widget behavior, and a custom widget in a library, is in the method of repurposing and distribution: Custom widgets are stored in special Axure library files (`.rplib`) that can be easily shared and repurposed in other projects.

The following screenshot illustrates the Custom Widget behavior feature: Message, alert, and information boxes are also good candidates to being constructed as masters, but most applications are likely to have several types of each and the flexibility to visualize various examples of messages in the prototype is important.

- Create a new master. Label it **M-Info Box** for example and change its behavior **Custom Widget**(A). Notice that the icon for custom widget masters is a slightly darker gray than that of **Place in Background** masters.

- Continue to wireframe the object (B). The location of the widgets on the wireframe (C) is not important.

- When you place the master on a page (D), the group of widgets that makes up the master has blue borders (E), and is not masked in pink, like a **Normal** master, or gray, like **Place in Background** masters. In fact, at this point, this group of widgets is no longer associated with the master **M-Info Box**.

- At this point, you can make changes to the widgets, just as you would with regular wireframe widgets (F):

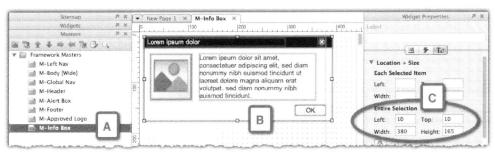

Finally, I want to mention the Flatten master feature which is related to Custom Widget behavior. Sometimes, you want to use a master with Normal or Place in Background behavior as a starting point for another control. You also don't want to modify the existing master. Therefore, we want to break the link from the instance of the master on the wireframe and the master in the Masters pane. This is what Flatten master does and the following screenshot illustrates the feature:

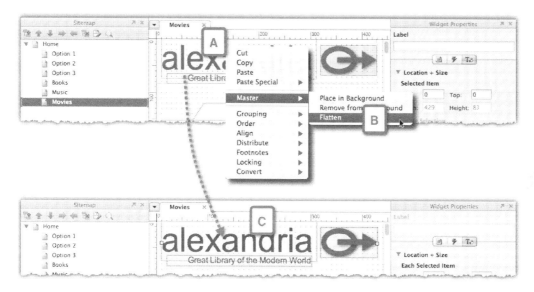

- On the wireframe you are editing, right-click anywhere over the instance of the master you want to "break" (A).

- From the context menu, select **Flatten** (B) from the **Master** option.

- This instance of the master will lose its tie to its parent master and will be converted back to being a collection of widgets (C), which you can edit freely on the wireframe. Changes that you make to the parent master will not be reflected here.

 You can set the behavior of a master when you create the master, or at any time later. If you change the original master behavior, then the new behavior will apply only to instances of masters you place from this point onward. Instances of the master that were placed in wireframes before the change will keep their original behavior.

Usage Report

Change is inherent to the iterative process. You may be working on a wireframe and realize that due to new or changed requirements, a change is needed in a master that is used on the wireframe. Before you proceed with the modification to the master, you remember that all instances of the master will change instantly anywhere this master is used.

The impact of changing a master hastily can be compounded if you are a member of a team that collaborates on an Axure-shared project file. You may not be intimately familiar with the details of wireframes that were created by your colleagues, or with the requirements that guide the design consideration in their part of the work. If you change the master in order to fit it to your page, then the update may come as an unwelcome surprise to your team members. The modification you made to the look and feel of the master, its functionality, or both, may 'break' their wireframes.

In order to solve this problem, Axure offers a useful feature, the masters Usage Report. Right-click on a master in the **Masters** pane (as shown in the following screenshot, A) and select **Usage Report** from the context menu (B). The **Master Usage Report** dialog (C) lists all the pages and other masters, where a particular master is used:

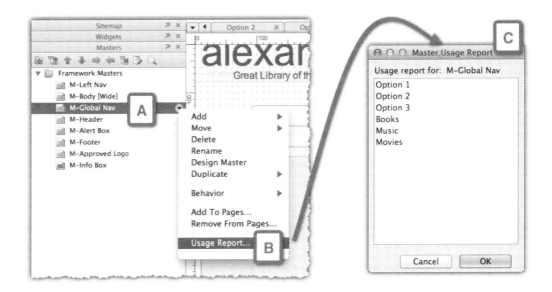

In a shared project situation, the list will help you identify if the master is used on wireframes created by other team members, so you can contact them to discuss changes. You can review the wireframes before making the change and determine the impact on the layout and functionality. Finally, if the list is empty, it means that the master is not used anywhere, and so is a candidate for deletion.

The Dynamic Panel Manager

The name **Dynamic Panel Manager** is a legacy from previous versions. In fact, since Version 6, the pane, which is contextual to the selected wireframe in the **Wireframes** pane, lists all the dynamic panel widgets and all the masters that are used on that wireframe.

Chapter 4, Interactivity 101, covers dynamic panels in depth, but a few words about these widgets are in order here. As its name suggests, Axure's **dynamic panel** widget has something to do with facilitating change, movement, and interaction. It is, in my opinion, the most unique of all Axure's features; the key to our ability to dream-up and communicate the user experience in an engaging way.

The dynamic panel widget stores and displays variations, or **states**, of a portion on the wireframe that needs to render differently based on some context. This widget saves the effort and redundancy of having to duplicate an entire wireframe, just to show several variations of a page section. Dynamic panels are used to construct sophisticated interactions that include animation, visual effects, drag-and-drop, and many others.

A dynamic panel widget is a container. Think about a deck of playing cards—a dynamic panel is the box that holds the cards. The **Dynamic Panel Manager** provides means to view, organize, and edit the individual's cards or states.

We will look at a simple example. The following screenshot illustrates an Axure HTML prototype in a Firefox browser. When the user clicks on the **Sign In** link (A), we want to show a **Sign In** pop up (B):

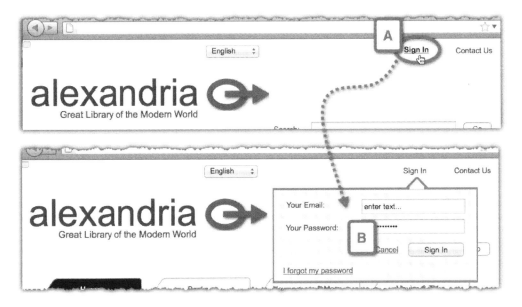

The preceding screenshot illustrates how this functionality is constructed in the Axure file and the role of the Dynamic Panel Manager, which we will shorten here to **DPM**:

- The header master M-Top HeaderBar (A) is open for editing in the **Wireframes** pane. It appears as the top node in the **Dynamic Panel Manager** pane. Notice the pink master icon (A).

- This master's wireframe includes a few dynamic panels and masters, but how can you tell what is going on? In the DPM pane, two items are nested underneath the master (B and C). Their icons indicate that these are **Dynamic Panel** widgets. A twisty next to each indicates that each of those dynamic panels is expandable.

- The **Dynamic Panel** widget (B) is the login pop up (see B in the preceding screenshot). On the master wireframe, it has a light-yellow mask, which indicates that it is a hidden dynamic panel. In the prototype, it becomes visible when the user clicks on the **Sign In** link (see A in the preceding screenshot).

- The **Dynamic Panel** widget (C) contains the Alexandria title and a tag line. On the master wireframe, it has a light-blue mask, which indicates it is a visible dynamic panel.

- Even in this very simple wireframe, dynamic panels and masters overlap and it can become difficult to isolate a specific widget. Use the **Hide** toggle (D) to reduce the visual clutter and focus on the widgets you want to edit. When you click an item in the DPM pane (E), it gets selected in the **Wireframes** pane (F):

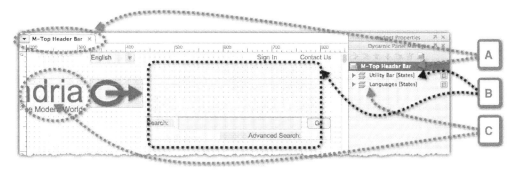

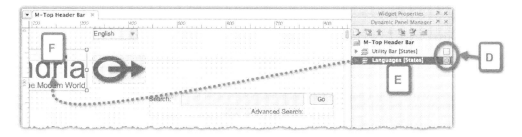

Using masters and dynamic panel widgets to construct wireframes is an efficient practice to create flexible, sophisticated prototypes, and good specifications. As you become more comfortable with the concepts of masters and dynamic panels, your wireframes are likely to become more complex, with nested masters and nested dynamic panels. Axure's **Dynamic Panel Manager** helps you negotiate the complexity by exposing the structure of dynamic panels in the wireframe you are editing.

The following screenshot continues our previous example, which illustrated a master wireframe, with two dynamic panels (A):

- When you expand each of those dynamic panels (B), their states are exposed. The first dynamic panel has two states. A twisty next to the top state (C) indicates that it too, is expandable.

- The second dynamic panel has three states (D).

- Expanding the nested state (C) reveals that it includes a nested dynamic panel (E), which has a single state (F).

Double-clicking on any of the dynamic panels, or their states, from the **Dynamic Panel Manger** opens them for editing, which is extremely convenient. Use the panel's button bar (G) to edit, and/or delete states, and change the order of states in the list:

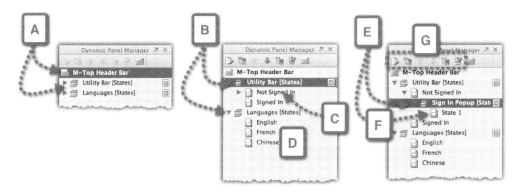

I mentioned at the beginning of this section that the name of this pane is somewhat inaccurate, because since Version 6, the **Dynamic Panel Manager** also exposes the masters that are included in your wireframe. Click on the master icon on the pane's button bar to toggle the visibility of the masters in the DPM (see the following screenshot, A):

- Click once on any of the masters in the list and it is selected in the **Wireframe** pane (B)
- Double-click on any of the masters in the list to open that master for editing in the **Wireframes** tab

In conclusion, when you open a complex wireframe after a few weeks of not working on it, or, if the wireframe was created by someone else, the **Dynamic Panel Manager** is your window to understanding the construction of the wireframe:

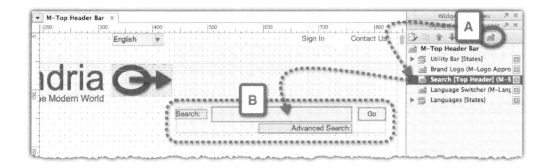

The toolbar and menu bar

Axure's toolbar and menu bar are where Axure's Mac and PC versions are native to their operating system. There is, however, little difference, functionality wise between Axure for Windows and Axure for Mac. Mac users can configure Axure's toolbar (see the following screenshot, A) by right-clicking and selecting **Customize Toolbar** (B) from the context menu. This is standard Mac toolbar behavior. On Mac, formatting functionality is located on the **Format** bar (C), whereas on the Windows side the functionality is organized in toolbars. The toolbar on Axure for Windows (D) has the pre-office 2007-ribbon look:

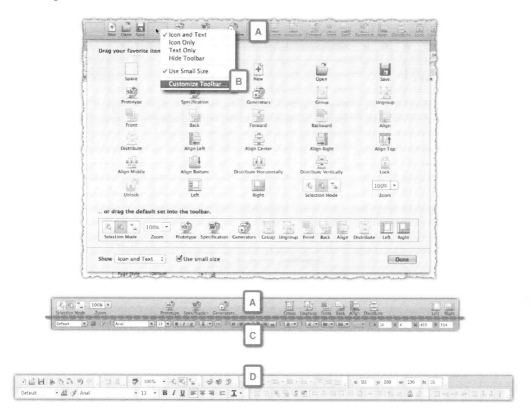

The menu bar is another interface element where the differences between the Mac and Windows version are related to conformity with the operating system. You can control the display of Axure's workspace panes from the View menu, as shown in the following screenshot, A and C with the **View** menu (B and D):

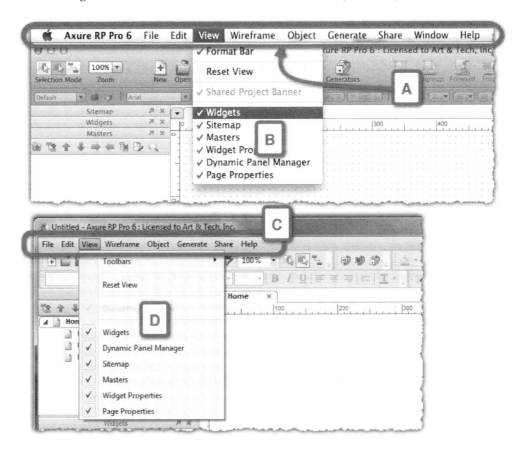

Finally, there is full compatibility between files created on Axure 6 for Mac and Windows. Note, however, that there is no backwards compatibility in either version. This means that, while you can open files created in Version 5.6, in Axure 6, you will not be able to use it again in Version 5.6.

Axure file formats

Axure supports two unique modes of prototype development workflows:

1. The first is focused on the needs of a single designer who is the sole author of the prototype in Axure. Axure's RP file format is the default when you create a new Axure project.

2. The other workflow mode facilitates team collaboration with built-in features such as controlled check in and outs and version control. Axure's RPPRJ file formats this. These powerful features offer so many benefits that a single practitioner should consider using this mode as well.

Earlier in this chapter, in the discussion on the Widgets pane we discussed a third file format, the RPLIB, which you use to create your own custom widget libraries.

The .RP file format (stand-alone)

This format is appropriate if you are the only person ever to need direct access to view or edit the file. In other words, if you are the sole practitioner working on a prototype using Axure, this is the default format to use. Prototypes saved in the RP format are stored as a single file on your local drive, for example, My Project.rp. This method is identical to any other file-based application such as Excel, Visio, or Word.

One of the challenges in UX projects is managing change. Rapid iteration is the essence of prototyping and so, the RP file you are working on will evolve from day to day, often dramatically. Sometimes, however, you need to go back to an older version. Perhaps, you messed something up, or some other reason.

The following screenshot illustrates a simple method I use to organize my Axure work and keep a history of previous iterations:

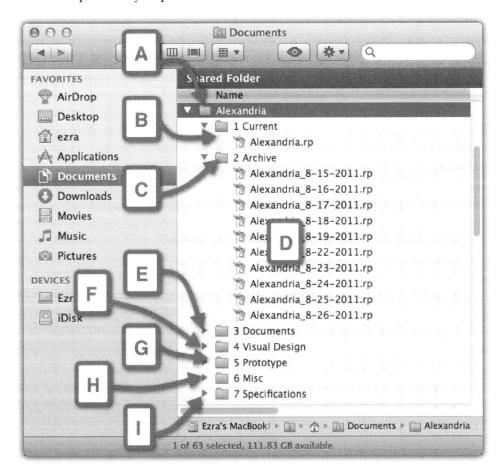

When I start a new Axure project, I create a directory for it (A) with the following subdirectories, which I number in order to control their sorting order:

- **1 Current** (B): This is where I keep the latest version of the file. At the end of the day, I use the **SaveAs** command to save a copy of the file in the `Archive` folder. I append the date to the name of the file. In this way, I have a history of my entire work and at the most may lose 1 day's worth of work.

- **2 Archive** (C): This is where all my previous versions of the project file are stored (D).

- **3 Documents** (E): This is where I use various project documents. I often have to divide it into additional subfolders.

- **4 Visual Design** (F): This is where I keep everything that relates to the visual design such as logos, style guides, and so on.

- **5 Prototype** (G): I generate the HTML prototype to this folder.

- **6 Misc** (H): Odds and ends that don't fit into any of the other directories.

- **7 Specifications** (I): Here I generate versions of the Word document, if specifications are part of the deliverables. I like to keep this directory last, because typically, specifications are the closing effort in the prototyping process, at least when it comes to the active participation of consultants in a project.

The RPPRJ file format (shared project)

This is the appropriate format for a team of UX designers who are collaborating on a UX project. The following screenshot illustrates the model in which the project repository (A) is hosted on a remote server, or a shared directory on the network:

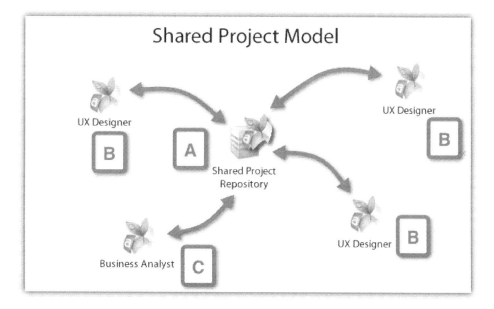

Several UX designers (B) and a BA (C) can access the files simultaneously from their Mac or PC clients, and collaborate on its construction and annotations. The ability to distribute work among multiple resources is very important, especially, for large enterprise projects. The topic of collaboration is discussed at length in *Chapter 9, Collaboration.*

Among the key features of this format are:

- Check out/check in controls
- Ability to cancel check outs, basically a form of undo, if you mess something up in the wireframe and want to start over
- Version control and the ability to restore previous versions

In order to create the shared project, open the `.rp` file in Axure and from the **Shared** menu, select **Create Shared Project from Current File**. Follow the simple wizard and you are all set. In order to create a shared project file from scratch, follow a similar path by opening Axure and using the blank file that opens.

Summary

If you are new to Axure, I hope that this chapter got you excited about wireframing with the tool. If you have been using Axure for a while, I hope that this review helped close a few gaps and informed you about some of the new features in Version 6. If you have not done so already, I highly recommend visiting the Axure's website. It offers a wealth of videos and tutorials that will help you master the tool's rich feature set.

Many users, me included, were able to do productive work with Axure within hours from downloading the trial version (offered for a 30 days evaluation). Axure is quickly becoming a de-facto industry standard for UX work, so it is a good skill to acquire and master. If you plan to purchase Axure, I am confident that you will get a return on your investment very quickly. Finally, if Axure becomes your primary prototyping tool, the more you know about it, the more freedom you will have to express your ideas in a powerful, compelling way.

In the next chapter, we lay down the foundations for the best practice prototyping construction. We cover the concepts of pages, masters and dynamic panels, as well as the methods for constructing scalable and reusable wireframes.

3

Prototype Construction Basics

User experience design is part art, part craftsmanship; the fusion of methodology and patterns with creative problem solving. The prototype plays a major role in the success of UX projects because it is simultaneously a concrete interactive preview of both the vision and the actuality of the application being designed. For the UX designer, Axure offers the ability to deliver simulations of rich interactive user experience, quickly, iteratively, and without having to know programming.

A few years ago, the cost of providing timely interactive prototypes was prohibitive for many companies. Most UX designers are not programmers and so have been limited to producing static wireframes in Visio or similar tools. Skilled developers had to be engaged in order to convert the static wireframes into interactive JavaScript, Dynamic HTML, or Flash simulations.

This was a mini development effort that required the UX designer to invest a significant amount of time to communicate interaction flows and the behavior of various widgets to the developer, and later help debug the simulation. Once a prototype has been coded, it typically reflected an outdated version of the actual static wireframes because in the meanwhile, the wires were subject to a number of iteration cycles.

With Axure, UX designers can create very sophisticated interactive prototypes without having to know how to code or having to engage developers in order to create the simulation. The gap between our ability to imagine the experience and articulate it in the prototype had closed. With this power also comes a demand for prototyping methods, techniques, and best practices. As projects have so many processes after all, why re-invent the wheel.

In this chapter, we cover how to set up a solid foundation for an Axure file.

Prototyping principles

I would like to propose three simple, project-agnostic guiding principles to prototyping, which you can keep in mind as you approach a new UX project and throughout the effort:

- *Estimate, plan, and keep re-evaluating* the prototyping and specifications effort. This will go a long way to help you deliver on vision, on time, and on budget while maintaining your sanity.

- *Master the tools you are using, including Axure.* The tools we master and the quality of our craftsmanship help shape our deliverables, and in turn increase the confidence of our clients and partners in our expertise and in the vision we help shape.

- *Just because you can do it in Axure does not mean you have to.* Be strategic about the amount of low-level high fidelity details to which you are committing.

Throughout the book, I will demonstrate the application of these principles to real life scenarios using a demonstration project or sample snippets, which you can download from `http://www.packtpub.com/support`. You will find that, although many of the ideas and best practices are presented in the context of Axure, they are in fact tool-agnostic and can help you in your work even if you use other prototyping tools.

Alexandria, the Digital Library Project

Elephants and mice share common ancestors and similarly, albeit oddly compared, UX projects for the global enterprise, share the DNA of much smaller UX projects. Core activities such as discovery, user and application research, requirements gathering, iterative design, and usability testing are fundamental to user-centered design despite potentially profound differences in the scale and complexity of the projects.

The book's sample project simulates the design process of a digital library web and mobile application, named after the city that was home to the largest library of ancient times, Alexandria. The choice of this subject matter was driven by the many opportunities to demonstrate numerous Axure features and techniques, in the context of an application that conceptually, is familiar to most readers.

Of course, there are many ways to skin a UX project and obviously, the demo project is a much simplified, abstracted version of what happens in reality, where the process involves rapid cycles of iterative design as we move from the concept to the detailed design. Still, the goal is to demonstrate the process of developing an interactive prototype and generating UI functional specifications with Axure from the ground up.

Any prototype incorporates many inputs that inform the design approach, including:

- Business requirements
- Feedback from users and stakeholders
- Intermediate usability tests to validate the proposed design

We begin the demo project by incorporating some high-level requirements and use cases, which serve as the foundation of a high-level, conceptual framework for the wireframing and prototyping phase. It will be an opportunity to discuss how Axure's diagramming capabilities feed the wireframing process. We will move to construction methods that include masters and dynamic panels, and include some examples of iteration and feedback that will require a rework of our initial construction.

As we dive into topics such as interactions, widget libraries, styling, and annotations, the demo project helps visualize various concepts and construction methods, when applicable. From a workflow perspective, we begin with a stand-alone RP file, Axure's default file format, and discuss collaboration extensively in *Chapter 9*, when we convert the project into a shared project RPPRJ file to demonstrate teamwork features and workflows. Throughout, we consider various prototyping and specifications activities in the context of the overall project plan, development methodologies, effort, and resources estimation.

Getting started—productivity in 30 minutes

Pardon the gimmicky header, but I want to emphasize Axure's value proposition as a primary UX design application. Any tool must balance its cost, feature set, and ease of use. If you purchase software with your own funds, clearly you ask: "If I invest time and money in this new tool, how soon can I be productive and do actual work?" In the case of Axure, the answer is days, often hours, and minutes, which will be the case for most of the activities outlined in this chapter.

In many projects, the initial use of Axure will be to develop a **vision** prototype, or a **proof of concept** (POC)—a high-fidelity, polished, and clickable prototype. More than anything else, it is a sales tool which plays a major role in rallying top management to support major investment in the next generation of a software product, or to persuade investors to bet on a new venture. Key attributes of the POC are:

- Not burdened too much by detailed business, functional, or technical requirements
- Highly interactive simulation that highlights new features of the proposed approach to innovative user experience
- Highly polished execution that incorporates branding and visual design

The POC articulates the appearance and behavior of the new software. It presents its "look and feel" in the best of all possible worlds. The closer the actual product ends up being to the vision, the better job we did as UX architects. It is an opportunity to think "out of the box", while keeping in mind the fact that a box does exist in the form of budgetary and technical constraints.

Therefore, let's assume you have already completed some of the initial project tasks, including:

- Strategy sessions with various stakeholders in the company
- Contextual interviews with end users
- Establishing a base line by conducting usability studies of the existing application
- Reviewing of competitive and related applications
- Analyzing the site's content
- Developing the taxonomy and global navigation
- Having a list of key features and user flows
- Developing personas and a matrix of user roles and their key tasks
- Having high-level business requirements

With this solid understanding of the product and its intended users, you are ready to dive into Axure and unleash your creative energies. In this chapter, you will learn how to use Axure to:

- Create use-case diagrams
- Create interaction flow diagrams
- Create Pages, Masters, and Dynamic panels

Initial requirements and use cases

Based on discovery activities conducted so far, you have a list of high-level requirements that provide a core set of guidelines and define the product offerings. In some projects, the list of business requirements is handed to you, and in other projects, you can play a key role in their development. Regardless, the requirements should not define the user experience. Rather, our contribution as UX designers is to translate the requirements into an excellent practical user experience.

Let's digest the first set of requirements:

1. From the home page, the user should be able to *browse* or *search* the library.
2. The user should be able to get more information about a title without leaving the home page.
3. Each title should have a dedicated page with full *details*, as well as preview capabilities.
4. The user should be able to search the library from any page, using either a *simple* Google type search box or an *advanced* search feature.
5. Search *results* will be presented in a list of matching titles.
6. The user should get more information about a title without having to leave the search results screen.
7. From the search results screen, the user should be able to access any title's *detail* page.
8. If no matching titles are found, then provide the user with a relevant *notification*.

Good requirements can be easily broken into short and unambiguous sentences with a syntax that includes the user, a user action, and the interaction outcome. In other words, each of these sentences becomes a **use case**. Use case methodology is beyond the scope of this book, but a wealth of information on this subject matter is available.

The high-level requirements with which we started, drive the following use cases:

*   *Browsing* items of the library
*   *Searching* the library for specific item(s) with Simple search
*   *Searching* the library for specific item(s) with Advanced search
*   *Viewing* search results
*   *Viewing* item details

Axure is an integrated wireframing, prototyping, and specifications system. It means that we can start developing the specifications document in parallel to the wireframing and prototyping effort. Diagrams are a good example of important documentation that can be created in Axure and generated in the Word specification document.

Use case diagram page

When you launch Axure, it opens with a blank new file with a home page and three nested siblings (see the following screenshot, A). I recommend keeping the structure and flow pages, such as use case and flow diagrams, in a section above the wireframe pages. Note that the order of pages in the **Sitemap** pane is the order in which those pages will appear the HTML prototype and Word specifications table of contents. By placing the structure and flow pages first, you control the logical narrative that provides high-level abstractions, such as user flows, before moving into the actual wireframes and interaction. This will work well in early review meetings, as you describe the prototype. Additionally, in a later stage, readers of the UX specification will be able to form a clear idea of the application by following the page progression.

In the **Sitemap** pane, add a **New Sibling** page above the **Home** page (B) as shown in the following screenshot:

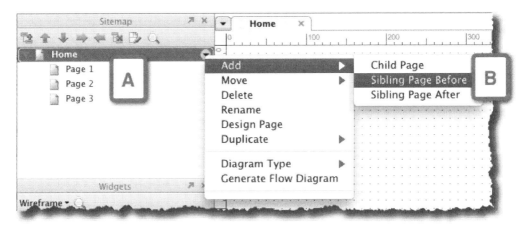

Double-click on this new page to open it as a tab in the **Wireframe** tab. Next, rename the new page **Use** Cases. (as shown in the following screenshot, A). Axure provides a method to differentiate between wireframe pages and diagram pages: Right-click and select the **Flow** option (B) from the **Diagram Type** contextual menu. Notice that the page icon (C) has changed making it easier to distinguish between wireframe and flow pages:

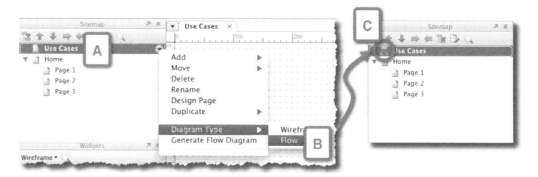

Wireframe and Flow pages are identical in all aspects except the icon to the left of their name.

Next, select the **Flow** widget library (see the following screenshot, A) in the **Widgets** pane. Drag out the **Actor** widget (B) to the page. This stick figure is the standard representation of users in **UML** and most diagramming methodologies. Drag out an **Ellipse** widget and label it **Browse Path** (C). The Ellipse is the UML notation for a use case. Continue to add and label ellipse widgets as needed:

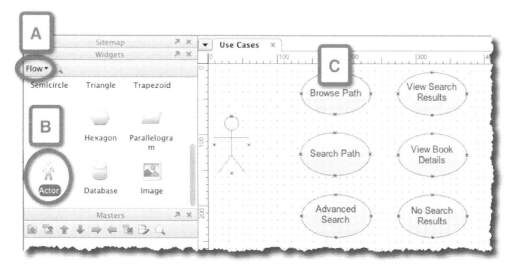

In order to complete the use case diagram, we want to connect the actor widget to the use cases and organize the widgets nicely on the page for a polished presentation. Begin with the layout and organize the cases in a vertical order that follows a logical progression of possibilities.

This is a great opportunity to get familiarized with Axure's three selection modes, which facilitate moving and arranging widgets on wireframe and flow pages. You can find the **Selection** Mode on the Axure's toolbar. (See the following screenshot, A for the Windows version, and B for the Max version.)

1. **Select Intersected Mode** (C): This is Axure's default mode. When you click and drag your mouse over the wireframe, all the widgets that are part of your selection area, even if they were only partially included in it, are selected.

2. **Select Contained Mode** (D): In this mode, only widgets that are fully included in your selection are selected.

3. **Connector Mode** (E): This mode is most effective when you work with Flow widgets because it generates connector lines that you can use to hook up the various flow widgets in your diagrams.

Personally, I prefer the **Select Contained Mode** over the default **Select Intersected Mode**, because it provides precision by including only items fully encompassed by my selection, leaving out others that are in close proximity:

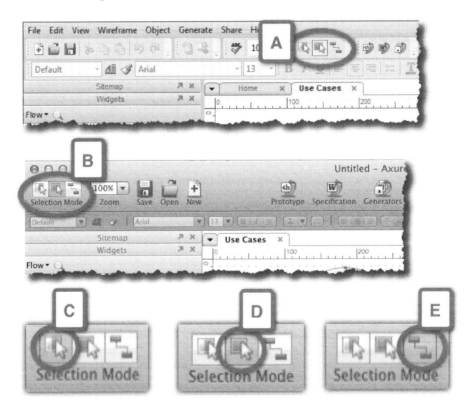

In order to organize widgets on a page, use the tools in the **Object** toolbar. The following screenshot shows the tools on the Mac version; the identical tools are on the Windows version:

- Group and ungroup objects (A)
- Move forward or backwards, top or bottom (B)
- Align objects left, right and middle and top, bottom and center (C)
- Distribute objects horizontally and vertically (D)
- Lock and unlock objects (E)

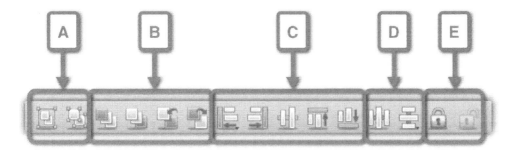

Select a group of widgets in the use case page, as illustrated in the following screenshot, and use the **Align** (A) and **Distribute** (B) options on the toolbar to balance the cases on the page:

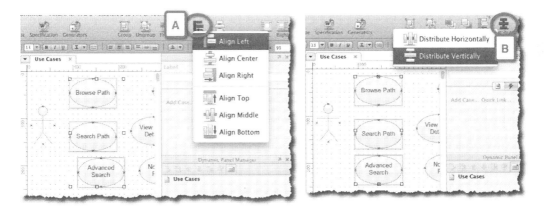

With all the use cases vertically aligned and evenly distributed, group them together using the **Group** option on the toolbar. Select this group and, while holding the *Shift* key, select the **Actor** widget. Use the **Align Middle** option to have the Actor facing the use cases.

Next, switch to the **Connector** mode and draw lines from the **Actor** widgets to each of the use cases. You should end up with a page that looks something similar to the following screenshot:

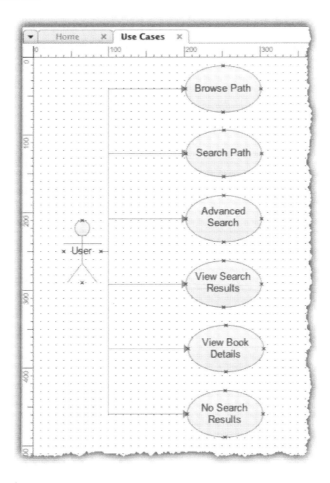

Saving the project file

To paraphrase the joke on Chicago elections: Save your work early and often. In my experience, Axure is very stable, but long ago, I developed the instinct to save my work frequently. In addition to the standard save, I recommend a strategy to support iterative design work: Use the **Save As** command at the end of each day to create an archive of daily versions of your RP file. It is also a good idea to use the **Save As** command before making dramatic changes to key wireframes.

Here is why: Your Axure file will evolve rapidly to incorporate a tremendous amount of detail, as you address increasingly finer requirements. Ideas that looked initially promising will not work as well as you thought. Feedback from stakeholders and users will require more changes, sometimes requiring that you backtrack to the previous version.

It is in your best interest then, to maintain an on-going history of your Axure file. When you work on a stand-alone file (.RP), this means that you are responsible for managing the revision history. I am not talking here about merely backing up your file, which is a given.

For managing the history of revisions, a technique or rather, a behavior that works for me is quite simple and easy to implement: At the end of each workday, save the file. Then, use **Save As** to save the file in an archive directory and append the date to the file name. The next day, open the file from the current directory. With this method, you will always be able to restore or find previous items and add them back to the current file, if needed.

First wireframe pages

With initial use cases in place, let's move forward to create relevant wireframe pages. The pages that immediately come to mind are:

- Home Page
- Search Results Page
- Item Details Page

As you might have noticed, when you launch Axure, it opens a new document similar to an MS Office application, such as Word or PowerPoint. You will see in the **Sitemap** pane that Axure places a **Home** page and three nested pages. This is the default for each new Axure file.

Rename the non descript **Page 1** and **Page 2** labels of the nested pages (see the following screenshot, A) to something more meaningful, and delete **Page 3**. Your **Sitemap** pane should look something similar to the following screenshot, (B):

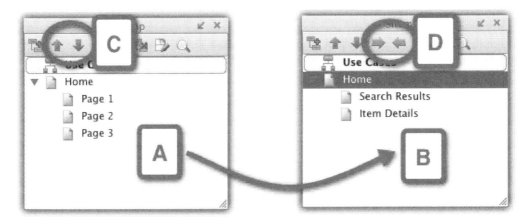

You can change the order of pages by using the move up and move down arrows (C), and change their nesting level by using the indent and outdent arrows (C).

Task flow diagram page

A prototype is tailored to visualize and demonstrate the user experience. Before we can develop the demonstration, we really need to nail down key user tasks which are, after all, the reason for the existence of the application. As the scope of this book limits our discussion of the topic to the context of Axure, I will focus on the aspect of creating task flow diagrams.

Task flow diagrams are a model, an abstraction of the Ping-Pong exchange that makes up user-system interaction. These diagrams also play an important role in:

- Validating the sequence and logic of each task with business and technical stakeholders
- Developing an agreement on which flows and parts of flows should be prototyped, and to what level of fidelity

The diagrams should be shaped by explicit context, which is determined by a combination of inputs, including:

- What the system knows about the given user
- The options afforded to the user by the system
- The user's actions

While there are no set standards for UX flow diagrams, keep in mind that clarity, precision, and organization would help you during joint sessions with stakeholders.

Axure provides a one-stop shop for creating both flow diagrams and the wireframes that are associated with them. The ability to use a single application for modeling, simulating and documenting the user experience, gives us a powerful work environment.

Two main flows that immediately come to mind in the context of Alexandria involve browsing and searching. In the first option, the user can browse titles on the home page and drill down for more details. The other path lets the user search for a set of titles, or for a specific title. Matches are presented in the search result list and the user can drill down to the details of a desired title. Thus, both paths may end on the same item-detail page.

Let's create a couple of task flow diagram pages, one for modeling the browse path and the other for search. In the **Sitemap** pane, add the two siblings below the Use Case diagram page. Label the pages and use the **Diagram Type** menu to change their icon to mark them as flow pages.

Browse path flow diagram

In order to compose the diagram, carry out the following steps:

1. Double-click to open the **Browse Path** page in the **Wireframes** pane.

2. From the **Widgets** pane, drag over the **Actor** widget.

3. Now comes the cool part: From the **Sitemap** pane drag over the Home page — it is the entry point to this flow. Notice that the widget inherits its label from its parent page on the **Sitemap** pane. Also note the document icon on the upper-left corner of the widget (see the following screenshot, A). It means that when you generate the HTML prototype, clicking on this widget will link to the actual Home page.

4. From the **Sitemap** pane, drag over the **Item Details** page.

5. Select the shapes and use **Align Middle** and **Distribute Horizontally** to clean up the presentation.

6. Change to **Connector Mode** to draw connectors from the Actor widget to the Home page and from there to the Item Details page. Use the **Arrow Style** options to add directional arrowheads to the connectors.

7. In order to add an interaction label to the arrow, add a glossary using the Wireframe library widgets and you have just completed your first flow diagram in Axure. It should look similar to the one shown in the following screenshot:

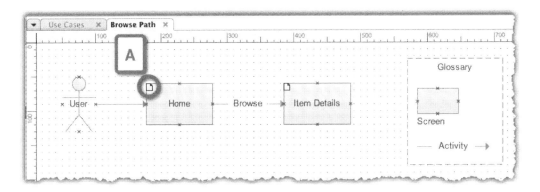

Search path flow diagram

The initial requirements call for two search features:

- Simple search
- Advanced search

Both methods take the user through a similar path: If any matches are found, they are displayed in the **Search Results** page (see the following screenshot, A) and the user can drill down to the **Item Details** page (B). If no matches are found, then the user can run a new search.

As you complete the search path, you realize that it exposes an important risk. If users run either a simple or an advanced search but do not find what they are looking for, then there is a possibility that the users would abandon the flow (C) and move on to another site. The justification for providing powerful, simple, and advanced search features should be tied to the strategic importance of Search in the application. This is an example of strategic insight that underscores the business value of developing supporting diagrams for the prototype:

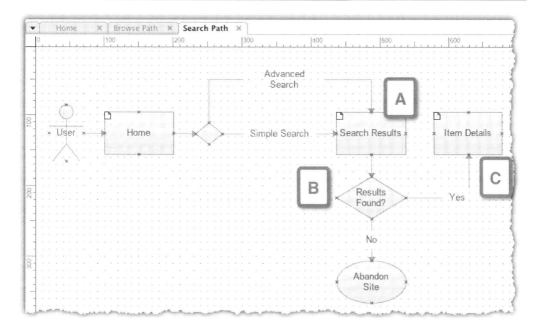

Link use cases to flow diagrams

In addition to being able to create and store diagrams and wireframes within the same application, you can link Axure diagrams and wireframes to create a seamless transition from the one to the other:

1. Open the **Use Cases** page in the **Wireframe** pane.

2. Right-click on the **Browse Path** use case and select the **Edit Reference Page** option (see the following screenshot, A) from the **Edit Flow Shape** submenu.

3. The **Reference Page** pop-up (B) lists all the pages in the **Sitemap** pane.

4. Select the **Browse Path** page to link the use case to the page and close the pop up.

5. Notice the reference page icon (D) that now appears on the upper-left corner of the use case. The behavior of the widget has changed: Before it is associated with a reference page, double-clicking on it enables the editing of the widget's label. By double-clicking on it, it references another page in the sitemap to open the **Reference Page** pop up. This is because the widget's title inherits the title of the referenced page and is no longer editable:

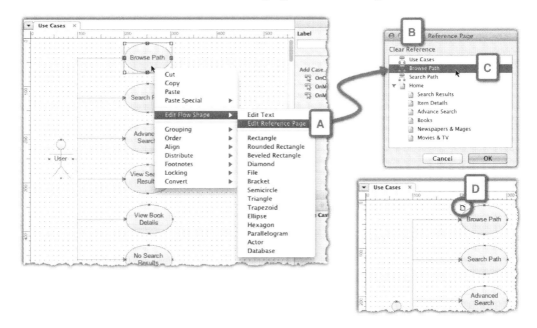

Generating the HTML prototype

It is now time to generate your first HTML prototype to review the work you have completed so far. As your prototype advances, you will find yourself generating previews quite often in order to validate that the HTML output works in the way you intended.

Accessing the HTML prototype generation feature is accomplished either from the toolbar icon or from the **Generate** menu. The **Generate Prototype** dialog (see the following screenshot (A) for the Windows version and (B) for the Mac version), allows you to specify various settings that impact the output. However, at this early point, you want to start with the **General** section (C) and let Axure know where to output the HTML prototype.

Either use Axure's default for the destination folder, a directory labeled "Axure Prototypes" in your `Documents` folder or keep all your project work under the same directory, as described in *Chapter 2*. This makes it easier to find all your project stuff, especially when you want to transport or backup up your work.

Firefox is the recommended browser, but you can specify your choice in the **Open With** section (D). Each time you generate the HTML prototype, it opens a new browser tab. It is a good idea to bookmark the page after the first time you generate the prototype, and from then on, use the **Do Not Open** option to reduce the proliferation of open tabs in the browser. Just generate and refresh the page:

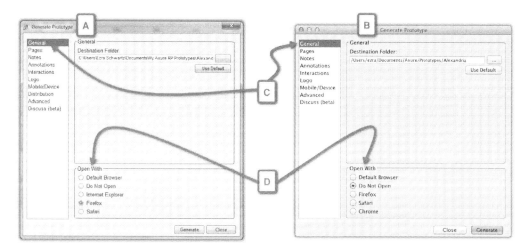

Hit the **Prototype** icon to generate the HTML prototype. The screen is divided into two sections:

- On the left, a pane with two tabs: the **Sitemap** and **Page Notes**. The **Sitemap** tab (see the following screenshot, A) is selected by default.
- The main body which displays the diagram or wireframe; the top page in the **Sitemap** is the default.

In our example, the **Use Cases** page (B) is selected in the **Sitemap** pane and displayed in the main section of the screen. As you roll your mouse over the **Browse Path** use case (C), notice that the cursor changes indicating an active link, which on click, will load the referenced **Browse Path diagram** page (D). Alternatively, clicking on the icon in the lower-right corner of the use case (E) opens the referenced page in a new tab. In our example, the **Browse** Path diagram shows the **Home** and **Item Details** page. The boxes in the diagram were made by dragging over the actual pages from the **Sitemap**.

Now, in the HTML prototype, these boxes too have a link icon (F), and clicking on the box of the icon links to the referenced wireframe page:

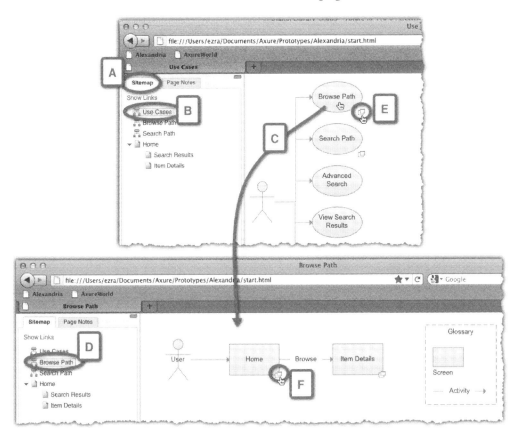

To summarize what we have covered so far:

- Creating use case diagrams
- Creating task flow diagrams
- Referencing and linking flow and wireframe pages from diagrams
- Generating an HTML prototype

Even an Axure novice can complete the activities we covered above in 30 minutes or so, and create a meaningful piece of work. As you continue to build the prototype, the underlying use cases and task flow will always be available for confirmation and validation.

Getting started with masters and dynamic Panels

With the foundation in place, we will now move on to develop some rough wireframes, focusing our attention to high-level requirements and the information gathered thus far. Here are some high-level, conceptual questions to develop:

- Information architecture: How is information organized and accessed on each screen?
- What are the main navigation systems?
- What are common components that are shared across screens?

The first wireframe

Often you might have a gut feeling about the general organization of the layout, based on experience and familiarity with similar applications. The header, footer, and body will serve as initial placeholders for deeper exploration.

Axure's HTML prototypes have fixed width. In other words, you cannot design an elastic wireframe which will adjust to the device's display. Therefore, it is important to decide what will be the wireframe's maximum width before placing widgets on the page. The decision can be simple, if the target device is known. iPhone, for example. If the application is device-agnostic, you are still likely to create wireframes for standard display and wireframes optimized for mobile experience.

Therefore, in our Alexandria Digital Library project, we start the home page by outlining three layout blocks with **Rectangle** widgets:

- Header
- Body
- Footer

The quick and dirty approach

This approach often does not bother with restrictions such as maximum wireframe width, widgets alignment and spacing, and other composition considerations. Wireframes are placed on the pages quickly and tentatively with a lot of copy-and-paste of similar widgets to speed up the construction. This approach can be compared to stream-of-consciousness writing, and for some, it is a great way to get ideas out.

The quick but structured approach

This approach is based on the principal that a small, upfront investment of time at the start of wireframe construction can pay off big-time later in the project.

Our first set of wireframes will be for a web-based application, so let's start by applying a new feature to Axure 6, the **Global Guides**, which is discussed in *Chapter 2*. The **960 Grid: 16 Column** option (see the following screenshot, A) establishes the maximum width for wireframes to 960 pixels. Additionally, the left and top margin for widgets is easy to maintain consistently at 10 pixels (B):

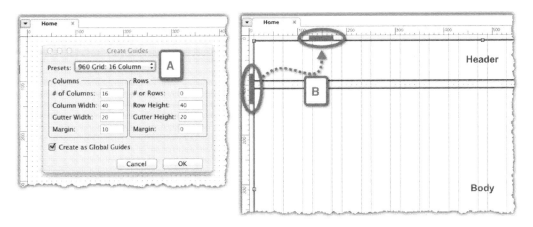

From the **Widgets** pane, drag over three **Rectangle** widgets. Resize and organize them as header, body, and footer blocks as illustrated in the following screenshot. With Axure's **Zoom** feature (A), you can adjust the display of the wireframe area, to get a better sense of the entire composition, a useful feature when you want to move or resize wide objects. Based on the **960 Grid** system (B), you can snap the blocks 10 pixels from the left and set their width to 940 pixels (C) leaving a 10 pixel margin from the right. Double-click on each widget to type in their label:

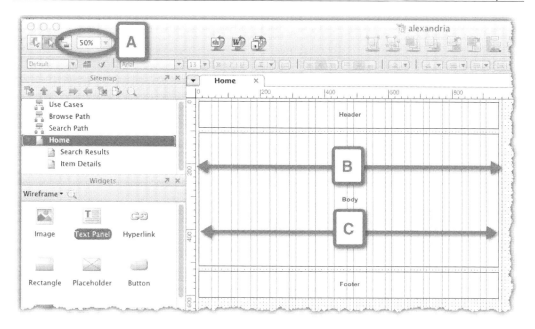

First masters: navigation systems

The home page is probably the most important page for websites just as it is for applications. However, in a world of deep links, the user's first interaction with a site often begins on other sites or search engines that link pages other than the home page. At a glance, the user should be able to discern:

- Where they are
- What the landing page is about
- Which actions are available in the context of the page and the site
- Where to navigate within the site

In order to develop the navigation systems for the application, we need to expand on the initial business requirements. The revised first requirement is:

1. From the home page, the user should be able to *browse* or *search* the library. For the Release 1, the library will offer subscribers three types of media:
    ° Electronic books
    ° Electronic newspapers and magazines
    ° Streaming movies and TV shows

2. For each type of media, the user should be able to select from a list of genres:
   ° Electronic books:
       ° Fiction
           ° Classics
           ° Humor
           ° Mystery
           ° Romance
           ° Thrillers
       ° Non fiction
           ° Advice
           ° Biography
           ° Cooking
           ° Sports
           ° Textbooks
   ° Newspapers and magazines
       ° Newspapers
           ° US Newspapers
           ° Chicago Tribune
           ° New York Times
           ° Washington Post
       ° World Newspapers
           ° The Hindu
           ° Le Monde
           ° Times of London
       ° Magazines
           ° (Release 1 US only)
           ° The Atlantic
           ° Popular science
           ° Wired magazine

3. The titles of newspapers and magazines listed in the navigation cannot be abbreviated.

In requirements discussions, business stakeholders emphasize the importance of listing the titles of available publications in a prominent way to draw the attention of potential subscribers.

We are obviously limited in space here and cannot continue to list all the subcategories for each of the media types. However, equipped with an initial taxonomy, we can begin the development of our global navigation.

Note the appearance of the phrase "Release 1" which helps define the scope of work planned for the initial launch. It also implies that future releases will expand on the initial offering, so scalability and flexibility should be an important design consideration.

Global navigation bar

In order to facilitate access to each of the media types offered in the library, you decide to try a horizontal navigation bar that will appear on all pages, thus making it a global element.

There are several benefits to this approach:

- It communicates very explicitly the type of offerings in the library
- It is very easy to navigate from one segment to another
- It is a common navigation element and most users will be familiar with it

There are also some drawbacks to consider, such as:

- There is a scalability limit of how many categories can be placed horizontally
- Where and how to present items of various media types

At this point, the benefits appear to outweigh the potential problems, so let's move to Axure. The navigation bar should be positioned between the header and main body, as illustrated in the following screenshot, A:

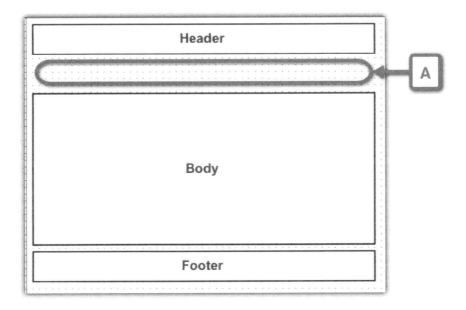

In order to construct the global navigation, carry out the following steps:

1. Drag over a **Rectangle** widget (see the following screenshot, A), right-click on it, and from the **Edit Button Shape** contextual menu, select **Tab Left** (B). The rectangle shape will turn into the familiar tab shape (C).

2. Resize the widget to fit the space between the header and body blocks (D). If you are using the 960 grid, then you will find it easy to size and snap the widget. Double-click and label the tab **Home** (E).

3. Copy the tab widget and paste it three times.

4. Distribute and align the widgets in a horizontal row. Again, the grid will be helpful.

5. Label the three tabs **Books**, **New & Mags**, and **Movies & TV**. (F)

6. Save your work:

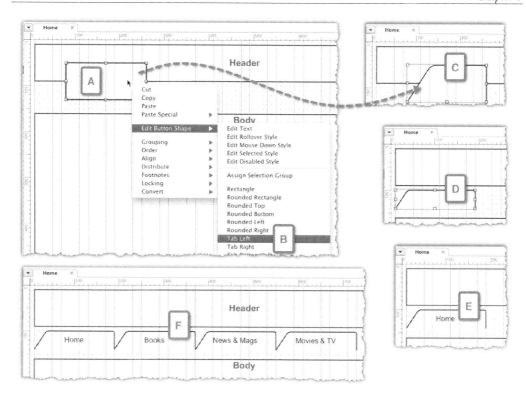

At this point, we have to add three main category pages to correspond to the tabs in the global navigation: Books, News & Mags, and Movies & TV. These, and the home page, will share the same global navigation element. We have two options to continue from here:

- Use the "quick and dirty" method to simply duplicate the home page, rename it, and adjust the widgets on each duplicated page. The drawback is that changes to repeating elements, such as the global navigation, will have to be applied manually to all wireframes. This approach is fast initially, but costly in the long run.

- Use the somewhat slower but structured method of converting all the repeating elements on the home page into masters, then duplicating it to create the category pages. The masters will be reused, thus saving time in the long run and ensuring construction consistency across pages. This is the approach which will be demonstrated next.

We are going to demonstrate the second approach, using masters. Masters are components of the user interface that appear on multiple pages. When you edit the master, all of its instances in the prototype are immediately updated. A twist that Axure has added to masters is that, while the look and feel of a master is identical wherever you use it, its behavior can be tailored to fit the context in which it is used. We will discuss this feature named **Raised Event** in *Chapter 5*, *Advanced Interactions*.

Therefore, our first master will be the global navigation bar:

1. In the **Wireframes** pane, switch off the home page select the group of four tabs that make up the global navigation bar (see the following screenshot, A).

2. Right-click anywhere within the selection and in the contextual menu select the **Convert To Master** option (B) from the **Convert** submenu:

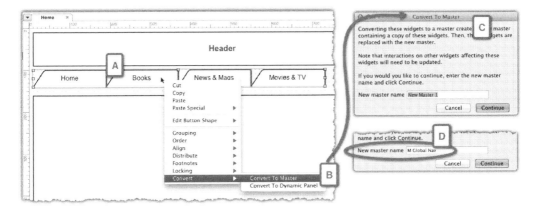

3. Axure will prompt you with a **Convert To Master** dialog as shown in the preceding screenshot (C). Take a moment to read the text:

   ◦ **Converting these widgets to a master creates a new master containing a copy of these widgets**: This means that a new master will be added in the **Masters** pane.

   ◦ **Then, these widgets are replaced with the new master. Note that interactions on other widgets affecting these widgets will need to be updated**: This means that a single item, the master, will replace the four discrete images that you placed in the wireframe. The master, which is an independent wireframe, now has those four widgets. When we discuss interactions later in the book, the impact of this procedure will become meaningful.

○ **If you would like to continue, enter the new master name and click Continue**: This is really important! Before you click on the **Continue** button, make sure to re-label the master, replacing the default and generic New Master 1, with something meaningful, and then click on the **Continue** button. We will discuss naming convention strategies in *Chapter 4*.

 Start the name of each master with an `M.` for example, `M Global Nav`. The prefix will make it easier for you to identify which open wireframes are masters.

You will immediately notice a change in the way the navigation bar looks: The following screenshot shows a visual comparison of the before and after states: The four selected widgets (A), are now grouped together (B) and the entire block now has a pink shade which helps you distinguish masters from other widgets.

The new master appears in the **Masters** pane (C). Keep in mind that the **Masters** pane is not contextual to a specific wireframe. Rather, it is the repository of all the masters you have in your project file. However, the **Dynamic Panel Manager** pane is contextual to the edited wireframe page. Clicking on the **Include Masters** icon (D) lists the new master (E) under the Home page. Note that the master is listed as: **Unlabeled (M Global Nav)**. We will deal with the naming issue shortly:

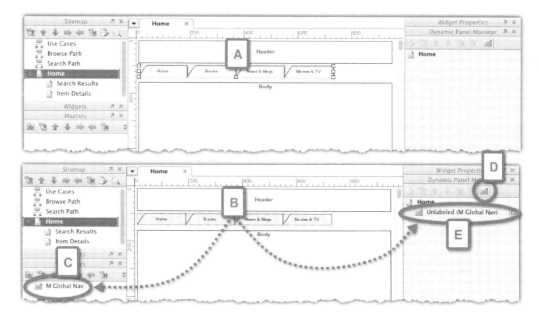

In the home page, continue to create masters out of the header and footer blocks as these elements too will appear on every page.

It is premature to convert the body block into a master because the home page, category pages, and other auxiliary pages that will be added later do not share the same layout and content.

New masters from scratch

You can also create new masters without converting existing widgets by using the **Add Master** option in the **Masters** pane. This is a good option when you know in advance that the wireframe will be used as a master.

Secondary navigation system

The global navigation bar addresses requirement R1/A, which deals with navigating between the three main media category types and the home page. Next, we want to develop a secondary navigation system to facilitate requirement R1/B, which lists the various subcategories within each media type.

Let's use the **Books** page as a model, which hopefully can be leveraged to the other pages. Begin by selecting the home page in the sitemap (see the following screenshot, A) duplicating it (B), and renaming the duplicate page from **Copy of Home** (C) to **Books**. (D). You may also consider the organization of the Sitemap, for example, keeping the category and other pages nested under the home page (E) or keeping, at least at first, a flat organization (F):

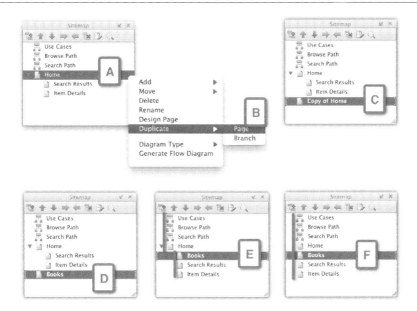

The page layout for the **Books** category page should look similar to the following screenshot. Construction wise we have three masters—the header (A), global nav (B), and footer (E). The body placeholder widget (D) has been resized to 75% of the page width to make room for the **Left Nav** widget (C). If you use the 960 guide, establishing the proportions is a little easier:

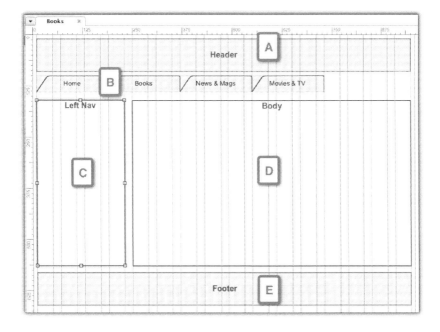

The left pane should communicate to the user all the content areas available in the library and make it very easy to access each content area. According to requirement R1.B1, the structure to model for Books should be:

- Electronic Books:
  - ◦ Fiction
    - ◦ Classics
    - ◦ Humor
    - ◦ Mystery
    - ◦ Romance
    - ◦ Thrillers
  - ◦ Non Fiction
    - ◦ Advice
    - ◦ Biography
    - ◦ Cooking
    - ◦ Sports
    - ◦ Textbooks

The **Tree** widget is a fast and efficient way to model a hierarchical navigation system in Axure. Before you drag the widget to the **Books** wireframe, lock the left pane widget to prevent it from moving while you edit the tree. The default tree widget (see the following screenshot, A) includes a parent and three nested siblings, all labeled **enter text...**, re-label the nodes and add additional items according to the requirements. For example, select the last node in the tree (B), right-click on it, and from the context menu select the **Add Sibling After** option. You can customize the tree widget in the **Edit Tree Properties** dialog (D), which you access from the tree's context menu:

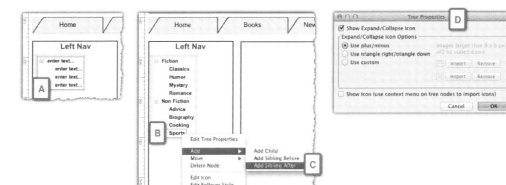

The first dynamic panel

The left navigation pane we just created for the **Books** wireframe (see the following screenshot, A), would be great for the other category pages: News & Mags and Movies & TV. We want the pane's location, dimensions, functionality, and visual design properties to stay consistent across all pages, which mean that the pane is a natural candidate for a master. However, how can we change the pane's content such that it fits the other category pages?

This is where Axure's **Dynamic Panel** widget comes into play. Here is how: If you locked the **Rectangle** widget (see the following screenshot, B), unlock it now. Select it from the tree widget (C) and convert this group into a master (D). Label the master **M Left Nav** and open it for editing in the **Wireframes** pane (E). In the master wireframe, select both widgets and convert those to a dynamic panel (F):

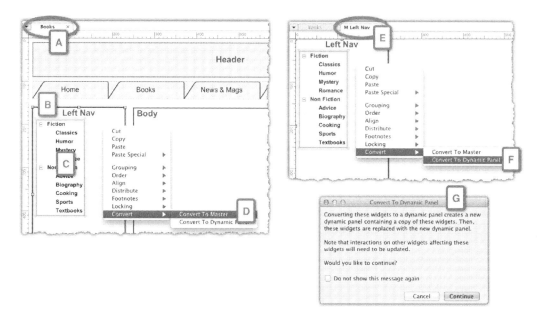

Axure will prompt you with the **Convert To Dynamic Panel** dialog (G). Take a moment to read the text:

- **Converting these widgets to a dynamic panel creates a new dynamic panel containing a copy of these widgets**: This means that a new dynamic panel will be added in the Dynamic Panel Manager pane. In addition, the panel will include a single state, which will contain a copy of the selected widgets.

- **Then, these widgets are replaced with the new dynamic panel. Note that interactions on other widgets affecting these widgets will need to be updated**: This means that the individual widgets which will be converted into a dynamic panel and will be replaced by the dynamic panel, which has copies of these widgets.

- **Would you like to continue?**: Well, yes.

- **Do not show this message again**: This is a checkbox, which I would leave unchecked for now.

Once you close the dialog box, notice the following changes to the master wireframe (see the following screenshot, A). The rectangle and tree now appear as a single box with a light-blue mask (B), which is how Axure helps you visually distinguish dynamic panels from other widgets.

The **Dynamic Panel Manager** pane, which is contextual to the selected wireframe, now displays the construction structure of the wireframe. The wireframe **M Left Nav** (C) is at the top. The icon to its left indicates that it is a master. However, note how easy it is to identify the master with the prefix M. In the following screenshot, there is the dynamic panel widget which is identified by a tri-color icon and is labeled by default as **Unlabeled** (D).

Now is the time to re-label it to something meaningful, such as **DP Category Tree**. I recommend using a prefix such as DP (short for dynamic panel) to help identify dynamic panels by their label. Finally, the node nested under the dynamic panel is of its single state, which is labeled by default as **State1** (E). Re-label the state to **S Books**. You got the naming pattern by now — the prefix S stands for S:

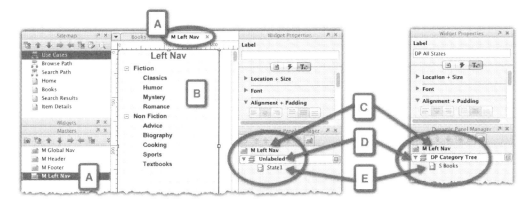

New dynamic panel from scratch

You can also create a new dynamic panel by dragging over a dynamic panel widget to the wireframe. Double-click on it for editing and the first state will open in a new tab in the **Wireframes** pane. Add widgets to this blank wireframe without convert existing widgets. This is a good option if you know in advance that the component you are going to wireframe needs to be a dynamic panel.

Adding states to a dynamic panel

Our next step is to add a couple more states to the dynamic panel, which correspond to the News & Mags and Movies & TV category pages. The following screenshot illustrates a couple of ways to do this:

1. In the **Wireframe** pane, double-click on the dynamic panel (A) or right-click on it and select **Manage Panel States** (B) from the context menu. In the **Dynamic Panel State Manager** dialog (C) that opens, click on the **Add** icon (D). A new state will be added below the Books state. Label this new state **S News & Mags** (E).

2. Another option to add new states is from the **Dynamic Panel Manager** pane (F). Click on the **Add State** icon (G) there and a new state will be added below the **News & Mags** state. Label this new state **S Movies and TV** (H):

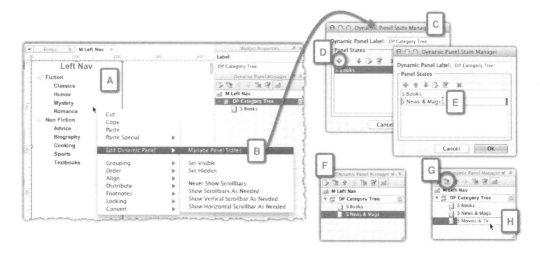

The two new states you added are basically blank wireframes. The next step is to create the appropriate trees for each state, in order to reflect Alexandria's categories for these media types. Open all states for editing either from the **Dynamic Panel State Manager** dialog or from the **Dynamic Panel Manager** pane. Copy the tree and rectangle widgets from the **Books** state wireframe and paste them in the other state wireframes. On each state, replace the generic **Left Nav** label of the rectangle widget with the label of the category page: Books, News & Mags, and Movies & TV.

In the **News & Mags** state, edit the tree to reflect the category structure as per requirements of R1.B2:

1. Newspapers and Magazines
2. Newspapers
3. World Newspapers
4. The Hindu
5. Le Monde
6. Times of London
7. US Newspapers
8. Chicago Tribune
9. New York Times
10. US News & World Report
11. Washington Post
12. Magazines
13. (Release 1 US Only)
14. The Atlantic
15. Popular Science
16. Wired Magazine

As you complete the tree structure for the News & Mags state, you hit a snag with US News & World Report: The long title extends the width of the left navigation object. Requirement R1.C specifically prohibits abbreviation of titles. The fastest way to resolve this design issue is to let the text wrap in the tree. However, Axure's tree widget does not allow wrapping. The second option is to widen the left nav and narrow the body section.

Before you act on the impulse to tweak the sizes of these two elements, follow requirements R1/B3 to finish the Movies & TV state, to see if there is a width issue there as well, and what is the maximum width needed to satisfy all states:

1. Movies
2. Action & Adventure
3. Children & Family
4. Drama
5. Foreign
6. Sci-Fi
7. TV
8. British Tube
9. Kids & Family
10. Comedies
11. Dramas
12. Mini Series

There are no width issues with the **Movies & TV** state, so we can tweak the width of the **News & Mages** state. Note the following important fact:

The width and height of a dynamic panel widget must be equal to, or greater than, the widest or highest state in the panel.

If you widen only the **News & Mags** state but do not widen its container, the **DP Category Tree** dynamic panel, the visible parts of the News & Mags state in the HTML prototype and in the Word output screenshot, will be determined by the width and height of the dynamic panel. In other words, the correct way to make the adjustment is to widen the dynamic panel first, rather than the states.

The original width of the left nav and body sections was set tentatively with the aid of the 960 grid, but without the specifics or constraints of content. We want to make the adjustments while continuing to benefit from the use of the 960 grid. The following screenshot illustrates the process:

- Open the master **M Left Nav** (A) for editing and show **Global Guides** (B). Move the widgets from their default position at 0 pixels from left and top (C), to 10 pixels from left and top (D). This adjustment will align the pane with the grid.
- The original width of the dynamic was 220 pixels (E). Widen the dynamic panel so it snaps to the 960 guide at 280 pixels (F and G).

Keep in mind that you widened only the dynamic panel, the outer container of the actual wireframes, which are the three states. The next step is to widen the rectangle shape in each of the states. The reason to apply the wider size to all the states is your desire to maintain structural and visual consistency in the layout framework of category pages. In other situations, it is perfectly ok that each state has different dimensions, as long as the size of the dynamic panel is equal to or greater than, the largest state.

When you open a state for editing (H), the width gap between the rectangle widget and the resized dynamic panel is clearly visible (I). Resize the rectangle, so that it snaps to the dotted blue line which marks the boundary of the dynamic panel:

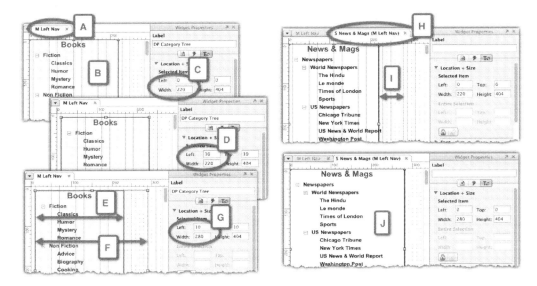

With the **Left Nav** adjusted to handle wide publication titles, the next step is to adjust the width of the body section of the **Books** page (see the following screenshot, A). The wider left nav section (B) covers the body section (C). Use the 960 grid to adjust the body width (D):

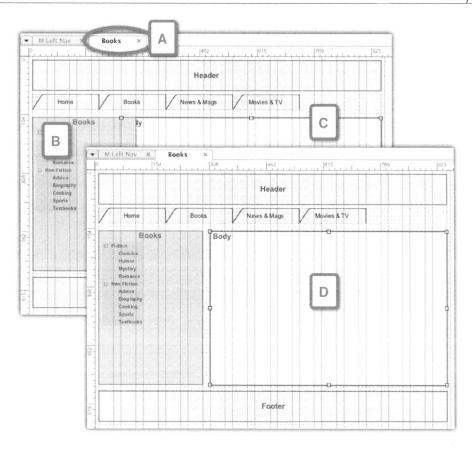

The first draft of the **Books** category wireframe now contains Alexandria's global and secondary navigation systems. In addition, with the exception of the body section, all other elements are masters. From a construction standpoint, we want to use this wireframe as a template for other media category pages: **News & Mags**, and **Movies & TV**.

Duplicate the "Books" page twice and re-label the copies **News & Mags**, and **Movies & TV**. The **Books** left nav state is visible on all pages, but don't get startled, because the first state is always visible on dynamic panel widgets.

Adding visual effects

Next, we want to enhance the user experience and provide visual effects in response to user actions. For example, when the user hovers over a tab in the global navigation bar, the tab should change its appearance. With Axure, you can create such effects effortlessly, which we will demonstrate on Alexandria's `Global Nav` bar:

- The **Global Nav** (see the following screenshot, A) is a master wireframe constructed from four **Rectangle** widgets, set to **Tab Left** shapes. Right-click on the left most widget, the **Home** tab (B), and from the context menu select the **Edit Rollover Style** (C) from the **Edit Button Shape** submenu. The other options for this widget include mouse down, selected, and disabled styles.

- In the **Set Rollover Style** Dialog (D) that appears, set the desired style attributes. In our example here, I will stick to a grayscale palette. The tab background will be black; the type will be white and bold. Note that in order to apply the bold style to the font, you have to press the **B** icon next to the **Click to toggle bold** property.

- Check the **Preview** checkbox (E), for a "live" preview of the widgets appearance on rollover. Click on **OK** when you are satisfied with the rollover style.

- Back on the wireframe, a new icon (F) appears on the upper-left corner of each widget. This visually indicates that the widget has one or more mouse states styles defined. Move your mouse over the square to preview the style (in our example, the rollover style) for this widget:

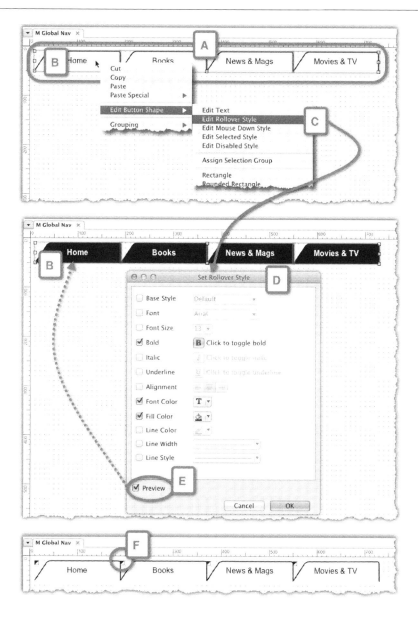

Next, we will add a rollover style to the **Left Nav** tree widget. The following screenshot illustrates the process:

- Open the master **M Left Nav** and the three states of the dynamic panel (DP) category tree. We need to apply styling to each of the trees, so start with the **S Book** wireframe (A). Right-click on the top node (B) and then select the **Edit Rollover Style** option (C) from the context menu.

- In the **Set Rollover Style** dialog (D) that appears, set the style attributes for the rollover: Check the **Underline** style and make sure to also click on the icon to the left of **Click to toggle underline**. Change the font color to blue.

- In the **Apply to** section (E), select the option named **This node, sibling and all child nodes**, which is a great time saver. Check the **Preview** option (F) to validate your choices on the tree widget (G) and if all looks ok, close the dialog.

- The style indicator (H) has been added to each of the items on the tree. Rollover the icon to see a preview of the style:

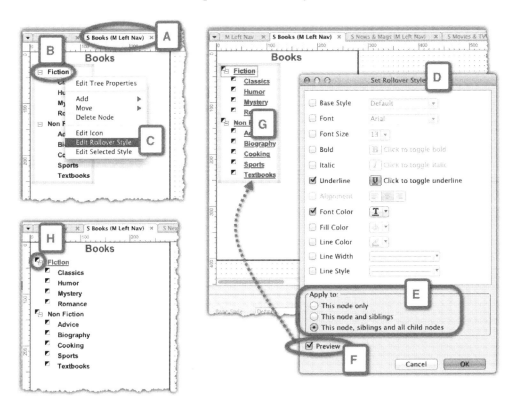

Repeat the steps on the tree widget of the other states. Generate the HTML prototype and use the **Sitemap** pane to review the rollover effects in the category pages you just finished.

Adding sketch effects

If you like to begin your design process for a project by sketching exploratory wireframes on paper or iPad, then you can achieve a similar tentative look by using Axure's **sketch effects** feature, which has been introduced in Version 6.

For early iterations of the prototype, this kind of treatment might help communicate to stakeholders that we are still looking at the initial concept. The effect can be applied on a page-by-page basis or to all pages as a global style. The latter makes it easier to remove the effect. In other words, Sketchiness affects the entire wireframe and not just selected widgets in a wireframe. The following screenshot illustrates the visual difference in the appearance of a wireframe page before (A) and after Sketchiness has been applied at 100% (B). Experiment with the **Sketchiness** slider (C) to find the level that works for you:

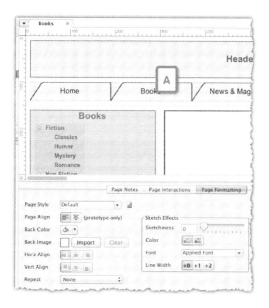
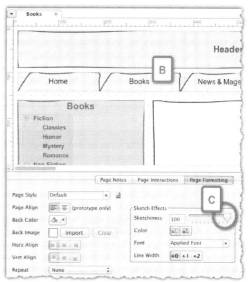

Updating task flow diagrams

Finally, it is a good idea to update the Browse Path flow diagram as the initial flow did not reflect the fact that the user can browse the media pages in addition to the home page. Your task now is to update the wireframe on your own, without a systematic description of the process. The end result, including linking to reference pages, should look similar to the one shown in the following screenshot:

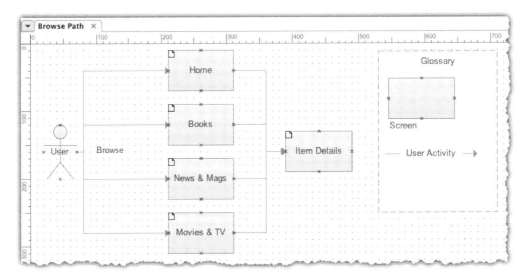

Practitioner's corner—Axure prototyping for mobile devices

Ritch Macefield, PhD, is a principal trainer and consultant at Ax-Stream, in U.K. He has graciously contributed his approach to Axure prototyping for mobile, which is presented here:

Mobile-friendly websites and mobile apps

There are a number of specific things you should be aware of when producing Axure prototypes for mobile devices, such as smartphones and tablets.

The first important thing to understand is the difference between mobile friendly websites and native mobile apps.

There are two basic types of system we use on PCs. Some systems run natively on the device and are specific to the PC's operating systems (for example, MS Windows, MacOS, or Linux) example of this are things such as Microsoft Outlook and Apple's QuickTime. These are sometimes known as desktop systems. There are also systems that reside on the World Wide Web (WWW), which are accessed through a browser, and are (largely) independent of what operating systems the PC is using.

The situation is exactly the same with mobile devices. There are native apps that run directly on the device, and are specific to the device's operating system (for example, iOS and Android). There are also mobile friendly websites. These are websites designed specifically to be used on the mobile device, within a mobile-based browser. Here, the site being accessed recognizes that a mobile device is being used, and provides a version of the site that is designed specifically for this type of platform. In rare cases, there may be many different versions of the site, which target a wide range of different mobile devices, but typically, there will just be a generic version for mobile devices or, perhaps, a version for smartphones and a version for tablets.

Of course, the nature of the systems we design for these two different types of platform is very different but, as we will explore throughout this section, this difference has implications for Axure mobile prototyping that may not be initially obvious!

Different device resolutions and aspect ratios

Websites targeted for PC-based browsers are designed for one, or just a few different, pages sizes. At the time of writing, 800x 600 pixels, 1024x768, and 1200x1024 are the most common of these. Some sites have liquid layouts so that the page size changes along with the browser window size (liquid layouts are not supported within Axure). The point here is that when prototyping for PC browsers, we typically only have to worry about a few different pages sizes, and it is both viable and common to produce different versions of Axure prototypes for more than one page size.

By contrast, mobile devices come in a very wide range of resolutions and aspect ratios. Even devices from the same manufacture, targeted at the same market can vary in the way. This means that it will not, typically, be viable to produce versions of the prototype for all the different types of devices on which the real system might run. In turn, this means that we need to think very carefully about what page size(s) we are going to prototype and what device(s) will be used when demonstrating and/or for usability testing the prototype.

Using the Viewport Tag

Whether you are prototyping a native app or a mobile friendly website, the Axure prototype will always be an HTML website. This once presented a significant problem in Axure mobile prototyping because mobile browsers typically scale web pages to ensure that pages fit completely within the browser window on the mobile device. However, this scaling was often inappropriate for (Axure) prototypes because it would shrink pages even when the page was already small enough to fit within the browser window!

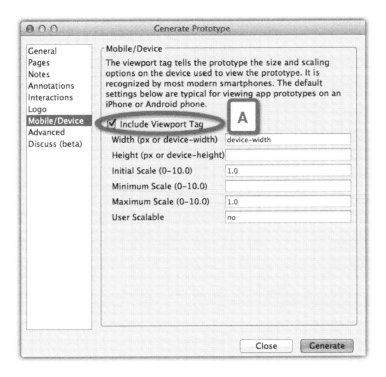

Axure 6 solved this problem using the "Viewport Tag" (see the preceding screenshot, A). This is a generic HTML tag that instructs mobile browsers how to scale web pages, and is recognized by most modern mobile devices. In Axure, you can set this tag when generating the prototype using the "mobile/device" option. In most cases, the default settings will work fine, but some devices will require special settings. In these cases, you will need to consult the documentation for the specific device(s) you are using.

Using a full screen browser

When prototyping native apps, we often also want to prototype various states of the device's status bar (this is usually at the top of the screen and shows things such as battery charge and signal strength). This presents an issue because, under normal circumstances, the device will always display its status bar, so, both the device and the prototype will have status bar, leading to a problem highlighted in the following screenshot (A):

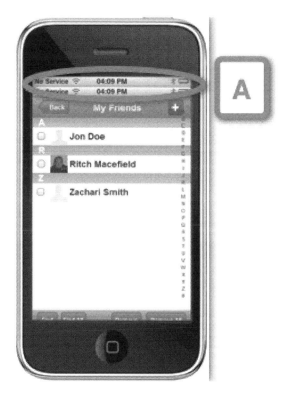

To get round this problem, the prototype needs to be viewed within a browser's full screen mode. Sadly, not all mobile browsers have such a mode; however, browsers are available for most devices that do have this capability. For example, Vanilla Surf is available for the iPhone/iPad and Dolphin Mini Browser is available for Android (there were free versions of both available at the time of writing).

Landscape and portrait page versions

Unlike systems that run on a PC, mobile device make extensive use of the ability to rotate the device, so that pages can be viewed in portrait or landscape mode. In turn, this means that we may have to prototype two versions of some, or all, pages in the prototype, as illustrated in the following screenshot:

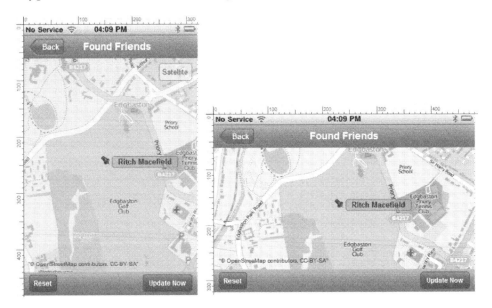

This feature of mobile prototyping also leaves us with the problem of being able to 'synchronize' the pairs of pages when demonstrating or usability testing our prototypes. In these cases, it can be useful to use a simulation tool, such as the one provided by ax-stream, which have the ability to keep pairs of pages 'in-synch'.

Event and gesture compatibility

The way in which we interact with a PC and mobile device are very different. For example, the following diagram illustrates how, for many type of interaction, there is no equivalency across the two platforms:

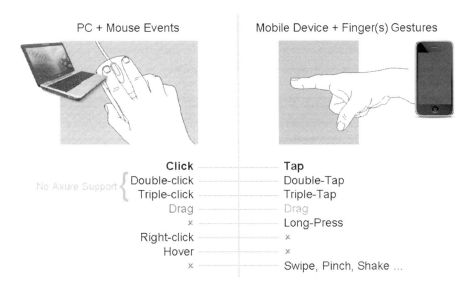

PC + Mouse Events | Mobile Device + Finger(s) Gestures

PC + Mouse Events	Mobile Device + Finger(s) Gestures
Click	**Tap**
Double-click	Double-Tap
Triple-click	Triple-Tap
Drag	Drag
x	Long-Press
Right-click	x
Hover	x
x	Swipe, Pinch, Shake ...

No Axure Support

The preceding diagram also illustrates two other important issues related to mobile prototyping with Axure. The first is that, although both type of platform support double and triple clicking/pressing, these two types of event/gesture are not presently supported in Axure.

The second issue is more subtle: although both platforms support the drag interaction, and drag is supported in Axure 6, the drag event creates an issue when prototyping native apps with Axure. This is because the Axure prototype is an HTML web page, so when it is run within some mobile browsers the drag event will act on the entire page, even if we coded the prototype to drag just part of a page using a dynamic panel. However, when we run the prototype on other mobile browsers and within a PC browser, we are able to drag just part of the page as intended. In summary, Figure 4 illustrates how, with Axure 6 mobile prototyping, the only event/gesture that is truly common to both PCs and mobile device is a single click!

This is just one of many examples of problems we get with Axure mobile prototyping related to events/gestures. To address this, ax-stream's mobile simulator (illustrated in the following screenshot) provides a way of mapping events to gestures so that, at least, we can 'represent' how the various mobile gestures would control the system being prototyped:

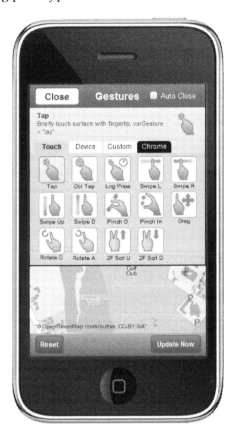

Browser limitations

As implied earlier, Axure prototypes can be run within a mobile browser on the device itself or within PC browser; perhaps by using some kind of simulator. With more complex prototypes (such as those using animation), we face an issue when running within a mobile browser, because mobile browsers do not necessarily support the more complex HTML and JavaScript present within an Axure prototype that include the more complex interactions. Sadly, the degree to which functionality within an Axure prototype is supported varies across both different mobile browsers and the device on which they are running!

Therefore, the only advice here is: do not assume that all of your interactions will work on your intended mobile devices, just because they work on your PC, and make sure you thoroughly test your prototype on the exact device and browser with which you intend to do demonstration and/or conduct usability tests.

Using widget libraries

There are numerous Axure widget libraries available, including libraries for mobile prototyping; at the time of writing, there are libraries available for iPhone, iPad, and Android devices. These range from simple 'dumb' Axure widgets to more complex widgets capable of, for example, supporting the Y-Axis rotation which is commonly used on mobile devices.

Loading prototypes onto the device

Mobile devices often access web pages through a 3G connection; which, of course, we all know can often be quite slow and un-reliable. Similarly, because mobile devices do not typically have the processing power, disk speed, or networking throughput capacity of a modern PC, browsing web pages can be slow, even with a strong Wi-Fi connection. This problem of download speed is exacerbated because real mobile websites have pages that are very deliberately coded to have a very small file size; specifically to optimize the download time. By contrast, the pages within Axure prototypes are not optimized in this way are typically relatively large!

In order to get round this problem with running Axure prototypes on mobile devices, the advice is to load your prototype onto the device itself and run it from there. In this way, your prototype will run as fast and as reliably as possible.

Summary

This chapter laid out the foundation for the project's interactive prototype and proposed a structured, pragmatic, and requirements-driven approach to wireframe construction. Taking advantage of Axure's unified wireframing and specifications environment, we covered:

- Constructing use case and task flow diagrams
- Basic wireframing aided by guides and grids
- Wireframe construction with Masters and Dynamic panels
- The importance of labeling of widgets, Masters, and Dynamic panel states
- Applying visual effects in response to mouse activity
- Applying the sketch effect

You were introduced to Alexandria, the book's demonstration project, and in a series of activities, created an initial set of diagrams and wireframes which included the use of wireframe and flow widgets, and Masters, and Dynamic panels.

The next chapter will introduce you to Axure interactivity fundamentals such as interactions, cases, events, and actions. We will also deepen the discussion on naming conventions and wireframe construction strategies.

4
Interactivity 101

In this chapter, we will cover Axure interaction basics and some of the simple, yet powerful features that empower non-programmers to develop high fidelity, clickable UX prototypes. We review the three components that make up an Axure interaction—events, cases, and actions, and how to compose both user-driven and automatic interactions.

Interaction design—brief history

Before we dive into the details of Axure interactions, a brief discussion of the evolution of user experience is in order, because historical perspective provides valuable insights into the reasons for, and nature of changes in, the way people interact with computers. These changes, in turn, define the methods, and the type of tools embraced, as a UX professional, in order to keep up with constant change.

Twenty five hundred years ago, Heraclitus observed: "Nothing endures but change", and this holds true until today. Axure emerged in response to a growing need for a UX-specific tool that could move us from the static to the dynamic—a tool that empowers a UX pro to create compelling rich user interaction quickly and without dependence on the services of a programmer or advanced programming skills.

Traditionally, user interface designers have been using basic tools to visualize the user interface. From the proverbial napkin, index cards, sketch books and other paper products, to general-purpose software such as PowerPoint, drawing software such as Illustrator, Photoshop or Fireworks and, of course, the all time favorite, Microsoft Visio. With the exception of visual design and branding related mockups, low fidelity static wireframes were the norm for user interface deliverables.

The 1950–60s

Many historical and practical reasons contributed to the predominance of the static wireframes approach. The chief reason is the fact that the discipline of **User Experience** as we think of it today, emerged only in the 1980s. In the 1950s and 1960s the reality was different, because there was no user interface! Input was loaded through punch cards or keyboards, and the computer made the software "run" from start to end. The user experience of that era could be compared perhaps to baking a cake—follow a recipe using the required ingredients, put in the oven, and hope that the outcome is edible. Logic and algorithms were paramount, placing programmers and analysts in a natural position to control all aspects of software development.

The general public had little exposure to, experience with, control over or expectations regarding computers in general and even less when it came to interaction with computers. The common perception was that working with computers was limited to smart people, and the idea that computers are difficult to use took root.

The 1970–80s

The Personal Computer (PC) began to trickle into the market in the 1970s and turned into a real commercial success with models such as the Apple II and, in 1981, the IBM PC. Human-computer interaction in these systems was facilitated by the keyboard and operating systems, such as Microsoft DOS. The PC, as these systems came to be referred to by the general public, marked the beginning of a dramatic transition from a user interaction that was strictly controlled by, limited to, and conducted in a business environment, to one that happens in home settings.

Once you got your new PC, there were very few software titles available to do anything useful. In order to use new software, or more importantly, play a new game, you had to write it yourself. So naturally, programmers continued to control all aspects of software creation. A new and hugely successful profession and business model—software development— had emerged.

While the size and cost of computing has placed the ownership of a computer within the reach of consumers, remaining hardware and software limitations has several implications on the user experience:

- Extensive use of abbreviations, such as file names that could be only eight characters long, truncated terms (*Ext P* instead of Extended Price), and the notorious Year 2000 fiasco.

- Extensive use of reference codes substituting entire words and phrases, with number or letters. For example:
  - ° 1 for exempt
  - ° 2 for non exempt
  - ° 3 for not applicable

- Finding the correlation between such code and its meaning, often required use of a bulky training document or user manual. As we know, few people bother reading these.

- Keyboard shortcuts and obscure key combinations were the only method for user input. The benefit was fast data entry and the drawback was the increased load on memorization requirements.

- 12 to 14 inches monochrome, and later color monitors at a resolution of 640x480 were the standard display hardware. This small real estate translated to proliferation of windows, dialog boxes, and horizontal scrolling. To complete a single task, a user was frequently required to negotiate many windows, dialogs boxes, and other prompts, which disrupted and slowed down the natural flow of relatively simple tasks.

This list includes some of the key ingredients for cryptic, ambiguous, and difficult-to-use software. The prevailing perception that software is complicated and hard to use was even further enhanced.

The 1980's moved the personal computer to new grounds in terms of user interactions although paradoxically, this had not, initially, resulted in improved usability. Several major breakthroughs contributed to a new paradigm of human-computer interaction:

- The GUI (Graphical User Interface)
- The Mouse (Direct Manipulation)
- WYSIWYG (What-You-See-Is-What-You-Get)

The **Graphical User Interface** that was born out of the pioneering work at the now legendary Xerox PARC, iconized by Apple Macintosh and much later popularized by Microsoft Windows, offered a new and exciting user experience that was much less dependent on keyboarding and memorization of key combinations and codes. Instead, representational metaphors such as the Desktop, the Trash, folders and icons, provided new cognitive facilities to bridge the gap between the user's mental model of the steps involved in performing a task, and the way the task was modeled in the software. The smaller the gap, the more intuitive the software was perceived to be.

A small input device, fondly named the **mouse**, further empowered users through the concept of **Direct Manipulation**: The ability to control the screen without the arbitration of a keyboard. Terms such as **Point-and-Click**, **Double-Click** and **Drag-and-Drop**, became an inseparable part of our daily lexicon. Another ground-breaking innovation of the era was **WYSIWYG (What You See Is What You Get)**. This gave the profound idea that the screen representation of a document, which the user sees and edits, is almost identical, in terms of size, positioning, and color, to a paper output.

For the first time since the beginning of computing, programmers were stepping into an unfamiliar territory—the graphic part in Graphical User Interface. Numerous decisions had to be made on issues such as layout and organization of information, colors palettes, typography, positioning, and alignment of UI widgets, choice of graphics for icons, and many others.

The impact on the life cycle of the software was that, as new features were added, a good programmer would look for the most logical place to add them, while others would be satisfied with any empty piece of screen real estate. Over time, the user interface would become increasingly bloated, confusing, expensive to extend or support, and ultimately, very difficult to use and support. Software further maintained its reputation as being complex, confusing, and not intuitive.

Yet, very often, attempts to improve the software by changing the user interface were encountered with great resistance—from users. A class of **Power Users** emerged in every organization. These were the people who figured how to *work* the system and knew its obscure and undocumented features. They internalized numerous key combinations, codes, and shortcuts, and felt in complete control. These people taught themselves and others how to be productive using an unproductive tool. With this mastery often came power and a sense of job security. An offer to change the software and improve it implied a real loss of investment and power.

The *user* part in Graphical User Interface emerged. However, it would take another decade and a half, and the introduction of a dramatic new invention, before the term **User Experience** would become synonymous with a discipline that today plays an integral role in the life cycle of software development.

The 1990–2000s

The World Wide Web, as it was known in the early days, initially proved to be a great setback to the user experience. Some of the reasons included:

- Narrow bandwidth facilitated through slow dial-up connections meant that screens could take a long time to render

- The entire page had to be refreshed upon clicking any hyperlink, leading further to poor performance

- Competing and incompatible flavors of web browsers meant that a page, designed for viewing on one browser, was not likely to render correctly on another browser

- The comforts of having familiar conventions for a GUI desktop client were gone, replaced by numerous user interfaces, as each website has its own design

These inconveniences were simply the unavoidable growing pains of an unstoppable progress. Innovations such as the Amazon Shopping Cart and Google's Search introduced new paradigms of powerful simplicity which turned the Internet from a somewhat naive democratic virtual environment to a fiercely commercial one.

The Internet proved to be the great equalizer, immortalized in a 1993 New Yorker cartoon by Peter Stiener, showing a dog using a computer telling another dog: "On the Internet, nobody knows you are a dog". In the context of user experience, two aspects of the reality depicted by this cartoon are especially relevant:

- Compared to traditional software development, creating simple websites was, and still is, lighting-fast and it does not require programmers, although programmers remain essential for more complex applications. Consequently, everyone and their grandmothers began creating websites.

- Whereas in the commercial world, the cost of changing software vendors was often prohibitive, website publishers soon found out a bitter reality: The abundant availability of alternatives meant that the competition was only one click away. Moreover, it could be difficult to distinguish between a site created in someone's bedroom, and one created by a global company. If the first was better, users flocked to it.

These two factors paved the way to effectively associating usability with revenue. The fledgling, disjointed, and little understood practice of user interface design began to emerge, sprouting methodologies such as Joint Development and User Centered Design. An argument emerged, that an investment in understanding users' needs may in fact yield better software.

The discipline of user experience has matured since the beginning of the new century. The web was transformed in the last decade, shedding many of its early-stage problems with user experience. Several factors played a role:

- The advent of high speed Internet
- Fast, affordable computers
- Browser compatibility

- Data interconnectivity via web services

- The Semantic web and increased decoupling of data from the way it is displayed

- Data updates without page reloading

Users developed much higher expectations for ease of use from commercial applications, and user experience has been placed front and center. Businesses began to see the user interface not as eye candy but as a strategic asset. New terminology, specifically addressing measurement of website effectiveness, has been introduced:

- **Analytics**: The tools and methodologies to quantify the traffic of users on a site

- **Conversion**: How many visitors actually complete a transaction

- **Retention**: How many users are loyal to the site and return with more business

More trends quickly emerged, most importantly, social networks, cloud computing, and mobile devices such as smartphones and tablets. The shift placed the user at the forefront of software development and focused on measurable, result-oriented design, and in turn, helped push the industry towards a formal recognition of **User Experience** as a revenue-generator as opposed to a cost center.

The present, future, and Axure interactions

Considering the history and evolution of user experience, it is clear that we are in a midst of an enormous transition in software design. Our ability to simulate highly engaging user experiences across diverse delivery platforms is critical, because UX is quickly taking a front and center position in the development life cycle.

Axure's interactions were game changing with respect to enabling UX designers to gain independence in the creation of high-fidelity prototypes. Over the years, Axure has expanded the vocabulary of building blocks that make up its interactions' features, yet delicate balance has to be maintained. On the one hand, Axure should not be too complicated or too similar to programming, and preserve its core mission. On the other hand, Axure is pressured to support increasingly complex interactions and devices. So far, Axure has been able to maintain a good balance between these two seemingly competing needs.

Axure interactions primer

Interactions are the feature that turns our static wireframes into clickable, interactive HTML prototypes. Axure shields us from the complexities of coding, by providing a simple, wizard-like interface for defining instructions and logic in English. Each time we generate the HTML prototype, Axure converts the interactions into real JavaScript code, which a web browser can understand.

Each Axure interaction is composed of three basic units of information: *When, Where,* and *What*:

- *When does the interaction happen?* The Axure terminology for *When* is events, and some examples include:
    - When the page is loaded in the browser
    - After a user clicks on a widget
    - After the user tabs out of a field

- *Where is the interaction?* An interaction is attached to either a widget, such as a rectangle, radio button or drop-list, or to a page or master wireframe. You can create widget interactions in the **Widget Properties** pane, and master interactions in the **Page Properties** pane.

- *What should happen?* It is the Axure terminology for what actions are. Actions define the outcome of the interaction, for example, when a page loads, set a dynamic panel to a specific state, when the user clicks on a button, link to another page, and so on. When the user tabs out of a form field, validate the input, and display an error message.

In addition, Axure interactions can be guided by conditional logic, which is an optional ingredient. We will cover conditions, variables, and other advanced features in *Chapter 5, Advanced Interactions*.

> **The W3C of Axure interactions**
>
> In addition to standing for the World Wide Web consortium, the acronym **W3C** also stands for When, Where, What, and Condition — the ingredients of an Axure interaction. It is an easy mnemonic to remember when you construct and debug interactions.

Guided example

We will start with a quick example, which builds on the static wireframes we created in *Chapter 2, Axure Basics – the User Interface*.

Step 1: Defining the interaction in simple words

When the user clicks on a tab on the **Global Navigation** bar, it links to the corresponding page. The new page will replace the current page.

As a learning device, use the W3C to break the sentence into the following building blocks:

- When: When the user clicks on it
- Where: A tab on the global navigation bar (widget)
- What: Link to the corresponding page
- Condition: No condition

Step 2: The Axure interface

Open the Global Navigation master (**M Global Nav**), for editing in the **Wireframes** pane as shown in the following screenshot. The navigation bar is made of four rectangle type widgets, styled to have a Tab Left appearance. Although each of these tabs will have an interaction attached to it, we will use the **Books** tab widget (B) for this example:

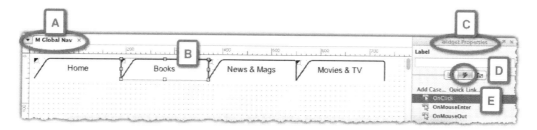

In the **Widget Properties** pane (C), click on the **Interactions** tab (D) to see the list of events that a rectangle widget can respond to. There are three events:

- **OnClick**
- **OnMouseEnter**
- **OnMouseOut**

The *When* part in Step 1 is: *When the user clicks*, so the **OnClick** event (E) is the event we need. Before moving ahead, however, we will review the following screenshot, which visualizes the contextual nature of widget-level interactions:

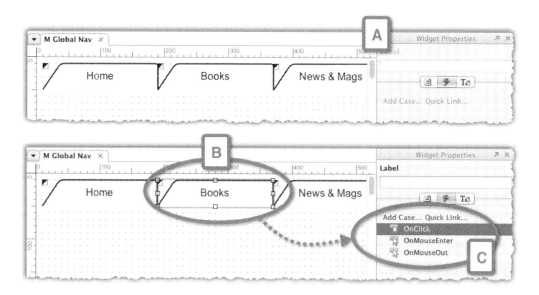

When no widgets are selected in the wireframe, the **Interactions** tab in the **Widget Properties** pane (A) is dimmed and no events are listed. When you click on a **widget** (B), the interaction section becomes active (C), listing contextual events to the selected widget type.

The primary interface for defining interactions is in Axure's **Case Editor** window, which we will discuss shortly. The following screenshot visualizes the ways to access this window from the **Widget Properties** pane:

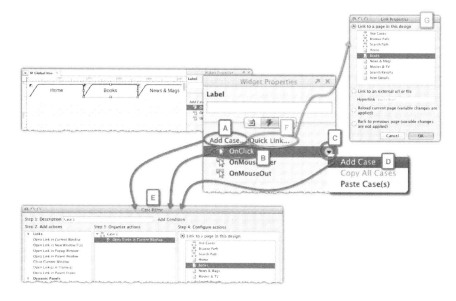

The following options will launch the **Case Editor** window (E):

- **Option 1**: Clicking on the **Add Case** link (A)
- **Option 2**: Double-clicking the **OnClick** event (B)
- **Option 3**: Clicking the context menu icon (C), which appears when you mouse over an event and select the **Add Case** option (D) from the menu

Moreover, if these options are not enough, Axure also offers a simplified method to deal with interactions that involve only linking:

- Click on the **Quick Links** link (F) to open the **Link Properties** dialog (G), where you can choose the appropriate linking target page

Step 3: Translating this requirement into an Axure interaction

Our example calls for a simple **OnClick** interaction. Although we hold off the detailed discussion on the actual structure of interactions until the next section of this chapter, it is very likely that you will be able to figure out yourself, how to link the **Books** tab to the **Books** page by using either the **Case Editor** window or **Link Properties** dialog.

However, I do want to point out a few subtle changes to Axure's interface that happen after you associate an interaction to a widget. The following screenshot visualizes the before and after states of various interface elements, which are detailed in the following table:

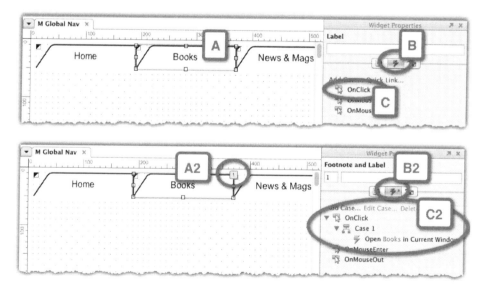

Axure UI	With interaction(s)	Without interaction(s)
The widget (A)	A yellow, numbered footnote icon appears on the upper-right corner of the widget (A2).	The footnote icon will also appear if annotations are associated with it.
Interactions tab (B)	An asterisk (*) is added to the right of the lightning icon on the tab (B2). This visual indicator is a useful reminder when the widget is selected, but you are working on either the Annotations or Formatting tabs.	No asterisk.
Interaction section (C)	A twisty icon appears to the left of the event. One or more cases are listed, and each case can also be expanded or collapsed. (C1)	

Step 4: Annotating the interaction (optional?)

There are two questions to consider at this point: Why bother with annotations to begin with, and why start with annotations so early in the prototyping phase? Here are some pointers to consider regarding the first question:

- Are you on the hook for delivering a UI specifications document?

- Are you planning to provide stakeholders with a link to the interactive prototype so they can review it?

- Are you part of a UX team of designers collaborating on the project?

If your answer was "Yes" to any of the preceding questions, the rationale is simple — because you have to, and because stakeholders will consume the prototype. While the reasons to annotate involve others, the reasons to start early involve you: Annotating wireframes can be tedious and time consuming, but let's face it — you will have to get to it eventually.

While you have the widget selected for editing (see the following screenshot, A), after you are done with the interaction, labeling the widget (B) and adding a description (C) will only take a few seconds.

Similarly, when you add an annotation to a widget to the **Interactions** tab, an asterisk appears to the right of the tab icon (D):

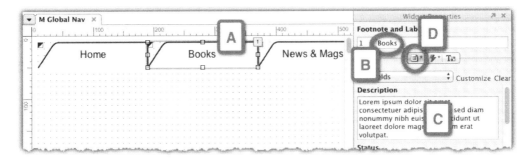

In order to complete this example, continue to add interactions to the other tabs that make up the Global Navigation. We will return to this master later in the book to demonstrate more advanced interaction features.

The purpose of this guided example was to familiarize you with the workflow involved in creating interactions, and Axure's interface nuances. Now we will cover interactions in more detail.

Axure events

Axure interactions are triggered by two types of events:

- When a page (and masters placed on a page) is loaded in the browser: These are automatic interactions that are triggered when the page loads.

- When a user directly interacts with a widget: These are triggered by the user.

Events triggered on OnPageLoad

Think about this concept as a staging setup, an orchestration of actions that take place behind the scenes and is executed as the page is rendered in the browser. Moreover, it is a setup to which you can apply conditional logic and variables, and deliver a contextual rendering of the page. In short, the OnPageLoad event, which can be applied to pages and on masters, is likely to become one of your frequently used methods to control your prototype.

Guided example: Changing the default landing page

When you generate a prototype, it always loads the sitemap's top-most page. In our Alexandria example, it is the **Use Case** page. However, as you move from modeling flows to wireframing—testing and presenting the prototype—it becomes desirable to start on the **Home** page, or some other page, depending on your needs. This example is an opportunity to demonstrate a simple interaction that is triggered when a page is being loaded in the browser.

The interaction objective is: As soon as the prototype loads in the browser, the top page in the sitemap redirects to a page you specified. We will break the interaction to its W3C components:

- **When**: The prototype launches
- **Where**: The top page in the sitemap
- **What**: Redirect to another page
- **Condition**: No condition

The following screenshot provides a visualization of setting up the interaction:

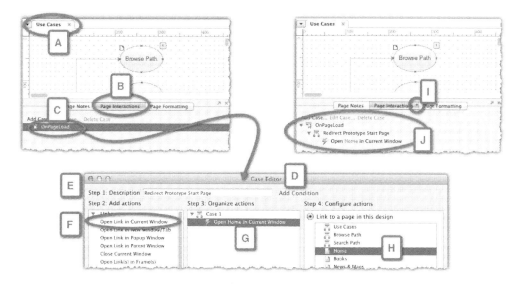

1. Open the **Use Cases** page for editing (A) and in the **Page Properties** pane, switch to the **Page Interactions** tab (B).

2. **OnPageLoad** (C) is the only interaction available, so double-click on it to open the **Case Editor** window (D).

3. Re-label the interaction in field **Step 1: Description** (E), from the meaningless **Case 1** to a more descriptive title, such as **Redirect Prototype Start Page**.

4. **Step 2: Add actions** lists all Axure's actions. The **Links** group of interactions is the one that handles navigation and the action **Open Link in Current Window** (F) is the most appropriate, so click on it.

5. The action now appears in the column **Step 3: Organize actions** (G), and all the pages in the sitemap are listed in the column **Step 4: Configure actions**. Click on the **Home** page (H), to identify it as the target.

6. We are done. Close the **Case Editor** window.

7. Notice the asterisk that was added to the **Page Interactions** tab (I), Axure's visual pattern is used to indicate that the page has interactions, and is a useful reminder when the **Page Properties** pane is completely minimized and only the tabs are visible.

8. The **New Case** (J) is now listed under the **OnPageLoad** interaction. Notice that you can easily interpret the interaction. Axure uses natural language to describe what should happen: When the page loads, open **Home** in the current window.

Generate the prototype. Although the top page in the sitemap is the **Use Cases** page, the prototype will open on the **Home** page, which was our objective.

Simulating contextual navigation

A trivial user experience requires that the global navigation object will clearly communicate to the user what page they are on.

When a page loads, the Global Navigation bar will change to reflect the selected page. We will deconstruct the interaction into its W3C components:

- **When**: A page loads
- **Where**: The Global Navigation master
- **What**: Reflects which page is presented
- **Condition**: No condition

What is interesting about this, and most requirements, is that there are many ways to execute the **What** component. The active tab can be larger, it can have a different color than the other tabs, and its label can have a font in bold and of a different color, and so on. While there are well-accepted UX pattern conventions, creativity and innovation are at the core of what UX designers contribute to the process.

As the interaction patterns of the application that you are designing will be tied to your interpretation of requirements, and to the application's visual design style guide, Axure's interactions are similar to Lego blocks—you mix and match standard pieces and end up with a unique creation. The following screenshot demonstrates this:

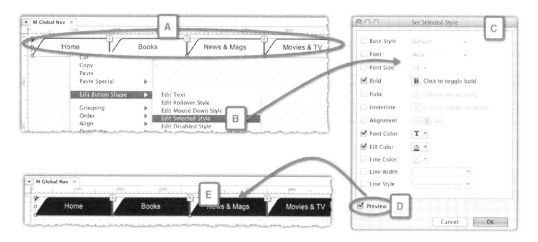

Back in *Chapter 3, Prototype Construction Basics*, we assigned a Rollover style to each of the tabs that make up the Global Navigation bar. Now, we will follow a similar path to assign a Selected style to the tabs:

1. Select all four tabs that make up the navigation bar, as shown in the previous screenshot (A).

2. Right-click and select the **Edit Selected Style** option (B) from the **Edit Button Shape** menu.

3. In the **Set Selected Style** pop-up (C), assign the visual attributes that you want the selected style to have. For example, a white text color over a black background color—the visual opposite of the non-selected tabs.

4. Check the **Preview** option (D) to see a live preview of the tabs in Selected style, and close the pop-up when done.

Next, we want to add an **OnPageLoad** interaction to each prototype page that is listed in the Global Navigation bar. When the page loads the interaction, it will set a tab on the Global Navigation to its Selected style:

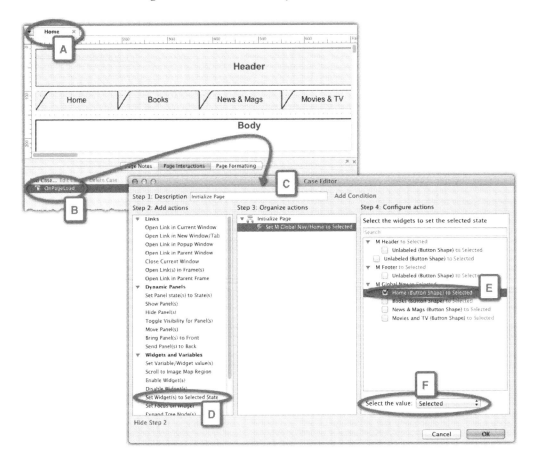

The preceding screenshot illustrates adding the interaction to the **Home** page, and you can apply the example to the other pages:

1. Open the home page for editing (A), switch to the **Page Interactions** tab in the **Page Properties** pane and double-click the **OnPageLoad** interaction (B). The **Case Editor** (C) window will open now.

2. Start by re-labeling the interaction with a meaningful name, such as **Initialize Page**. Then, review the actions listed in the column **Step 2: Add actions**.

3. In the **Widgets and Variables** section, you will find the action **Set Widget(s) to Selected State** (D), which is the one we need. Click on the action and it will be added to the column **Step 3: Organize actions**.

4. All the widgets that are part of the home page wireframe are listed in the column **Step 4: Configure actions**. Find the **Global Nav** section, and check the **Home (Button Shape) to Selected** (E) checkbox.

5. At the bottom of the column, select the option **Selected** from the **Select the value:** drop-down (F).

Generate the prototype. The **Home** page loads first and the **Home** tab (shown in the following screenshot (A)) has the **Selected** style applied. As you rollover the other tabs, they change their visual appearance to the Rollover style (B), as shown in the following screenshot:

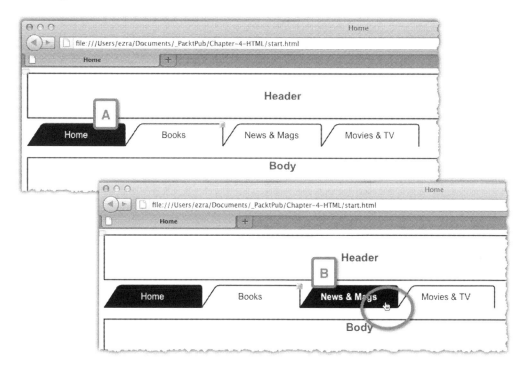

Labeling Widgets

If you want to assess the value of labeling your prototype widgets, rebuild the Home page, and the three media pages and their associated masters, but don't label *anything*—just keep pages, masters, widgets, and interactions with their default label. You will find that as your prototype evolves, creating interactions become nearly impossible because nothing can be easily identified.

OnPageLoad events and dynamic panels

With the Global Navigation bar wired, it is time to focus our attention on the left navigation pane, which we have on the **Books**, **News & Mags**, and **Movies & TV** media pages. In *Chapter 2, Axure Basics – the User Interface*, we constructed the **Left Nav** master using a dynamic panel widget. Each media page has a corresponding state that lists categories that are relevant to that medium.

Currently in the prototype, however, each of the media pages is displaying the **Books** categories on the left pane, because, as a default Axure will always display the top-most state of a dynamic panel.

Our objective is to get the **Left Nav** to display the correct categories on the page on which it is located. In addition, **Media Nav** is a more descriptive name for this interface component, so let's rename it in the Axure file.

The interaction into its W3C components is as follows:

- **When**: A medium page (**Books**, **News & Mags**, **Movies & TV**) loads
- **Where**: The Media Nav master
- **What**: Display the relevant categories for that medium page
- **Condition**: No condition

The easiest method to get the dynamic panel to load the appropriate state is to use the OnPageLoad event. The following screenshot illustrates the construction process using the **News & Mags** as an example, which you can apply to the other two pages:

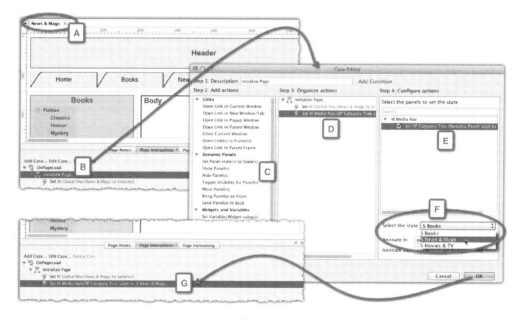

1. Open the **News & Mags** page (A) for editing and switch to the **Page Interactions** tab in the **Page Properties** pane. We want to add an action to the existing **Initialize Page** case (B), which we created in the previous section.

2. Double-click on the case to launch **Case Editor**. In the column **Step 2: Add actions**, find the **Dynamic Panel** group of actions. As we want to change the state of a dynamic panel, the action **Set Panel state(s) to State(s)** (C), is the one we need. The action appears in the column **Step 3: Organize actions** (D), but we focus our attention on the next column.

3. The column **Step 4: Configure actions** shows the dynamic panel **Set DP Category Tree (Dynamic Panel) state to** (E) nested below the master **M Media Nav**. It is the only dynamic panel on this page. From the **Select the state** drop-down (F) select the relevant state.

4. Generate the prototype to make sure that the OnPageLoad works as you expected, and if everything looks fine. Repeat these steps on the other two pages.

The generated prototype is illustrated in the following screenshot. The **Home** page loads first and when you click on the **Books** tab in the Global Navigation bar, the **Books** page appears. The **Books** tab (A) is set to its **Selected** state, and the media pane lists books of related categories (B). Clicking on the **News & Mags** tab loads the page and its Global Navigation (C) and media pane (D) are set accordingly:

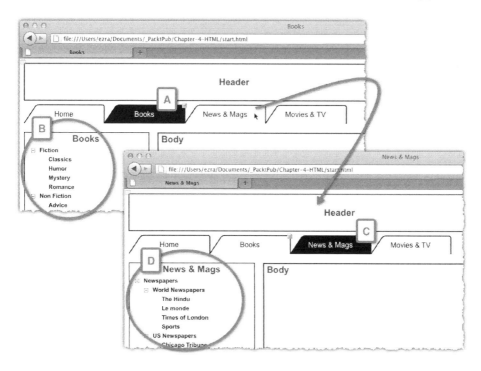

OnPageLoad event in detail

I hope that by now you have developed a taste for the OnPageLoad event. As we can see from the examples, it is a powerful, and quite a simple mechanism. It enables you to reduce the number of redundant wireframes in the prototype by using masters and dynamic panels, which can be controlled by the OnPageLoad event to display the appropriate state. In *Chapter 5*, we will discuss the use of conditional logic and variables, which further increases the usefulness of this event.

In order to conclude this section, here is a detailed review of Axure's OnPageLoad event, which can be used on pages and masters:

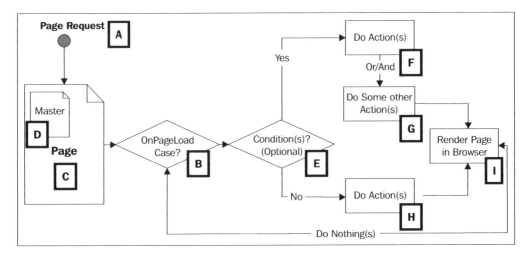

- The browser gets a request to load a page (A), either because it is the first time that you have launched the prototype or as a result of the navigation from one prototype page to another.

- The browser first checks for OnPageLoad interactions. An OnPageLoad event (B) may be associated with the loading page (C), a master used on the page (D), or both.

- If an `OnPageLoad` exists, the browser first evaluates page level interactions, and then master level interactions. As we will see in *Chapter 5*, the benefits of this order of operations is that you can set the value of a variable on the page's `OnPageLoad` interaction, and pass that variable to the master's `OnPageLoad` interaction. It sounds a bit complicated though!

- If the OnPageLoad interaction includes condition(s) (E), the browser will evaluate the logic and execute the appropriate action (F and/or G). Otherwise, if the `OnPageLoad` event does not include a condition, the browser will execute the interaction (H).

- The requested page is rendered (I) per the interaction.

User triggered events

Like the real application, an Axure prototype can respond to user actions. The closer the prototype simulates the systems' response, the easier it is for stakeholders and participants in usability testing, to predict how the application is intended to work in production. We achieve a higher fidelity in the prototype by simulating the widget's behavior in response to user-initiated events such as click, rollover, drag, and so on. While the `OnPageLoad` event is triggered automatically when the page loads, widget interactions are triggered when the user acts.

Guided example: Sign-in

Earlier in the chapter, we had an opportunity to create a user-driven interaction, when we attached an `OnClick` event to each of the tabs on the Global Navigation master. The interaction involved a simple linking action triggered when the user clicked on the tab. This is the tip of the iceberg for Axure interactions.

In the following example, we will expand widget interactions, by adding a **Log In** object to the header section.

It is, of course, impossible to cover in detail the evolution of the entire demo application, so let's pretend that in subsequent iterations, the application's name, logo, and tagline were added to the Header master. The following screenshot illustrates the evolution of the **Header** from a simple rectangle (A) that served as a placeholder for initial wireframes to replace the rectangle with the application's name, logo, and tagline (B), to the point where we are ready to articulate our design of the **Subscribe** and **Log In** experience (C):

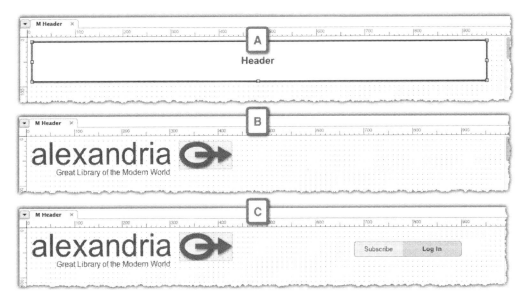

The subscription and log in interaction design is informed by meetings with business stakeholders who repeatedly emphasized that they want the header bar to be very minimalist, much like an iPhone or iPad app. The focus should be on getting visitors to the site to subscribe or log in.

In our example, we will build the login prompt and demonstrate some more actions on widget possibilities.

The following diagram shows the login flow and its basic requirements: When the user (A) clicks on the **Log In** button, a pop up with a username, password fields, and assistance should appear (B). The user needs to provide their e-mail ID and password. Upon a successful log in, provide links to the user's profile, and account information. In addition, display special promotions offered to the user (C):

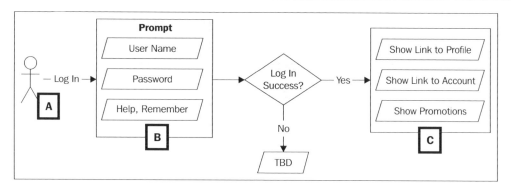

Compared to the previous requirements that we have used so far in our examples, this requirement is quite detailed, as it covers an entire user interaction flow. I am leaving out an alternate path purposely, which deals with a user who needs assistance to log in, as we will cover conditional logic in *Chapter 5*.

Construction strategy

Before wiring the interaction, we need to wireframe the Login pop-up, and there are some construction issues to consider. For example, should the entire **Subscribe/Log In** control (button and pop up) be a part of the **Header** master, or an independent master nested in the Header master? The following screenshot shows the Header master (A) inside which the **Subscribe/Log In** component (B) was constructed:

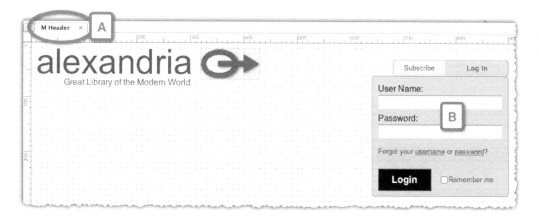

It is always a good idea to keep the construction as modular as possible, to reduce both the complexity and redundancy of wireframes. As the functionality and behavior of the **Subscribe/Log In** component is distinctly separate from the header, it makes sense to detach it from the header, by converting it to an independent master.

In addition, we know that for the login pop-up to appear when the user clicks on the **Log In** button, the pop up must be a dynamic panel. That is because it is the only Axure widget for which you can control the visibility attribute.

The following screenshot visualizes the construction steps needed before we can create the interaction for the **Log In** button:

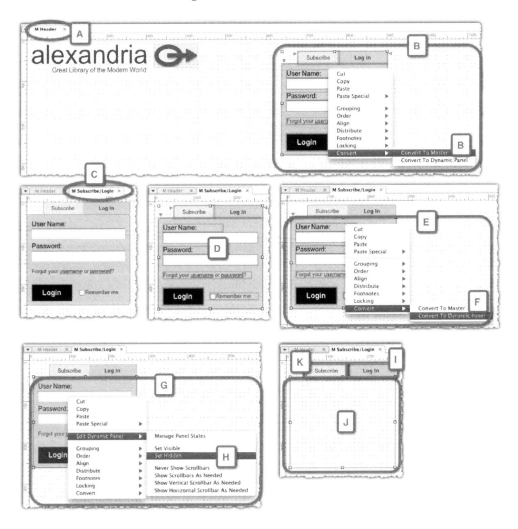

- We start in the **Header** master (A), by selecting all the widgets that make up the **Subscribe/Log In** component (B) and converting the selection to a master. As we do the conversion in the **Header** master, an instance of the new master will replace the widgets that were converted.

- After opening the newly minted **Subscribe/Log In** master for editing (C), we select all the widgets again, and set the position of the entire selection to 10 pixels from the left and top of the wireframe's upper-left corner (D). This is an optional step, which gives you a visual control that all the widgets are within the visible parts of the wireframe and not bleeding outside.

- Next, we select all the widgets except the **Subscribe** and **Log In** widgets (E), and convert the selection to a dynamic panel (F).

- We select the dynamic panel (G), and set it to **Hidden** (H).

- The **Subscribe/Login** master is now composed of the **Log In** button (I), the hidden dynamic panel of the Login prompt (J), and **Subscribe** button (K).

Finally, we label all the widgets in the **Subscribe/Log In** master.

Adding the interaction

We are now ready to add the interaction that is triggered when the user clicks on the **Log In** button widget. The W3C components of the interaction are:

- **When**: The user clicks the **Log In** button
- **Where**: The **Log In** button (Rectangle widget)
- **What**: Show the login prompt
- **Condition**: No condition

This interaction, as shown in the following screenshot, does not cover the entire flow, of course, it covers only what happens after the user clicks on the **Log In** button:

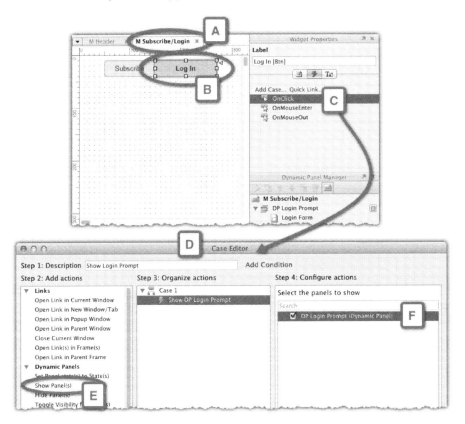

1. The master **M Subscribe/Login** master should open for editing in the **Wireframes** pane. Click on the **Log In widget** (B) and in the **Widget Properties** pane, double-click on the **OnClick** event (C).

2. In **Case Editor** (D), give the interaction a meaningful name, for example, **Show Login Prompt**, and in the column **Step 2: Add actions**, select the action **Show Panel(s)** (E) from the **Dynamic Panels** section.

3. The only dynamic panel in this master's wireframe is listed in the column **Step 4: Configure actions**. In our example, it is labeled as **DP Login Prompt (Dynamic Panel)** (F). Check it to indicate your selection.

That seems to be done. The following screenshot illustrates the generated prototype after you click on the **Log In** button:

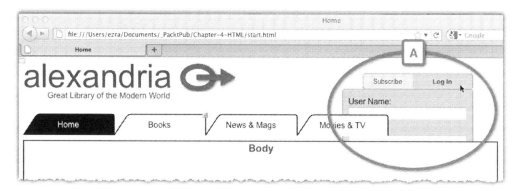

Something does not look right! While the login prompt becomes visible when you clicked on the **Log In** button, it appears behind the Global Navigation and body sections. That is because the way Axure manages the Z-axis, or the depth relationship of wireframe widgets.

Although Axure does not provide a formal layer management feature such as those common in drawing applications, it supports ordering of widgets using the **move front**, **back**, **forward**, and **backward** options. In addition, the first widget you place in the wireframe will be at the very background, and following widgets will be in front. This is not something you might notice, unless the widgets overlap.

What has happened in our example is that the **Header** master was placed first on the wireframe, and the login prompt—which is nested in it—is obscured by the Global Navigation and **Body** sections that were added after the **Header** and so are in front of it.

In order to repair this problem, carry out the steps shown in the following screenshot:

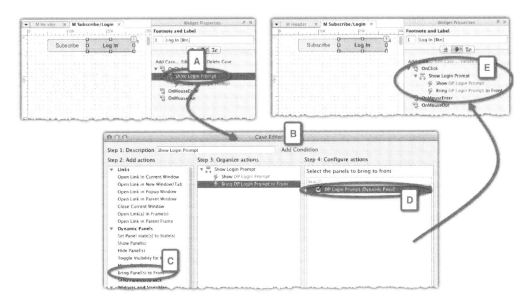

- Back in the **M Subscribe/Login** master, select the **Log In** button, and double-click the **Show Login Prompt** interaction (A).

- In the **Case Editor** (B), find the **Bring Panel(s) to Front** action (C), in the **Dynamic Panels** section of the column **Step 2: Add actions**.

- Check the checkbox to the left of the DP **Login Prompt (Dynamic Panel)** (D) — the single dynamic panel in this wireframe. Close **Case Editor**.

- Now, the interaction created for the **OnClick** event includes two actions — making the hidden dynamic panel visible, and placing it in front of all other widgets in the wireframe where the master is placed.

The following screenshot illustrates the result after you generate the prototype again:

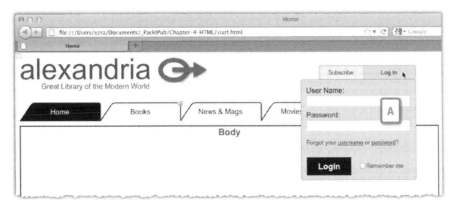

The interaction now works just as intended, and the **Login Prompt** (A) now appears on top of the other elements. Prototyping the login interaction, however, has just begun. Now that the login prompt is visible, we need to simulate a successful and unsuccessful login. We will get back to these flows in *Chapter 5*, but one tweak that we can apply now, will afford the user to dismiss the login prompt.

There are a couple of ways to hide the panel if the user chooses not to log in at this point. The fastest method is to replace the action **Show Panel(s)**, with the action **Toggle Visibility for Panel(s)**. When the user clicks the **Log In** button for the first time, the **Login** prompt will become visible. Clicking on the button again will hide the prompt, and so on.

Organizing actions

As you composed your initial interactions in the **Case Editor**, you may have wondered about the role of the column **Step 3: Organize actions**. As it turns out, once you have two or more actions associated with a case, their order is important. The following screenshot explains the modification of the Show Login Prompt interaction, which includes two actions:

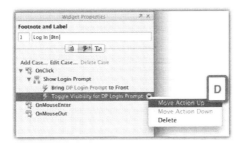

- Our initial interaction (A) listed the **Show Panel(s) action** first, and then **Bring Panel(s) to front** as second. This makes total sense.

- In order to replace the **Show Panel(s)** action with the **Toggle Visibility for DP Login Prompt** action, we have to delete the **Show action first** (B).

- The **Toggle Visibility for DP Login Prompt** action is added below the **Bring DP Login Prompt to Front** action (C).

- You may not be sure if the order matters in this case, but, because in the initial interaction the **Bring DP Login Prompt to Front** was last, you may want to maintain the same order that proved to work. To change the order, select the **Move Action Up** option from the actions context menu (D).

- You will end up with an order that is similar to what you had originally (E).

- In this specific case, it turns out that the order of actions in the **Step 3** column did not matter much. However, as your interactions become more advanced, one of the first troubleshooting techniques is to check that the order of actions make sense.

Widget, Events, and Context

Each of Axure's built-in widgets, with the exception of the iFrame, can be assigned an interaction. No single widget can perform all possible actions, which is a good thing, because most user interface widgets have inherent, well-established constraints. For example, a radio button can be selected or deselected, enabled or disabled, and in or out of focus. So, Axure events and widgets are contextual. In order to see, which actions are associated with a widget, drag-over the widget to the **Wireframes** pane, and while it is selected, switch to the **Interactions** tab in the **Widgets Properties** pane.

Note that you don't have to create interactions to enable some widgets for interaction. Form input widgets such as text fields, radio buttons, or drop-downs will respond to the user without any interactions, although no follow-up action will take place. For example, the user will be able to type in a text field, but actions such as evaluating the contents of the field, or actions once the user exits the field will not happen unless you create the appropriate interactions. Other widgets, such as rectangle or image widgets without an interaction, will appear as part of a static image when the wireframe is rendered in the browser.

The following figure is a visualization of Axure's Widget/Actions groupings:

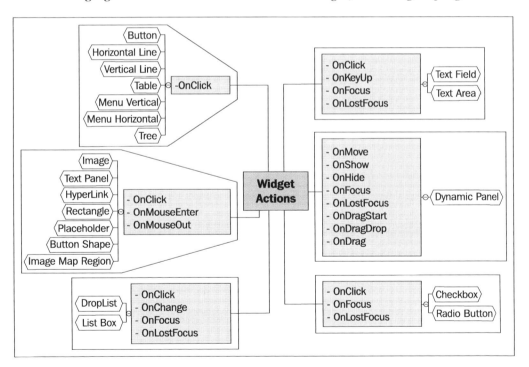

Widget Events in detail

The OnClick event is one of the fundamental triggers of modern user-computer interactions. In Axure, it is one of several actions you can associate with a widget and, as discussed earlier, widgets and events are contextual.

The following diagram gives a detailed look at Axure's widget level events:

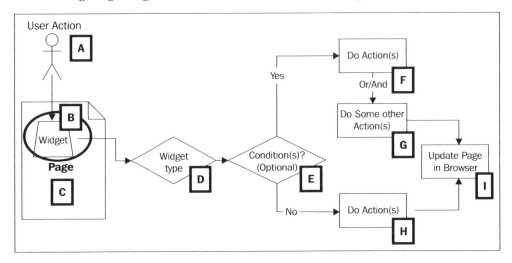

- The user interacts with a widget by initiating an event (A), such as an OnClick event that is associated with that widget (B).

- The type of widget (button, checkbox, and so on) constrains the possible response the user can expect (D). For example, before clicking on a button, the user may move the mouse over it, and the visual appearance of the button will change in response to the OnMouseEnter event.

- The browser will check if conditional logic is tied to the widget event (E). For example, you may have created an interaction in which a rollover event will display different states of a dynamic panel based on some variable. The browser will evaluate the condition and execute the action(s) (F and G).

- If no conditions exist, the browser will execute the action(s) associated with the widget (H).

- Based on the actions tied to the event, the browser will update the screen, or load some other screen (I).

Axure cases

You are familiar with cases from modeling and diagramming the user experience. **Cases** are abstractions of interaction flows the user has with an application. Each case encapsulates a discrete path the user can take. Typically, we are asked to prototype the primary case and often alternate paths, which are either contextual to the user or to some other conditions that may cause the same task to have variable flows. Multiple cases of the same task infer some conditional logic that affects which path of the task will be followed.

Axure cases are a way to build alternate paths for the same task. In all of the examples that we constructed so far, we encountered cases as a part of the process of creating interaction. However, other than labeling the case in a meaningful way, we had no real use for cases. That is because our interactions so far involved single cases and no conditions were involved.

The following diagram illustrates the structure of an Axure interaction and where Axure cases fit in:

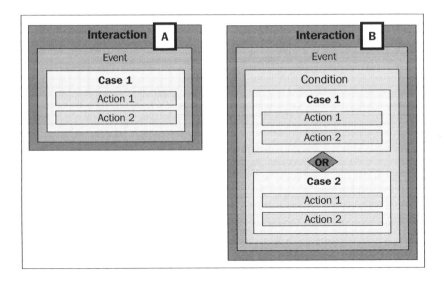

Cases are typically used in one of two ways, in both page and master `OnPageLoad` events, or in widget events:

- A single case with one or more actions (A) per single interaction event; no conditional logic is involved

- Multiple cases, each with one or more actions (B) per single interaction event; conditional logic is used for manual selection of the prototype to determine the execution of the interaction

An Axure case is basically a container of actions, and it is what makes it possible for us to simulate alternate interaction paths. The higher the fidelity of the prototype, the higher is the number of multicase interactions.

Guided example: Construction and interactions

Back to our Alexandria example, we want to continue our work on the **Login** section. We want to simulate a successful login flow. However, the wireframes are not complete. In this example, we first go through some wireframe construction and tweaking, which is necessary before the actual interactions can be built.

Part 1: Construction tweaks

Due to limitations of space, and in the interest of keeping the flow of reading as smooth as possible, some minor details have been omitted. If you choose to follow this exercise, it is an opportunity to experiment.

We start with the following screenshot, which illustrates where we had left off with the **Subscribe/Login** master:

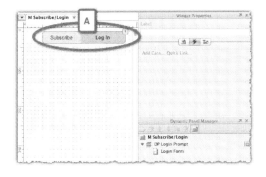 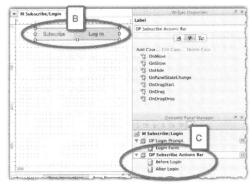

Objective: Upon successful login, **Subscribe** and **Log In** buttons should be replaced with the following:

1. **Welcome** <First name of user>

2. Links to **Profile**, **Account**, and **Support**

3. In the current wireframe of the master **M Subscribe/Login**, the buttons for **Subscribe** and **Log In** are made of rectangle widgets that are placed directly on the wireframe (A). Let's convert the widgets into a dynamic panel with two states. The top state is these two buttons, so label the state something like **Before Login**. The second state will show the new links as per our objective, so label it **After Login**. Also, label the dynamic panel that contains those two states as **DP Subscribe Actions Bar** (DP stands for Dynamic Panel).

    The following screenshot continues the construction process:

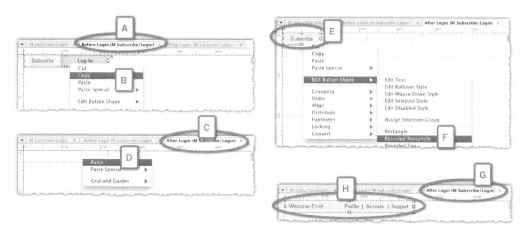

4. Open both states for editing. From the **Before Login** state wireframe (A), select and copy the widgets (B). Switch to the **After Login** state wireframe (C), and paste the widgets (D) using the context menu.

5. For reasons of visual consistency, the welcome notice and new links will appear in a rounded rectangle widget that has the same height as the buttons in the first state, but is a bit wider. In the **After Login** state, change the style of one of the pasted links (E) from a **Rounded Left** widget to a **Rounded Rectangle** (F). Proceed to change the text to **Welcome** <name> and the new links (H).

The following screenshot continues the construction process:

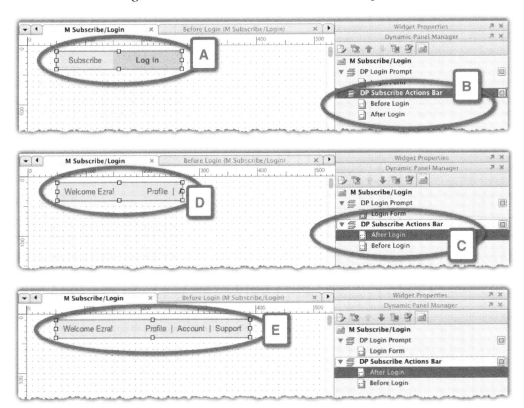

6. Return to the master wireframe. The **Subscribe** and **Log In** buttons (A) in the dynamic panel **DP Subscribe Actions Bar** (B) fit the width of the dynamic panel. However, you want to adjust the panel's width, so that the wider state in the **After Login** state will fit as well.

7. In the **Dynamic Panel Manager** pane, move the **After Login** state so it is above the **Before Login** state (C). Now, you can see the state's wireframe (D). It is easy to adjust the width of the dynamic panel (E) quickly and accurately.

The following screenshot continues the construction process:

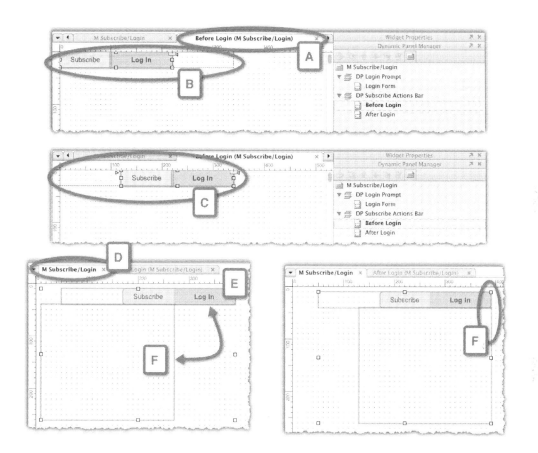

Now that the dynamic panel which holds both states of the login buttons has been adjusted to the size of its largest state, we can switch the order of the states in the Dynamic Panel Manager, so that the **Before Login** state is visible by default.

8. Open this state for editing (A), and move the buttons from the left side of the dotted blue boundary of the dynamic panel (B), to the right (C). Why? Because these buttons are positioned close to the right margin of the **Home** and other site pages. After login, we want to avoid the wider state from extending to the right of the right margin.

9. Switch back to the master wireframe **M Subscribe/Login** (D). It is now composed of two dynamic panels. One of the buttons (E) and the other which we created in the previous example of the login prompt (F). Right align them so that that the login prompt will appear below the **Log In** button (G).

The following screenshot concludes this construction process:

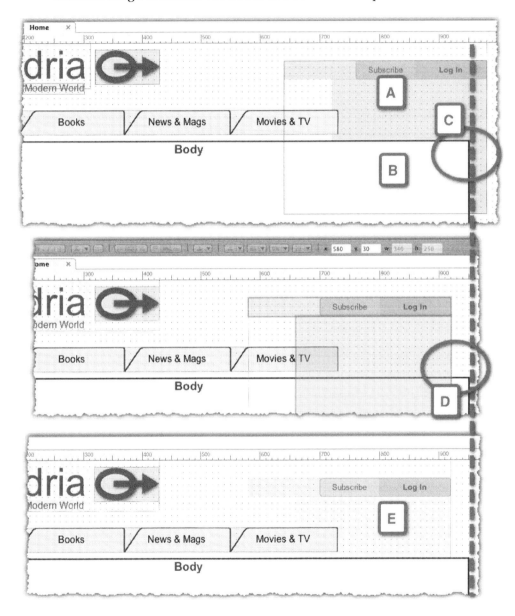

We did a lot of widget shifting on master level wireframes and now it is critical to check the impact of these tweaks on the page wireframes which will be generated in the prototype.

1. When we open the **Home** page wireframe for review, it appears that the **Subscribe/Login master** (A) has shifted to the right and is now extending beyond the body section (B), which marks the right margin of the wireframe (C).

2. We initially placed the **Subscribe/Login** master in the Header master, but given the latest tweaks to the **Subscribe/Login** master and the potential of further tweaks, perhaps it makes sense to place the master directly on the page wireframe. Cut the master out of the Header master, and paste and position it on the **Home** page master (D).

3. As we will have to place the master on practically all other pages of the application, there is a risk that future repositioning of the master on one wireframe, will have to be repeated, with a risk of position inconsistencies between pages.

4. In order to avert the risk, apply the X position of the **Subscribe/Login** master placement on the **Home** wireframe, to the placement of the dynamic panels in that master's wireframe. Then, change the master's behavior to **Place in Background**.

5. Switch back to the **Home** page wireframe, delete the instance of the **Subscribe/Login** master that is there, and drag-over a new instance of the same master. It will automatically snap right into the appropriate position (E). The effort of placing and maintaining a consistent position for this master has now been greatly reduced.

Part 2: Adding interactions

After a well-deserved coffee break, it is time to complete what we set out to do at the beginning of the example, which is, to simulate what happens when the user signs in.

Our objective: When the user clicks on the **Log In** button after providing a username and password (if the credentials are correct), replace the **Subscribe** and **Log In** button with a welcome message and links to the user's profile, account, as well as a link to support. At this point, we don't want to elaborate on failed logins, so we will provide a placeholder until the wireframes for this path are updated.

The following screenshot illustrates the initial steps in the process:

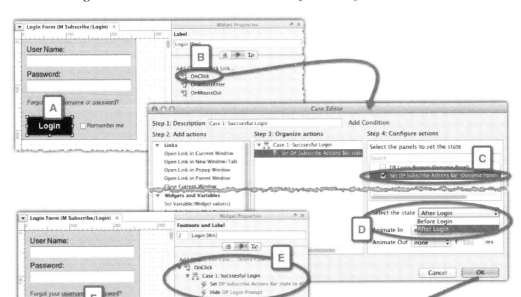

We will start with the interaction that simulates a successful login. This will be very basic, and we will not evaluate if the fields actually have any data, nor will we compare the input to some expected credentials (but no worries, we will get to this in *Chapter 5*).

1. Open the **Login Form** state of the login prompt dynamic panel and select the **Login** button (A). Double-click on the **OnClick** event (B) and select the action **Set Panel state(s) to state(s)**. Rename this case. In the column **Step 4: Configure Actions**, two dynamic panels are listed—the **Login Prompt** and the **Subscribe Actions Bar**. Check the latter, and from the **Select the state** drop-down select **After Login** (D).

2. After you close the **Case Editor**, the new interaction is added (E), and a yellow footnote tag is added to the **Login** button (F), indicating that an interaction (or/and annotation, or both) is associated with it.

The following screenshot continues the process:

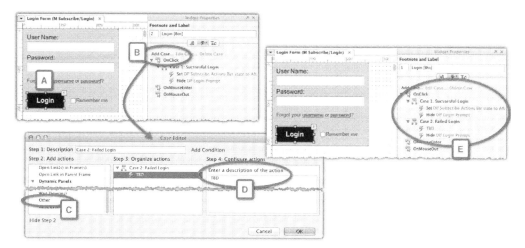

Next, we will add the alternate login case, when the user does not provide valid credentials:

- With the **Login** button still selected (A), double-click the **OnClick** event, or click on the **Add Case** link (B) to launch the **Case Editor**.

- As we did not prepare the wireframes needed to support this flow, let's use a place holder: The action **Other** (C) lets you describe in words the intended interaction. In many cases, this is good enough to get a conversation going. Type the description in the column **Step 4: Configure actions** (D), and close the editor.

Two cases are now nested under the **OnClick** event (E). It is time to generate the prototype and see what we get! The following screenshot illustrates the result generated in the browser:

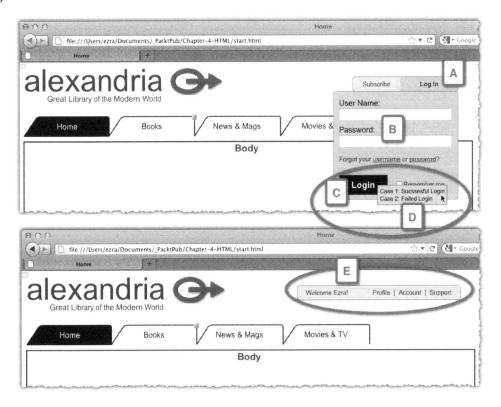

Axure actions

Earlier in this chapter, we looked at Axure events, which trigger actions. We described cases, which are the organizational units for one or more actions triggered by an event. Hopefully, as you went through the guided examples throughout the chapter, you have noticed the richness of functionality we can simulate with Axure and the fact that no programming skills are needed—just a bit of common sense.

Axure currently supports twenty-five actions, organized in the following four groups:

1. Links
2. Dynamic panels
3. Widgets and variables
4. Miscellaneous

The following diagram shows Axure's action groupings:

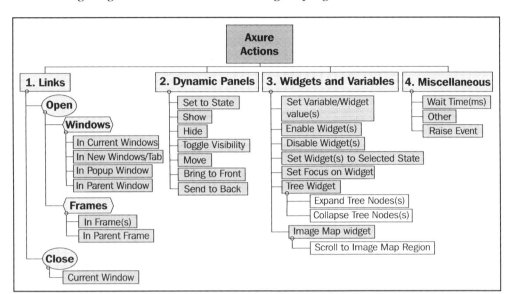

Links actions

These actions are parallel to the HTML `<a>` target attribute, such as `_self`, `_parent`, and so on, which specifies where to open the linked document. They are mostly self-explanatory and used to facilitate navigation. The frame actions allow you to take advantage of the iFrame widget and load a page within a page, or even multiple pages within a page.

Dynamic panel actions

Dynamic panels are the widgets that are responsible for the prototype "magic". The actions afford control over horizontal, vertical, and depth position, visibility, and movement.

Widgets and variables actions

Wherever applicable, you can enable or disable widgets, for example, fields, radio buttons, or checkboxes. You can set focus on a widget, which is great for placing the cursor in a particular form field when a page loads. As we demonstrated earlier, you can set a widget to a selected state and this will work as long as you create a selected state for the widget. Finally, there are some specialized actions for the tree and image map region widgets.

Miscellaneous actions

- **Wait Time (ms)** is self-explanatory and extremely useful for setting up timed interactions.

- **Other** is basically a text placeholder, where you can articulate in writing some action that should take place.

- **Raise Event** is an action that is applicable only to widgets that are placed in a master wireframe. We will discuss raised events in detail in *Chapter 5*.

Summary

In this chapter, we covered the fundamental aspects of Axure interactions. Interactions can be associated with pages, masters, and contextually with widgets. It is up to you to determine which elements in a prototype should be interactive, and to what level of fidelity these interactions should mimic in the planned application. As a rule of thumb, focus on your deliverables, and on the value that each interaction can provide, to make the prototype communicate your intention for a better user experience.

If you are expected to deliver a specifications document, the higher the fidelity and complexity of your interactions, the more difficult it gets to generate a clear and easy-to-digest specifications document. Start experimenting very early with the output of your prototype as a Word document and final words to conclude this chapter—label widget and interaction elements in your wireframes!

In the next chapter, we will cover more advanced aspects of Axure interactions such as conditional logic, variables, raised events, and so on. However, don't let the word *advanced* scare you, because the investment in learning some more intricate aspects of interactions and wireframe constructions will help you create really compelling high-fidelity prototypes.

5

Advanced Interactions

Don't let the word "advanced" scare you away from this chapter! I am going to cover a set of features such as raised events, conditional logic and variables, introduction to a terminology which is usually associated with programming and suggests complexity. It is understandable if you are not interested in, or are intimidated by, the prospect of coding, and wish to avoid using this set of Axure features as long as possible. You should not.

First, rest assured that no coding is involved. By now, you are familiar with Axure's **Interactions** and the **Case Editor** features, which require you only to select from a contextual selection of options and construct interactions by pointing and clicking. The only typing required is the labeling. You will find a similar easy-to-use interface when you use features such as the **Condition Builder** or simulate "drag and drop".

Secondly, think about some of the terminologies and methods we use in interaction design. We use branching logic to determine use cases, scenarios, and how functionality responds to user interaction under certain conditions. Axure makes it fairly easy to model the logic we need, in order to visualize branching paths, and express it in the interactive prototype.

Finally, not only will you maximize your investment in Axure, you will also enhance your own professional skills and have an opportunity to express your creativity. Much like learning a new language, the greater your vocabulary the more expressive will be your communication. It is the same with professional tools; and like any professional tool, Axure, more than anything else, is an enabler for your creativity. So, let's dive right in.

Conditions

When you incorporate conditional logic into your prototype, you save yourself from a great deal of overhead work. If you don't use conditional logic, you are limiting your ability to simulate conditional interactions in your prototype. Let's face it, we use logic all the time, even if the results are not always logical. Moreover, in computer science and interaction design, we must use conditional logic in order to accommodate variable situations and exceptions. Yet, there seems to be a general reluctance to deal with direct use of logic when it comes to using software. A good example is the so-called "advanced" search feature that most search engines, including Google, offer, and the reason why Google's concept of a single search field and no operators has become the standard search interface.

If-Then-Else

Programming languages employ a variety of syntaxes for creating and evaluating conditional statements. Axure simplifies things by using the very common syntax of If-Then-Else, which essentially looks like this:

- If A is true, then do X
- Else, if B is true then do Z

This kind of decision-making is very natural to UX designers because we use a similar logical approach to model task and interaction flows. When we create a conditional interaction, we reflect the flow's logic in the prototype. As it is best to learn by doing, let's dive into a quick example:

Sandbox files for learning and experimenting

Sometimes, the most effective way to figure things out is by experimentation. In the course of prototyping, you will find yourself wondering how some Axure feature works, or wanting to explore a new interaction. This is where the sandboxing technique can help: Create a blank new Axure file on your desktop, work through your explorations on this file, and then apply your learning to the project file. In the sandbox file, you don't have to worry about "breaking" any of your previous work and can focus instead just on the mechanics of the feature you are trying to figure out. The technique will also keep your production file clean and free of experimentation wireframes.

Guided example—conditions and dynamic panels

Axure makes it very easy to apply conditional logic to the prototype, as you will see in this example. We will use a "sandbox" file to explore the feature, and later, apply the learning to the Alexandria project file.

Step 1: Defining the interaction

Our goal is to change the state of a dynamic panel based on the user input. This is one of the most commonly used conditional logic interactions in the construction of Axure prototypes, and a great illustration of If-Then-Else.

In this simple example, the user selects a shape from a list of shapes and the appropriate shape appears. As we established in *Chapter 4, Interactivity 101*, the first step is to define the desired interaction. Now that the conditional logic is involved, this is also the opportunity to spell out the logic:

- When: When the user *changes* the selection
- Where: A *droplist* widget
- What: *Change the state* of a dynamic panel to show the corresponding shape
- Conditions: On entry, the droplist should show the option "Select from List", and no shape should be visible
- If the user selects the value "Rectangle" from the droplist, show the rectangle state
- If the user selects the value "Triangle" from the droplist, show the triangle state
- If the user selects the value "Circle" from the droplist, show the circle state
- If the user selects the value "Select from List" from the droplist, hide the shapes

The logic here is simple, because each selection in the droplist has a corresponding dynamic panel state. We instruct Axure to evaluate which option is selected in the droplist, and then change the state of the dynamic panel accordingly.

Notice that the first sentence in the condition section specifies the entry state, in this case, the option "Select from List". This is the **default state** when the screen loads. When you plan interactions that involve conditions, always make sure you account for a default state of that UI control.

Step 2: Constructing Wireframe

We will start by preparing a sandbox environment. Create a blank directory on your desktop and label it Axure Sandbox. In this directory, create another directory named HTML—this is where we will generate the prototype. Finally, create a new Axure file named Sandbox and save it in the Axure Sandbox directory. The following screenshot illustrates the steps:

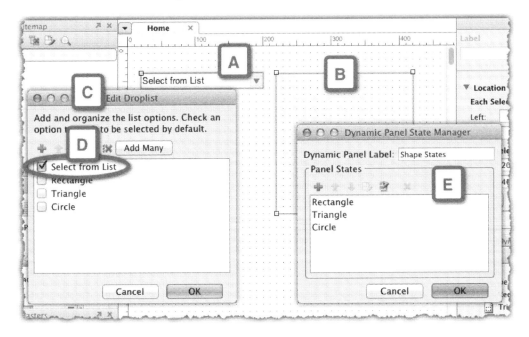

- From the **Widgets** pane, drag over a **Droplist** (A) and a **Dynamic Panel** (B) widget. Label them **Droplist** and **Shape States**, for example.

- Double-click on the droplist and in the **Edit Droplist** dialog (C), add the values specified in *Step 1*, and check **Select from List** to make it the default value (D).

- In the dynamic panel, create the states for the three corresponding shapes. This does not need to be an elaborate production. Make sure you label each of the states (E).

- Right-click on the dynamic panel and select **Set Hidden** from the context menu.

Step 3: Setting the first condition

When you start with interactions, having the flow pre-planned helps in creating the wireframe and in adding the interaction. Now that we covered both in *Steps 1 and 2*, we will set the conditional logic for the interaction. The following screenshot visualizes the process:

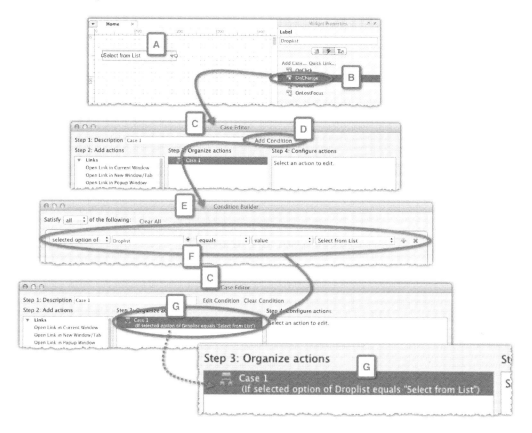

- With the droplist selected in the wireframe (A), switch to the **Interactions** tab in the **Widgets Properties** pane, and double-click on the **OnChange** event (B) to launch **Case Editor** (C).

- Before clicking on **Case 1**, we want to create the conditions. Click on the **Add Condition** link (D) to launch the **Condition Builder** window (E).

- We will discuss Condition Builder later in this chapter, but for now, notice that the *first* condition row already appears in the builder. It is contextual to the selected widget, and is structured like an equation: "The selected option of droplist equals the value Select from List." (F). As this is one of the conditions that needs to be evaluated, each time the user changes a value in the droplist, we can use it as is. Click on **OK** to close the builder.

- Back in **Case Editor** (C), notice that the condition has been added to **Case 1**, and Axure presents it in a human-friendly way: **If selected option of Droplist equals "Select from List"** (G).

Step 4: Adding the first interaction

Now we need to instruct Axure about the action to apply when the condition we have just set is met. In this case, when the value of the droplist is "Select from List", the shapes should be hidden. As the shapes are in the dynamic panel widget, we want to hide that widget. Now, you might ask yourself, "Why hide the dynamic panel, if it is already hidden?"

When you create conditions, always make sure to account for ALL the possible cases that are applicable to the interaction.

It is true that in the wireframe, the dynamic panel is hidden by default. However, once the user selects a shape from the list, the dynamic panel will become visible, until the user changes the value in the droplist to "Select from List". Moreover, this is where the **Set Hidden** action will come into play. The following screenshot illustrates the process:

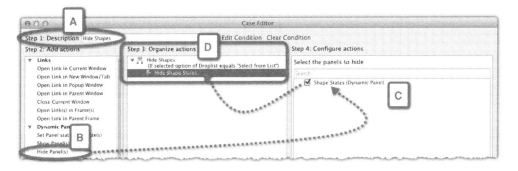

- First, label **Case 1** to something meaningful such as **Hide Shapes** (A).

- Select the **Hide Panel(s)** action (B), and click to check the dynamic panel widget which is listed in the column **Step 4: Configure actions** (C).

- The complete interaction is now listed under the column **Step 3: Organize actions** (D).

Step 5: Completing the interaction

At this point, the interaction includes a single case, which handles a single condition. In order to complete the interaction, we need to capture additional cases when the user picks various shapes from the droplist. The following screenshot illustrates the first half of the process involved in adding the condition and interaction for the first shape:

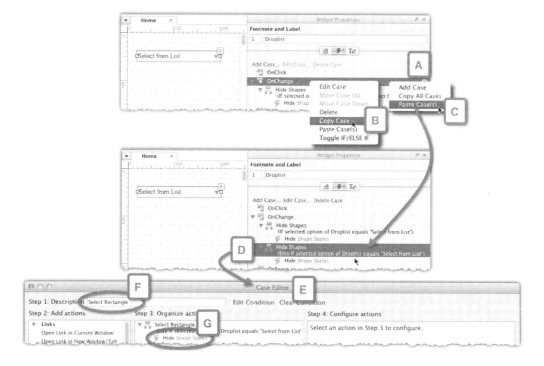

- As we are evaluating the selected option of the same widget, the only variable to check is the value of that option. This means we can use a shortcut: Right-click on the initial case created in *Step 4* (A), select **Copy Case** (B), and then **Paste Case(s)** (C) from the context menu.

- Double-click on the new case (D) to open **Case Editor** (E), where the first things to do are to rename the case (F), and delete the Hide action (G).

Using one case as the starting point for another case is common. The following screenshot illustrates the process of tweaking the duplicate case to fit a new condition:

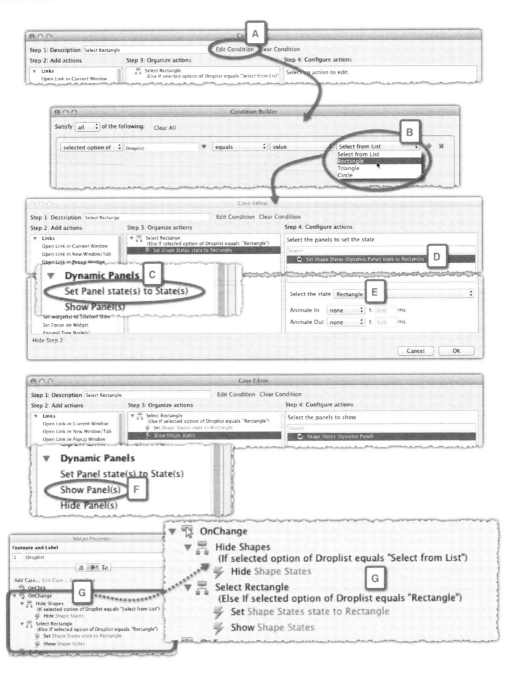

- In **Case Editor**, click on the **Edit Condition** link (A). All there is to do next is to change the copied selection from **Select from List** to **Rectangle** (B), and close the **Condition Builder**.

- Back in **Case Editor**, set the action to **Set Panel state(s) to State(s)** in the column **Step 2: Add actions** (C) and in the column **Step 4: Configure actions** (D), check the dynamic panel widget (D) and select the **Rectangle** shape (E).

- We need to add a **Show Panel(s)** action (F), because the dynamic panel widget is hidden by default and it is also hidden when the selected option in the droplist is **Select from List**. With this action set up, close **Case Editor**.

- The interaction for **OnChange** case (G) now covers a couple of the conditions we specified in *Step 1* of this example. Add the additional cases using the process outlined in *Step 5*.

The following screenshot illustrates what the complete conditional interaction should look like:

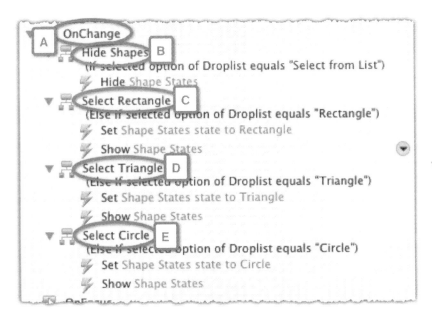

When the user changes an item in the droplist, the **OnChange** action (A) evaluates the selection and:

- If the user selects the value **Rectangle** from the droplist, show the rectangle state (C)

- If the user selects the value **Triangle** from the droplist, show the triangle state (D)

- If the user selects the value **Circle** from the droplist, show the circle state (E)
- If the user selects the value **Select from List** from the droplist, hide the shapes (B)

It is time to generate the HTML prototype. Make sure you set the path for the prototype to Axure Sandbox | HTML, as discussed in *Step 2* of this example. The following screenshot (A through E) illustrates the generated result:

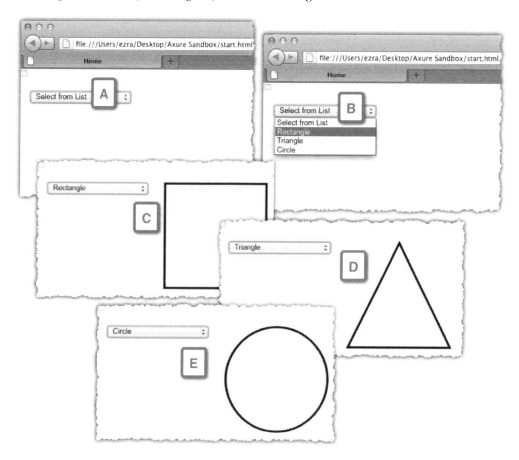

The Condition Builder

Let's take a closer look at a simple conditional statement from the previous example. The interaction for the Rectangle case is composed of the following two sentences:

1. If the selected option in the Droplist equals **Rectangle**
2. Set **Shape State** state to **Rectangle**

The first sentence is the condition being evaluated, and the second sentence is the action that takes place if the condition is met. Now let's focus on the condition sentence itself, and the flexibility afforded by the modular nature of Axure's Condition Builder.

Although the condition is composed of five droplists, what we are looking at is an equation in which we compare the first two droplists to the last two droplists. The following screenshot illustrates how the segments are assembled in the builder:

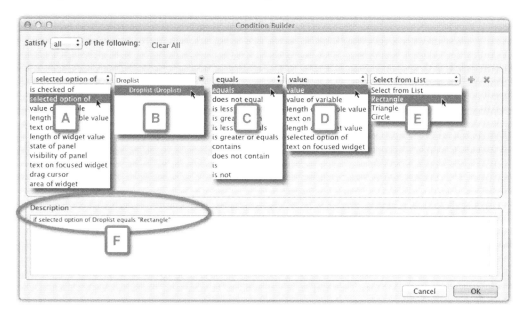

- **selected option of** is one of eleven choices in the first droplist (A). The selection made here affects the other droplists. Note that, although in our example, we have the interaction tied to the OnChange event of the droplist widget, the condition we add does not have to be limited to evaluating the selected value of the droplist. We could add other conditions to the OnChange event that evaluate any of the other choices in the builder's droplist A.

- Our choice in the first droplist narrows the options in the second droplist (B) to droplists and listbox widgets. Our example wireframe has only a single droplist widget and so **Droplist (Droplist)** is the only item listed.

- The third droplist (C) is where we set the comparison choices in droplists A and B to the choices in droplist D and E. In addition to the option **Equals**, there are nine more options to construct the equation.

- In the forth droplist (D), we specify what type of value the comparison will evaluate. In our example, we want to know what is the selected option in the wireframe droplist. However, we could also set a comparison to the selected option of some other droplist and create contextual droplists (example is coming below).

- The last droplist (E) is contextual to the selection we make in D. In our example, as we opted to look at the value of the **Droplist** widget (B), Axure lists the values we entered for that widget.

- Finally, the **Description** section (F) is automatically generated by Axure to reiterate the condition in plain English.

Guided example—multiple conditions

We often have to evaluate multiple conditions before we can determine which action to take. For example, simulating validation of the required form or authentication fields, or simulating a contextual rendering of an application screen, based on the user login, status, and other parameters. The Condition Builder is a significant time saver because with relatively few wireframes, mostly variations within dynamic panel states, it is possible to create multiple conditions and simulate sophisticated interactions.

For this example, we will continue with our Alexandria project. Specifically, we will complete the login validation which we constructed in the previous chapter.

Step 1: Defining the interaction

Our goal is to evaluate if the user entered their username and password, prompt the user if there is missing or wrong information, or log them into the site. This interaction is broadly used, although interaction patterns vary slightly. Successful sign-in is a critical task because in most sites and applications, it affords access to the most valuable features.

It is sometimes tempting to postpone, or skip altogether, simulating the sign-in task, because it is so trivial. However, without an explicit directive from UX about this flow, we are leaving the interpretation and design to the developers.

In this example, we will use Condition Builder to compose several conditions and the first step is to define the desired interaction. As with all interactions that involve conditional logic, this is the opportunity to spell out the logic:

- When: When the user *clicks on the* **Login** *button.*
- Where: The *Login rectangle* widget.

- What: Validate the username and password. Alert the user if there is an issue, or log the user in.
- Conditions: On entry, the **User Name** and **Password** fields are *empty*, and the **Login** button is *disabled*.
- The **Login** button is enabled only if both fields are populated.
- When the user clicks on the **Login** button.
  - If the provided credentials are ok, change the screen to reflect a successful sign-in screen.
  - If any or both credentials are wrong, notify the user and disable the Login button.
  - If the user re-typed the credentials, reactivate the Login button.

The logic here is a bit more involved compared to the previous example, as we need to account for the interaction in multiple widgets: The form fields, the **Login** button, and the notification to the user in the case of an authentication problem.

The following screenshot illustrates the current state of our **Login** wireframe and its interaction, as it was created in *Chapter 4*:

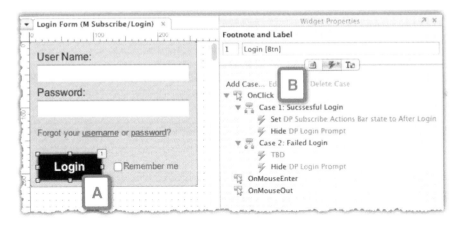

- The **Subscribe/Login** master is a dynamic panel with two states
- **Login Form** is on the second state, and the only widget with an interaction is the **Login** button (A)
- The interaction is triggered by an **OnClick** event which does not evaluate the **User Name** and **Password** fields

Step 2: Constructing Wireframe

We will start by iterating on top of what we have already created, and make adjustments to the wireframe according to the new requirements. The following screenshot illustrates the tweaks:

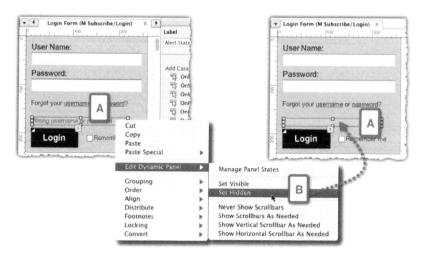

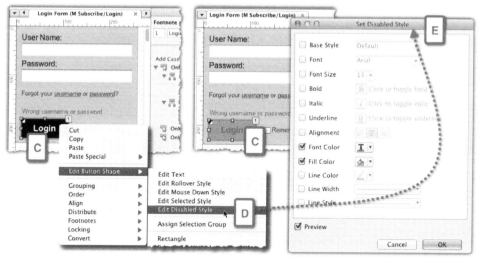

- It appears that in the current wireframe, there is no room for providing the user with feedback if there is an issue with the username or password.

- Right above the **Login** button, we will add a dynamic panel which will contain the error message (see the preceding screenshot, A) and set it to **Hidden** (B). Remember that dynamic panel widgets are the only widget type for which you can control the visibility properties:

    ○ The height of the current pop up needs to be adjusted to accommodate the added alert, and remember to increase the height of the dynamic panel that holds the state.

- The **Login** button (C) needs to have a disabled state. There are at least a couple of ways to approach the constructions.

    ○ Converting the widget into a dynamic panel and adding a disabled state:

    ○ Use the styling feature to add a **Disabled Style** (D) in the **Set Disabled Style** editor (E) and use actions to switch between normal and disabled styles. In this example, I will use the second option because it involves maintaining a single wireframe widget and the use of styles which is faster to update.

With the wireframe updated to support the interaction, we can now move on to the next step.

Step 3: Interaction tweaks

A quick review of the flow of interactions, as it pertains to the wireframes, is illustrated in the following screenshot:

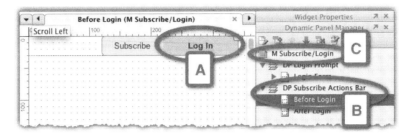

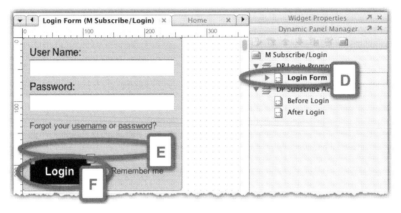

- The entire interaction is triggered when the user clicks on the **Log In** button (A), a widget in the **Before Login** state of the dynamic panel **DP Subscribe Actions Bar** (B), which is part of the master **M Subscribe/Login** (C).

- The dynamic panel **Login Form** (D), which is also in the master (C), will become visible.

- The alert dynamic panel (E) will be hidden. This is taken care of by setting the default visibility of this dynamic panel to hidden:

  - The **Login** button (F) needs to be set to show its disabled state.

As setting the **Login** button to a disabled style cannot be defaulted on the widget, it needs to be set in an action. The process is illustrated in the following screenshot:

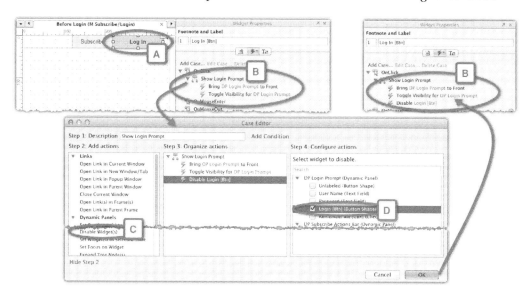

The logical place to have this action is on the button that triggers the interaction, the **Log In** button (see the preceding screenshot, A). Moreover, as we already created an initial interaction for this widget in *Chapter 4* (B), we only need to add the action **Disable Widget(s)** (C and D) to that interaction. Generate the prototype and test this out. The styling of the **Login** button will be set to the visual style you assigned to the widget, and although the widget has an **OnClick** interaction associated with it, it will be disabled.

Step 4: Evaluating multiple conditions

Now that we have established an initial state for the **Login** button in the prompt, we can move on to composing the interaction that will enable the button and allow the user to continue with the login process.

As the **Login** button should only be enabled if there is some content in the **User Name** and **Password** fields, let's assign each of the fields with an interaction to evaluate just that. In this example, our evaluation will not be too elaborate.

- For the **User Name** field, we will check whether the user typed in at least four characters. We will not look for a specific value.

- For the **Password** field, we will check whether the user typed in at least six characters. We will not look for a specific value.

Both fields are **Text Field** widgets. This type of widget can support the following events:

- OnClick
- OnKeyUp
- OnFocus
- OnLostFocus

How can we decide which event should trigger the interaction? The truth is that you can accomplish the requirements in several ways, and in some cases, it is a matter of trial and error. In this example, I will use the OnKeyUp event to trigger the actions that evaluate the fields, because this event provides an instant feedback to the user if the entered credentials satisfy the requirements.

The following screenshot illustrates the conditions and interactions for the **User Name** field (A):

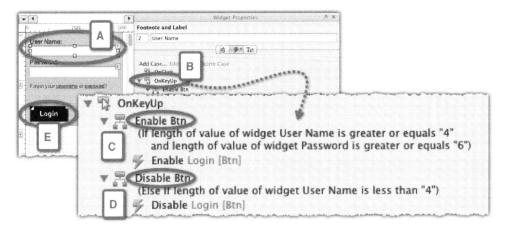

- We need to create two cases for the **OnKeyUp** event (B):
  - The first case (C) will evaluate whether the length of the input in this field is at least four characters, and whether the length of the input in the **Password** field is at least six characters, because the user must provide both pieces of information. If the length of the input for both meets the conditions, the **Login** button (E) will be enabled.
  - The second case (D) will keep the **Login** button disabled, if the length of input to the **User Name** field is less than four characters. We don't need to evaluate the length of the **Password** field, because the **User Name** must meet the condition and so it does not matter if the **Password** field is ok.

This example was a demonstration of the frequent need to evaluate multiple conditions in a single case. Let's take a closer look at the Condition Builder:

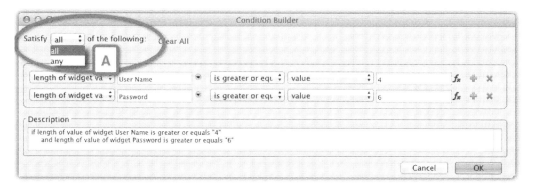

Satisfy all or any

The preceding screenshot illustrates the Condition Builder's **Satisfy** droplist (A) which has only two values, **all** and **any**. By default, it is set to **all**, which is fine if you have a single condition in the builder. With two or more conditions, it becomes critical that this droplist is set to the correct value. To help you make sense of the condition, the droplist is set as part of a sentence. Always read the entire sentence when you consider which option to set:

- Satisfy all of the following:
- Satisfy any of the following:

In our example, the conditional logic controls whether or not to activate the **Login** button, and because BOTH fields must be validated, the selection of "all" in the **Satisfy** droplist is the correct one.

Step 5: Final conditional touches

Complete the interactions and conditions for the **Password** field and generate the prototype to test whether the login control works as intended. The companion Axure file for this chapter includes the complete interaction, but I encourage you to try to figure it out yourself, because, as with anything else, we learn best by first-hand experimentation.

It will also be nice to demonstrate the alert field, which notifies the user when either of the fields is invalid. This condition is tested when the user clicks on the active **Login** button.

In this example, we will only evaluate the **Password** field and the process is illustrated in the following screenshot:

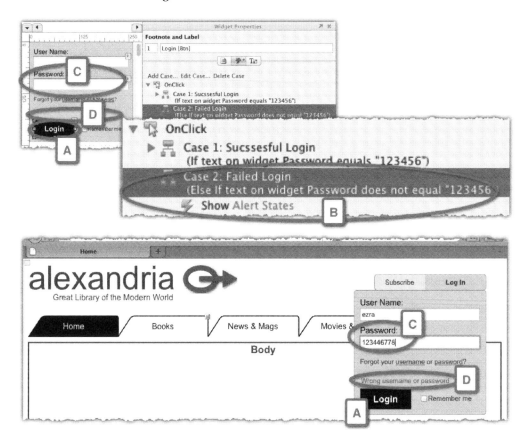

- We have already created an interaction for the **Login** button (A) in *Chapter 4*. The initial version did not evaluate anything, and the two cases for the **OnClick** event were to be triggered manually.

- The revised interactions for the **Successful** and **Failed** Login cases will evaluate a specific password value. While the conditional logic in the **User Name** and **Password** fields evaluates the length of the input, here, we want to simulate the system response if the value of the **Password** field (C) is incorrect.

- For convenience, set the password to something that is easy to remember and type, because as long as the conditional simulation of the login is in place, you will have to go through the flow each time you generate the prototype. This can become very tedious. Our password will be simply be 123456. If needed, however, you can use Axure to simulate very rigorous password verification conditions.

- The alert line (D) appears only if the password is incorrect. The **Successful Login** case will test if the password equals to 123456 and will change the state of the entire dynamic panel.

Troubleshooting conditions

As ease as it is to set up many interactions and conditions in Axure, I can guarantee that there will be cases where your interaction will not work as expected. The following are some basic troubleshooting ideas:

- The most common culprit—a simple copy and paste issue—might explain inexplicable behavior of a widget. The problematic widget may have inherited the interactions and conditions of the original widget. Clean up as needed.

- Are you evaluating the correct widget? Axure presents all the widgets that are placed on the page (or master). The list can be very long and so picking the wrong widget is understandable. If you are having a hard time finding the widget, re-label it temporarily as XYZ, which will make it much easier to spot. Remember to restore to the original label after you fix the interaction.

- Take a moment to write down the conditional logic and review it against what you have in Axure. Make sure to review in order. Sometimes, just writing the logic, especially if it is a bit more complex, makes it easier to spot the problem in Axure.

- Check the **Satisfy all/any** droplist if you have multiple conditions. Depending on how you want the logic to work, the setting may be wrong.

Raised events

Can a tiger change its stripes? Can an Axure master change its size or shape from one page to another? The answer to both is, unfortunately, no. However, you *can* control the behavior of a master, so that each of its instances, across multiple pages, would have a different behavior for the same event. Raised events greatly extend the usefulness of masters and once you learn this feature (easy, I promise), you will find yourself using it often.

There are three important things to remember about raised events:

- Raised events can be created *only* for widgets that are on masters
- A master may have multiple raised events
- Creating a raised event is a two-step process:
    - Step 1: Create the raised event on the master
    - Step 2: Create the interaction for the raised event on the page where an instance of the master is placed

Why do we need raised events? A one-word answer is **Context**. The longer explanation goes something like this:

- Masters would be of very limited use for an interactive prototype, if there was no way to allow the master exhibit different behaviors, based on the page on which the master is placed.
- When a master is placed on a page, it is not possible to edit or assign interactions from the page to any of the master's widgets. The master's wireframe has to be edited in its own page. A raised event affords a way to create an interaction on a wireframe, which can be applied to widgets within masters.

Guided example

Our first example will demonstrate the use of raised events to manage the behavior of a Global Navigation master, such that a tab that corresponds to the current page will not respond to an OnClick event.

In *Chapter 4*, we set a basic interaction for each of the four tabs that make up the master **M Global Nav**. Each of the tab widgets links to its corresponding page when an OnClick event is triggered. For example, on the **Home** page, clicking on the **Books** tab links to the **Books** page; quite straightforward.

The problem is that the **Books** tab continues to be clickable on the **Books** page because the tab is part of the master. It performs its built-in interaction on each page on which the master is placed. In this example, we will make the behavior contextual.

Step 1: Creating a raised event on the master

For this example, there is no need to make any construction changes to the wireframes, just adjust the interactions. The following screenshot illustrates the wireframe *before* using raised events:

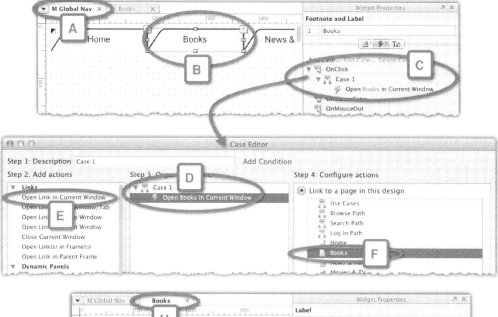

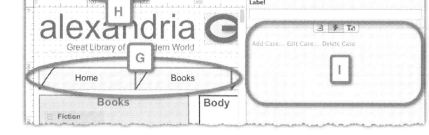

- On the master **M Global Nav** wireframe (A), the **Books** widget (B) has a single interaction tied to the **OnClick** event (C).

- The interaction, as seen in **Case Editor**, is **Open Books in Current Window** (D), composed of the action **Open Link in Current Window** (E) pointing to the **Books** page in the sitemap (F).

- An instance of the master M Global Nav (G) is placed on the Books page wireframe (H). Notice that the **Interactions** tab in the **Widget Properties** pane (I) is disabled and empty.

As you can see in the preceding screenshot (I), widgets on the master cannot be assigned interactions once the master is placed on a page. Moreover, depending on the interaction, it is complex or impossible to create an interaction context in the master wireframe that is assigned to master widgets. The following screenshot illustrates the first of the two parts in the process of creating raised events:

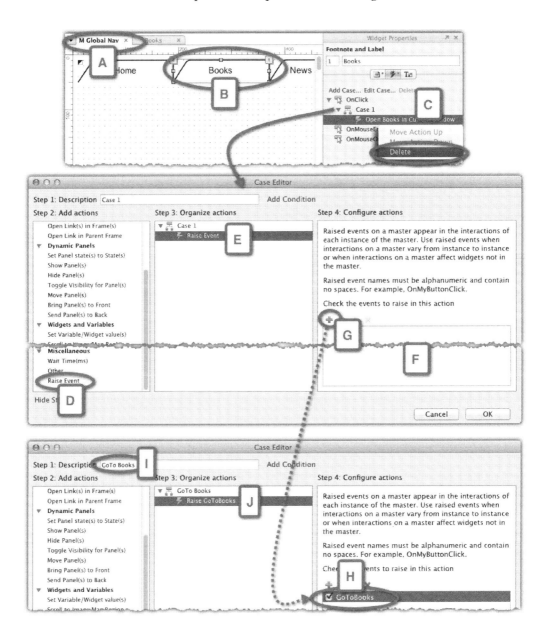

As raised events can only be created in a master wireframe, we start by opening the Global Navigation **M Global Nav** (A). I will focus on the **Books** tab widget (B), but the process should be repeated for all widgets.

- The **Books** widget has one interaction triggered by the **OnClick** event. We start by *deleting* the existing action **Open Books in Current Window** (C).

- Double-click on **Case 1**, and in **Case Editor**, scroll all the way to the bottom of the column **Step 2: Add actions**, where you will find the **Raise Event** action (D) nested under the **Miscellaneous** section.

- While the **Raise Event** action is added to the column **Step 3: Organize actions** (E), the column **Step 4: Configure actions** (F) is empty.

- In order to add a new raised event, click on the **Add** icon (G) there. You may have noticed that Axure provides a description of raised events in the top part of the column. The important part of the description pertains to labeling raised events:

    ◦ Raised event names must be alphanumeric

    ◦ Spaces are not permitted in raised event names

- Label the raised event something like **GoToBooks** (H), and, very important: *make sure you check the checkbox to the left of the raised event name!*

- While you are at it, and if you did not do it before, label the generic **Case 1** to something meaningful such as **GoTo Books** (I).

- Notice that now, because of labeling, the interaction in the column **Step 3: Organize actions** is easy to figure out.

Troubleshooting Raised Events

The first thing to check if a raised event does not work is to make sure that the checkbox next to the raised event name in **Case Editor** (see the preceding screenshot, H) is indeed checked!

Finally, the following screenshot illustrates an alternative way to create raised events on the master:

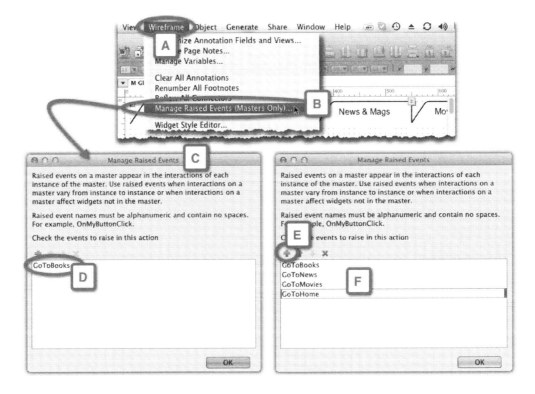

- From the **Wireframe** menu (A), select **Manage Raised Events (Masters Only)...** (B). This menu option is contextual and you do not see it on the **Wireframe** menu when you work on pages or dynamic panel states (unless those are part of a master).

- The **Manage Raised Events** dialog (C) pops up and it is identical to the one that appears in **Case Editor**. Existing raised events, such as the one we just created in the example, will be listed (D).

- Use the **Add** icon (E) to create additional raised events (F). These raised events will then be available for you to use in interactions for widgets within that master.

The following screenshot illustrates how to associate these raised events with master's widgets, this time using the **Home** tab widget as an example:

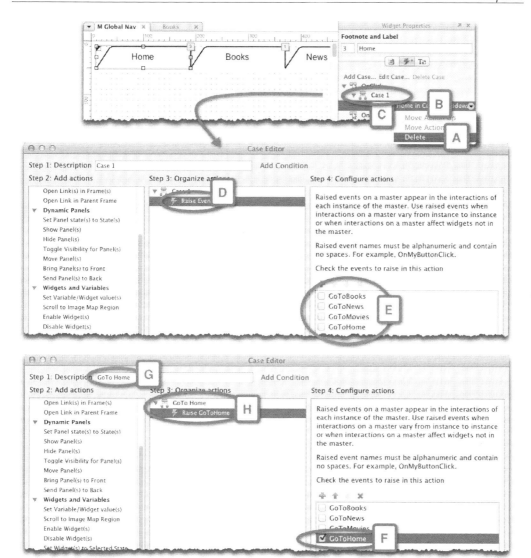

- Follow the step that we took in the **Books** tab, and start by selecting the **Home** tab in the master wireframe, and use the **Delete** option (A) to clear the original action **Open Home in Current Window** (B).

- In **Case Editor**, as soon as we select the **Raise Event** action, it appears in the column **Step 3: Organize actions** (D), and all four events we just added are listed in the column **Step 4: Configure actions** (E).

- After checking the box next to the raised event **GoToHome** (F) and labeling the case with the meaningful name (G), the interaction in the **Step 2** column is updated (H).

Repeat the process for the **News & Mags and Movies & TV** widgets to complete the conversion of the master **M Global Nav**. At this point, each of the widgets on the master can respond to an `OnClick` event which will trigger the corresponding raise event. However, we created the labels for those raised events. The names could be very arbitrary. So how does Axure know that the label **GoTo Home**, for example, is supposed to link to the **Home** page? How do we assign an actual Axure action to the raised event? For the answer, let's move on to the next section.

Step 2: Applying interaction to raised events on a page

The following screenshot illustrates the "before" and "after" use of raised events on the **Books** page wireframe:

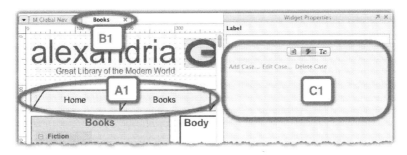

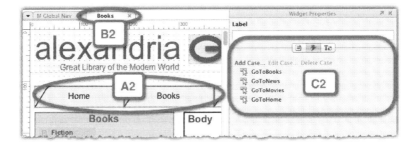

- Without raised events: In the **Books** page wireframe (A1), there is an instance of the Global Navigation master (B1) in which the tab widgets have conventional link actions. When you click on the master on the page wireframe, the functionality of the **Interactions** tab in the **Widget Properties** pane is disabled (C1), because the master's widgets are not exposed to the page.

- With raised events: In the **Books** page wireframe (A2), there is an instance of the Global Navigation master (B2) in which the tab widgets have interactions that involve raised events. When clicking on the master on the page wireframe, the functionality of the **Interactions** tab in the **Widget Properties** pane is enabled, and the raised events are listed (C2). Now, it is possible to create interactions on this page, which will be triggered by widgets on the master.

Therefore, here is the fascinating and powerful aspect of raised events, and why the time investment in understanding raised events will pay off. As masters are placed on multiple pages, the list of raised events will be exposed on each page, including the wireframe pages of other masters. In each page, you can create *different* interactions for the same raised event. Moreover, this is how the same master can have different behaviors on different pages.

The following screenshot illustrates the interactions assigned to the four tabs in the Global Navigation on the **Books** page:

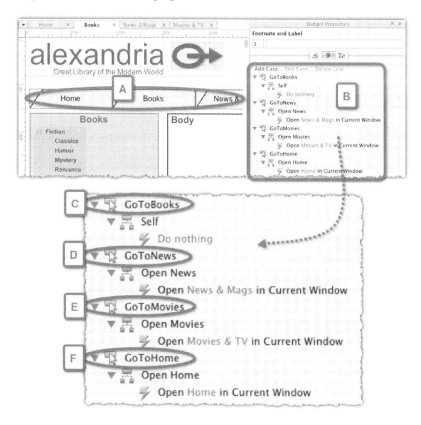

- When the master **M Global Nav** (A) is selected in the **Books** page wireframe, all the raised events associated with the master are listed in the **Widget Properties** pane's **Interactions** tab (B).

- The OnClick event for the raised event of the **Books** tab widget (C) is only assigned an "Other" type action, with some verbiage that basically says that when the user clicks on this tab, nothing happens. Creating a case for this raised event is optional, and here I also demonstrate how to user the "Other" action as a way to document the prototype.

- Note that for usability testing, you may want to clear the interaction, so that the tab will not respond to a mouseover.

- The OnClick events for tabs **Home**, **News & Mags** and **Movies & TV** (D, E, and F) involve the simple link action to the corresponding page of each of the tabs.

Repeat the assignment of interactions to the master's raised events on each of the other pages.

Nested masters: Amplifying the raised event

It is common to include one master within the wireframe of another master. The raised event of the nested master, however, will not be exposed when the enclosing master is placed on page wireframes. The following screenshot illustrates an example of the nested master:

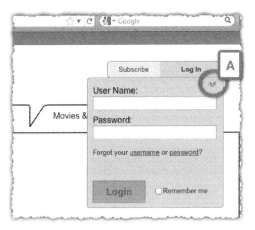
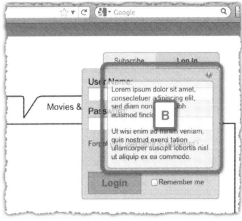

- One of the requirements for Alexandria is to provide a contextual help. Your proposed approach is to include a small help icon where needed. In this example, the icon appears in the login prompt (A). Clicking on the icon shows a transparent help pop up (B), which can be dismissed by clicking it.

The following screenshot illustrates the underlying construction in Axure, and the issue of raised events in nested masters:

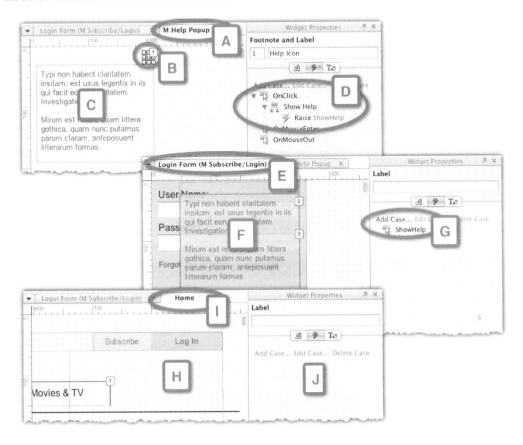

- The help pop-up is constructed as a master **M Help Popup** (A), composed of an image widget that holds the help icon (B) and a dynamic panel widget (C) where each state contains the relevant help content. In order to visualize the example, the dynamic panel is shown as visible, but in the actual construction, it should be set to hidden by default.

- The interaction for the help icon (B) is triggered by an **OnClick** event, which includes the raised event action **ShowHelp**. As the help pop-up master will be placed on multiple pages and masters, the plan for the raised event is to do the following:

    ○ Show the help pop-up dynamic panel

    ○ Bring the pop up to the front

    ○ Set the dynamic panel to the state which contains the help content that corresponds to its placement on the page wireframe

- Place an instance of the help pop-up master on the **Login Form** master wireframe (E). When the pop-up master is selected (F), its raised event is visible in the **Interactions** tab (G).

- However, when you click on the **Login** master (H) on the home page wireframe (I), the raised event of the nested help pop-up is not visible (J).

What to do? The following screenshot illustrates the issue and solution using a simple method which I call **Amplify Raised Events**:

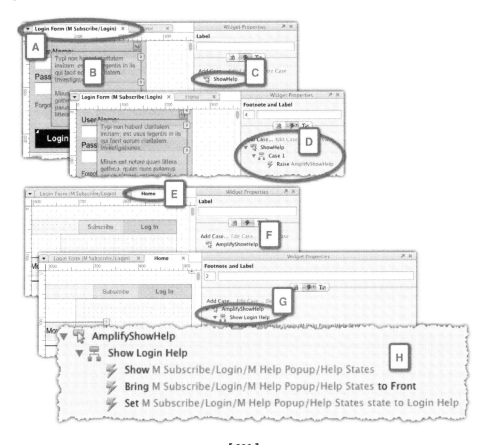

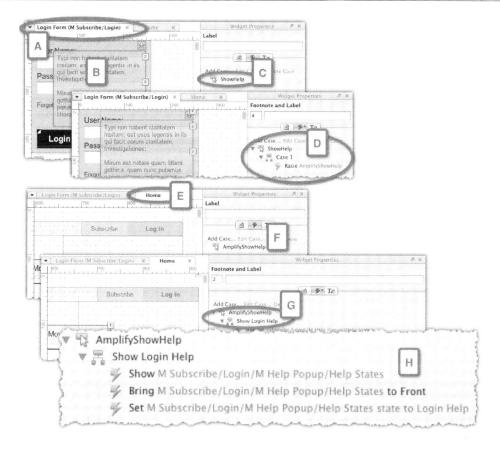

- While we cannot see the help master's raised event on the **Home** page wireframe, we *can* see it on the login prompt of the master wireframe (A). So, click on the nested help master (B) to show the raised event in the **Interactions** tab (C).

- Create a new case for the raised event **ShowHelp**. The action for this case will be a raised event which you will name **AmplifyShowHelp** (D). Essentially, the nested raised event will trigger a new raised event. In essence, it will amplify or repeat the call to the original raised event action.

- Switch to the **Home** page wireframe (E) and click on the **Login** master (F). The raised event **AmplifyShowHelp** will be visible in the **Interactions** tab (G).

- Now create a new case for this raised event, name it **Show Login Help** and assign it relevant actions, as discussed above. Generate the prototype to make sure that the interaction is working as intended.

To conclude the raised events topic, I want to re-emphasize the tremendous usefulness of this feature to the construction of high fidelity prototypes. While masters help us enforce visual consistency and reduce the number of redundant wireframes, raised events help assign contextual behaviors to those masters.

Variables

About two thousand years ago, the Greek philosopher Epictetus said that:

The materials of action are variable, but the use we make of them should be constant.

The ancient Greeks loved deep concepts, such as atoms, so it is not surprising that they invented information architecture and the notion of separating a reference to data from the actual data it contains. Wikipedia has a good definition for a variable. In the context of computer science, it is "A symbolic name given to some known or unknown quantity or information for the purpose of allowing the name to be used independent of the information it represents."

We use variables all the time. For example, when we think (or perhaps prefer not to think) about our account balance, the term "account balance" is a name for a variable. The actual dollar amount of the balance changes, but our way to reference it does not have to. As Epictetus said, the variable is constant, its value changes.

In addition to storing data, variables are used to pass this data around, from one event that sets their value, to another event that consumes that value. As a result, variables are very useful when you have conditional logic, because it is possible to check the value of a variable in order to determine which path to take.

We can also control the scope in which variables can be used:

- Local variables are limited to a certain function in a certain area of the application, and are not available to other functions in other areas of the application.
- Global variables are "visible" or available to all functions across the entire application.

A simplified analogy is human memory. We are equipped with a "working" or "short term" memory, a limited storage capacity that enables us to complete specific tasks. For example, it helps us to remember that we put water to boil, or where we left our phone. There is no need to store this information after the activity ended and the information is replaced by new transient information. We also have long-term memory, which enables us to retrieve information on demand long after its acquisition.

Guided example—creating context with variables

A personalized and contextual user experience is a core tenant of modern apps and applications. Thus, it is highly probable that you will be expected to prototype such adaptability in your projects. The following example demonstrates a use of variables to support a contextual rendering of the prototype based on the user login.

Step 1: Defining the interaction

The Alexandria project has a business model that is based on revenues from advertising and paid subscriptions. In order to keep things simple for our example, there are only two subscription tiers:

- Free: Registered users have free access to most content, but each item is wrapped in advertising and there are limits on the number of items the user can consume in a given day

- Unlimited: No advertisements, no daily limits and access to all content

Our goal is to have the prototype present the appropriate home page content based on the user login. Specifically, how the home page renders to visitors, and how, after login, it renders to Free or Unlimited subscribers.

Step 2: Construction considerations: Dynamic panel or pages?

The **Home** page wireframe needs to be updated to account for three variations:

- The **Home** page before the user logged-in.

- The **Home** page after a user with a free subscription logged-in. Need to show the placement of advertisements on the layout.

- The **Home** page after a user with an unlimited subscription logged-in. Need to show the placement of promotional offers on the layout.

The number of ways to come up with the appropriate design is obviously limited only by your creativity. The key construction to consider, however, is how to implement the three different home pages in the prototype. The following screenshot illustrates the current construction and helps review the options:

- **Option 1**: In addition to the current **Home** wireframe (A) which is needed for a generic home page which is displayed to visitors, add a dedicated page for free and unlimited subscribers.

- **Option 2**: Convert the **Body** section into a dynamic panel. Each state will reflect a different rendering of content for visitors, or based or signed-in users.

Which option is better? Here are three issues to consider:

- Are you designing a complex application where the body section of the page is complex and variability of each page is significant?

- Are you on the hook to deliver UI specifications?

- Are you part of a UX team of two or more designers who may need to work on this page?

If your answer to any or all questions is yes, then you might be better off taking option 1, the dedicated page route. Here is why you should preferably choose the dynamic panel option:

- A complex body section means that each state of the dynamic panel is likely to be composed of nested dynamic panels and masters. In other words, a body section composed of a dynamic panel can yield a page which is very complex, harder to manage and edit, and perhaps slow to load.

- Only one full rendering of the home page will be generated in the Word specification document, and that of the top most state, or the state specified in an **OnPageLoad** interaction for the page. All other variations of the body section will appear as dynamic panel states, making it much more difficult for developers or other consumers of the specification to get a sense of the entire page. A dedicated page for each context will yield complete screenshots of each variation, which you will be able to annotate as relevant.

- It is easier to distribute the work among team members, as checking out one of the home page wireframes will not prevent another designer from working on another **Home** page wireframe.

Finally, because with the exception of the body section, all other elements of the **Home** page wireframe are masters, maintaining consistency where it is important is not going to be an issue.

Duplicate the home page and rename the following pages:

- **Home [Visitor]**
- **Home [Subscriber]**

As the focus of this example is variables, we will not bother elaborating on the construction too much. In the wireframe **Home [Subscriber]**, convert the body rectangle widget into a dynamic panel with two states: Free and Unlimited. At this point, they should be identical, except their label.

Step 3: Adjusting existing conditions

Back in *Chapter 4*, we set the prototype to load by default on the **Home** page. That assignment has not changed despite the fact that we just duplicated and renamed the page. Now we are going to add some logic that will determine if the logged-in user has a free or an unlimited subscription and link to the appropriate state of the **Home [Subscriber]** page.

The user needs to provide two bits of information in order to login: a username and a password. The fidelity of the prototype will not be compromised if we only use the password to evaluate the user's subscription type. After all, this is only a prototype, not the actual application!

The following screenshot visualizes the process of setting the variables that will help us determine the type of account associated with the logged-in user:

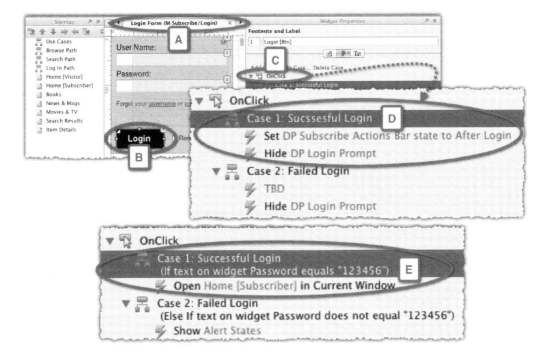

- In the master **M Subscribe/Login** (A), tweak the interactions associated with the **Login** button (B). We already have a case for a successful login (C), with a condition that evaluates the content of the password field for the string 123456 (D). That initial interaction, however, does not really do anything other than changing the state of the login master.

- Instead, **Successful Login** should link to the **Home [Subscriber]** page [E]. However, this is only half of the solution. How do we know which state of the body to show on the **Home [Subscriber]** page?

- All that is needed here is to add another condition that checks if the password equals 654321 — this will be our method of forking the interaction:
  - ○ The password 123456 will be now associated with the free subscription login
  - ○ The password 654321 will be associated with the unlimited subscription login

Of course, you can set whatever passwords you want, but it is important to keep them easy to memorize and enter — we will have to enter those passwords each time we want to walk through any of the screens associated with logged-in users.

The following screenshot visualizes that adjusted logic:

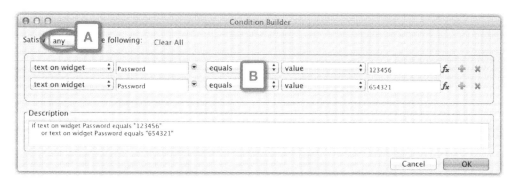

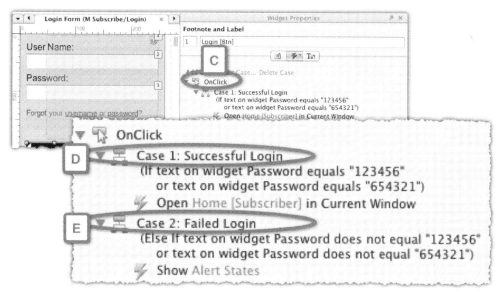

- We are checking if the **Password** field equals 123456 or 654321 (A), and if any of those values are found (B), the **OnClick** event (C) will link to the **Home [Subscriber]** page. This is the **Successful Login** case [D].

- We also need to adjust the **Failed Login** case [E]. If the **Password** field does not equal any of the two values, then an alert will be displayed.

Step 4: Variables and the order of actions

How will the **Home [Subscriber]** page know which state of the body's dynamic panel to display? With variables, of course, using the action **Set Variable/Widget(s) value**.

The following screenshot illustrates the most important aspect of adding variables to an interaction—the order of actions:

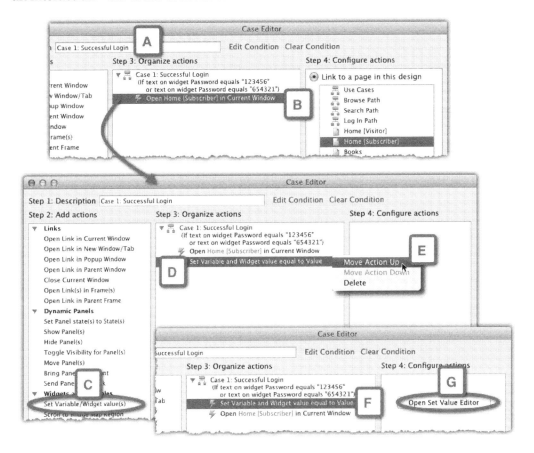

- The current **Successful Login** case (A) has a single **Open Link in Current Window** action (B). When the action **Set Variable/Widget(s) value** (C) is added, it is listed in the column **Step 3: Organize actions** *below* the existing action (D). The interaction *will not work* as intended if you keep the two actions in this order, because the new page will load before the variable value has been set.

- In the column **Step 3: Organize actions**, click on the set variable action (D) and use the contextual menu (E) to move it to be the first action in the case (F).

Now that the order of actions is set, click on the **Open Set Value Editor** button (G) in the column **Step 4: Configure actions**.

Step 5a: Setting variables (and possible snags)

Moving forward in this prototype, it is important to keep track of what type of subscriber is interacting with the application in order to present the appropriate content, and demonstrate the difference in the user experience for visitors and subscribers.

In other words, we need to know the user type. The user type is determined by two facts:

- Has the user logged-in or not
- What is the subscription level of a logged-in user: free or unlimited

The user type is an example of a variable. In Axure, variables have basic naming rules. A variable name must be:

- Alphanumeric
- Less than 25 characters long
- Without spaces

Our first variable can be named UserType, and its possible values can be expressed as:

- Visitor = 0
- Free Subscription = 1
- Unlimited Subscription = 2

Using numbers to reference variable values has the advantage of being short, less prone to typos, and easier to remember. However, whenever variables are involved, I highly recommend that you write down those values. It can get confusing when the number of possible values are higher.

The following screenshot illustrates the process of creating the variable **UserType**, and assigning it values in the context of the **Login** button. Or rather, attempting to set it a value, and discovering that an interaction needs to be tweaked in order to accommodate the added logic. We will continue from where we left off in the preceding screenshot:

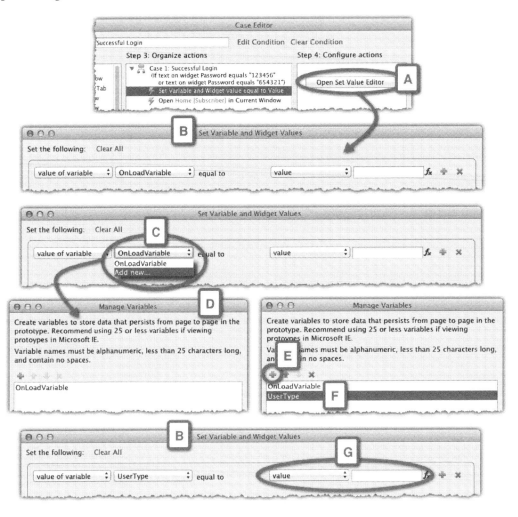

- Click on the **Open Set Value Editor** button (A). The **Set Variable and Widget Values** dialog (B) contains a default row which is conceptually similar to the rows in **Condition Builder**. We can construct a variable value assignment phrase by selecting or typing values in each of the four columns.

- Axure's built-in variable **OnLoadVariable** is the default value in the second column. However, as we want to create a brand new variable, use the **Add new...** option (C) from the droplist.

- In the **Manage Variables** pop-up (D), use the **Add** icon (E) to add the **UserType** variable to the list that initially has only the built-in variable, and close the pop up.

- Back in the **Set Variable and Widget Values** dialog, we hit a snag: Our current Successful Login case includes a condition that considers both 123456 and 654321 as viable options.

This means that our Successful case is too general. We need to break it into explicit cases, one that checks if the value is 123456, and the other, if the value is 654321. Only then, will we be able to assign the variable **UserType**, the values 1 or 2.

I wanted to take you through this path of hitting a snag during work on interactions, because it illustrates the inherent iterative nature of prototyping. Previous wireframes and interactions have to be constantly adjusted, to support higher fidelity. With experience, you will learn to predict such situations.

Step 5b: Setting and initializing variables

The following screenshot illustrates the process of finalizing the variable assignment after adjustment has been made to the **Login** button's **OnClick** interaction:

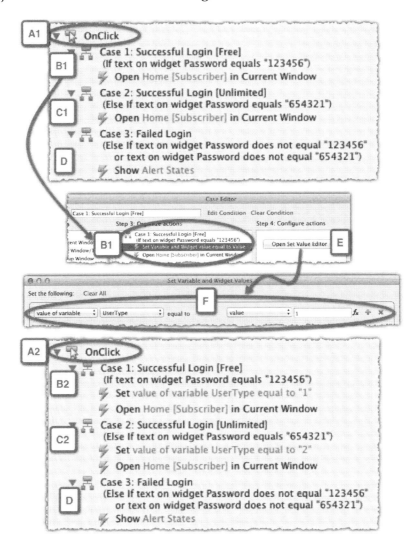

- For the **OnClick** event (A), we now have a dedicated case that checks if the password is 123456 (B1) and another that checks if the password equals 654321 (C1). Both are cases for successful login. We did not have to modify the case for unsuccessful login (D).

- Open the first case (B1) in **Case Editor** and click on the **Open Set Value Editor** button (E) to launch the **Set Variable and Widget Values** window. Now it is easy to complete the variable value assignment: In *Step 5a*, we have established that for the condition password that equals 123456, the variable will equal 1 (F).

- Repeat the step for the condition password that equals 654321, where the variable should be set to 2.

The revised **OnClick** event (A2) now includes two cases that can set the variable UserType based on the value in the **Password** field.

Initializing, passing, and resetting variables

The bad news about variables is the fact that you are responsible for making sure they function correctly. The good news is that there are basically only three steps to remember about proper handling of variables, and as long as you keep those in mind, troubleshooting should be easy, or unnecessary.

Remember that when you create a variable, you are only creating an empty container, so it is important to ensure that some event, triggered by some widget or page load, actually populates the variable with a value. This is the step of *initializing* the variable.

It is common to mistakenly think that some value, such as zero, will be automatically placed in the variable by the software. The meaning of "no value" is "Null", which is different from zero. Zero is an actual, explicit value. Null means that there is no value. In the case of Axure an empty variable is noted by two quote marks with no space between them: "".

There are circumstances where it is helpful to set the value of a variable immediately at the time of prototype generation. It is easier to *troubleshoot* changes in the value of a variable, when you can track its change from the start, or, *initialize* it.

Think about your variables as a herd of sheep: You want to know their condition at all times. Maintain a running list of variables you use in the file, their possible values, and the resulting path based on the values. One method is to keep such a list in Axure, as a dedicated page on the **Sitemap** pane. This is especially beneficial in shared project files because all team members can easily share and learn about the variables used in the file.

The following screenshot illustrates how we initialize the variable **UserType** in a continuation of our example:

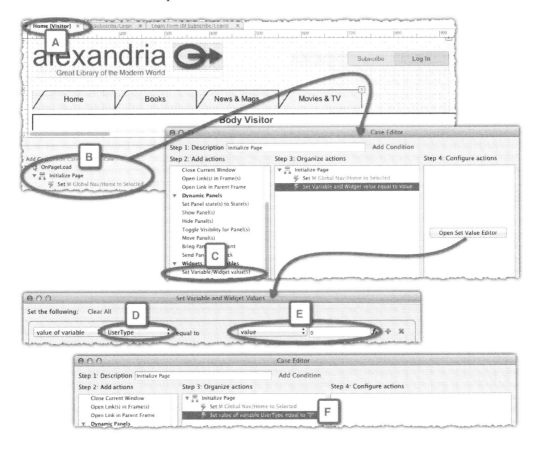

- Earlier in this example, we have established the page **Home [Visitor]** as the prototype's default landing page. Therefore, by default, the user who interacts with this page is a visitor, until they login. This is an opportunity to formalize this fact by initializing the value of the variable **UserType**.

- Open the **Home [Visitor]** page (A) for editing and double-click on the **OnPageLoad** interaction (B). In **Case Editor**, add the action **Set Variable/ widget value(s)** (C). In the **Set Variable and Widget Values** dialog, set the value of the variable **UserType** (D) to **0** (E).

- Each time the prototype is generated, the updated **OnPageLoad** event (F) on the **Home [Visitor]** page will set the value of the variable **UserType** to **0**.

Step 6: Using variable values to determine appropriate cases

Upon successful login validation, the page **Home [Subscriber]** is loaded. This is when we will use the value stored in the variable **UserType** to determine which state of the Body's dynamic panel to display. The following screenshot illustrates the process:

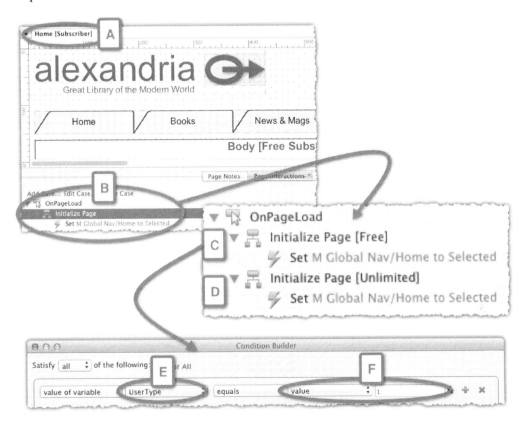

- As the page **Home [Unlimited]** (A) is a duplicate of the original **Home** page, it includes the original **OnPageLoad** event (B) which has a single action for the Global Navigation.

- Similar to what we did in *Step 5b*, we need to have a case for each of the possible user types. Duplicate the original case and rename the two cases:

  ○ **Initialize Page [Free]** (C)

  ○ **Initialize Page [Unlimited]** (D)

- Double-click on the first case and add to it a condition that checks if the value of the variable UserType equals to '1', which stands for free subscription.

In order to complete the condition, we set the appropriate actions and adjust dynamic panels on the page, so they show the relevant state. The following screenshot illustrates the process for the **Initialize Page [Free]** case:

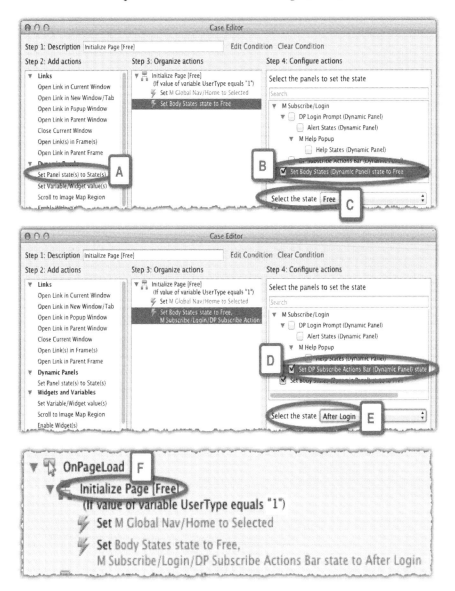

- We add the action **Set Panel state(s) to State(s)** (A) and set the state of the **Body** dynamic panel (B) to the **Free** state (C).

- As this page can only load if the user has successfully logged-in, we also need to set the dynamic panel **Subscribe Actions Bar** (D) to its **After Login** state (E).

The completed **Initialize Page [Free]** case (F) is set. Apply similar modifications to **Initialize Page [Unlimited]**. The following screenshot illustrates the generated prototype for the **Free Subscription** home page, where the value of the variable UserType equals '1':

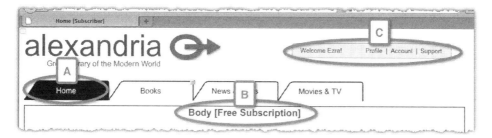

- The **Home** tab (A) in the Global Navigation is set to its selected style

- The **Body** section is set to the **Free Subscription** state

- The **Subscriber Action Bar** (C) is set to its **After Login** state

This concludes the guided example on variables. While on paper the process may appear long and complex it is, in actuality, quite fast and straightforward. Many of the steps mentioned here are basic and take seconds to perform. The key for success with this type of advanced interactions is to think through the entire flow. Remember what it is that you are trying to simulate, and be practical about it.

Variable types

Axure supported variables in previous versions, but Axure 6 has some significant enhancements that improve the practical use of variables in your prototype and open up new possibilities for creating high fidelity prototypes. Axure offers three types of variables which are discussed in the following sections.

Global variables

As their name suggests, global variables, once set, are available to any page throughout the browser session. In other words, they will expire only when you close your browser tab or window.

Axure's built-in variable

Axure comes with one built-in variable: the OnLoadVariable. It is a very useful container when each page in the prototype loads. As page load is a guaranteed event you can use this variable to initialize, set, or reset the value of widgets and other variables. One thing to keep in mind is that just because the variable is called OnLoadVariable, it will work even if not used exclusively on a page load event. It will work anywhere. However, in keeping with the principal that variable names should be meaningful and relevant to the event that triggers them, it is not a recommended practice.

Create your own variables

Axure supports unlimited variables, but like everything good in life, there are some limits. First, if you are using Internet Explorer to test and socialize your prototype, Axure recommends limiting the prototype to a maximum of 25 variables. In practice, 25 variables can satisfy a great number of advanced prototyping.

If you use Firefox (Axure's recommended browser for viewing HTML prototypes), the sky is the limit if you want to use variables to the max. Variables are passed through the URL, and the limit of Firefox URL is 64,000 characters. In other words, when you add the characters that make up the names of your variables, and their values, the sum total should be 64K or lower. Therefore, while there is a limit, 64,000 characters should be more than enough. In any case, the phrase "Less is more" applies to variables as well.

Special variables

Displaying the current day, date, or page name in the prototype is a valuable capability and another welcome enhancement to Axure 6. Just like the other topics discussed in this chapter, don't let the terminology hold you from using this function. Think about special variables as the "Insert" feature in Microsoft Word. You can insert today's date into a document or display the page number in the footer. Similarly, Axure provides a form of built-in access to useful parameters which you can incorporate into the prototype when relevant.

Currently, these built-in variables include attributes of the current day, or the name of the current page. Most likely, items such as current time and other attributes will be added to Axure in the future. The following table shows a list of special variables offered in Axure 6:

Variable Name	Description	Example in editor	Result in prototype
PageName	Name of the current page as it appears in the **Sitemap** pane.	This is the [[PageName]] page	This is the Home page
Day	The numeric value of the current day in a range of 1 to 31	Today is day [[Day]] of the week	Today is day 17 of the week
Month	The numeric value of the current month in a range of 1 to 12	This is month [[Month]] of the year	This is month 5 of the year
MonthName	The name value of the current month	This month is [[MonthName]]	This month is May
DayOfWeek	The name value of the current day	Today is [[DayOfWeek]]	Today is Friday
Year	The current year in 4 digits	The year is [[Year]]	The year is 2011
GenDay	The numeric value of the day in which the prototype was generated in a range of 1 to 7	Generated on day [[GenDay]]	Generated on day 15
GenMonth	The numeric value of the month in which the prototype was generated in a range of 1 to 12	Generated on month [[GenMonth]]	Generated on month 8
GenMonthName	The name value of the month in which the prototype was generated	Generated in [[GenMonthName]]	Generated in January
GenDayOfWeek	The name value of the week in which the prototype was generated	Generated on [[GenDayOfWeek]]	Generated on Tuesday
GenYear	The year in which the prototype was generated	Generated in [[GenYear]]	Generated in 2011

Usage examples

Here are some examples of combinations you can make with variables:

In the editor	Result in prototype
Today is [[DayOfWeek]], [[MonthName]] [[Day]] [[Year]]	Today is Thursday, August 24 2011
Prototype generated on [[GenMonth]]/ [[GenDay]]/[[GenYear]]	Prototype generated on 12/28/2011

Local variables and functions

Both of these features are new to Axure 6 and add a significant boost to our ability to create sophisticated interactive prototypes. However, a serious discussion of these topics is beyond the scope of this book, and a shallow explanation of how these features work can be more confusing than helpful. Complementary materials about these features will be posted online.

Naming variables

Axure variables have basic naming rules. A variable name must be:

- Alphanumeric
- Less than 25 characters long
- Without spaces

Here are some best practice suggestions to keep in mind:

- As you cannot use spaces, and are limited to alphanumeric characters, use the "CamelCase" convention, which makes it easy to parse words within the variable string. Basically, you need to capitalize the first character in each word. For example, use "WishListCount" instead of "wishlistcount".

- Use descriptive names so that you, or others who work on the file, will understand what the variable stands for. Avoid names such as Var1, Var2 and so on because I can guarantee that within days or weeks, you yourself will not remember what these names stand for.

- If you are working on a shared project file, each team member should add their initials at the end of the variable name, in all caps. For example, "WishListCountES". Note the potential for redundant variables, as each designer creates their own version of the same variable. This is an example of a collaboration process issue which we will discuss in *Chapter 9, Collaboration*.

How variables can help in usability testing

One of the key attributes of any high-fidelity prototype is the degree by which its look and feel mimics the "real" application. In UX prototyping, in addition to the visual treatment, it is the *responsiveness* to user input that makes a big difference in reducing the gap between the mockup and the actual software.

The higher the fidelity of your prototype, the higher the quality of feedback you get from participants in usability studies. Historically, however, prototyping has been limited to hard-coding data to the wireframes, thus, inherently reducing the responsiveness and dynamic qualities of the simulation. Short of hiring a programmer to code a prototype, and the effort that introduces its own massive problems, there was no practical way to easily demonstrate the true dynamic responsiveness and how data changes from one screen to another in response to a user input, under varying conditions.

As a result, usability studies were, and still are, often hindered by the fact that we need to ask the participant to ignore hard coded information or continuity issues. In other words, we ask the user to ignore the "brains" part of the user experience, that is the data and context associated with task flows. At least in my experience, I find that most participants get the fact that they are looking at a mockup and understand why the data does not really reflect the flow they were supposed to follow, or why they are restricted to a script.

It can be difficult to distinguish between valid usability issues in the design, and "noise" which is a result of the participant getting confused by mechanics and data presentation limitations of the prototype itself. Thus, the following example demonstrates a technique which is based on the use of some variables to personalize the experience for the UT participant.

Guided example—contextual usability testing

The following example demonstrates a basic method for personalizing the prototype for participators in a usability test. Review the construction of the sample file hSandbox_Chap-5b.RP. The following screenshot illustrates the first half of the concept:

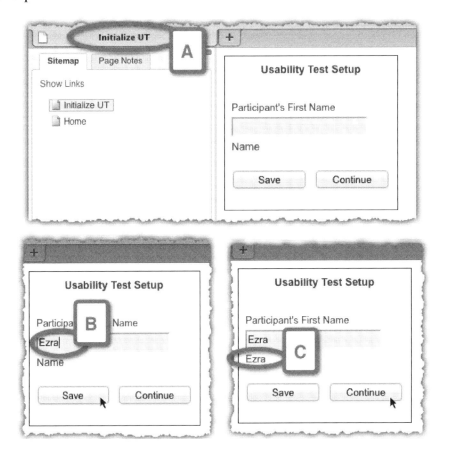

- Our example contains two pages. The first, **Initialize UT** (A), is intended to be used by the person who facilitates the test—perhaps yourself. A couple of minutes before starting the text, enter the person's name (B) and hit the **Save** button.

- The **Save** button triggers an OnClick event that sets the value of a variable that you created to the value of the text in the **Participant's First Name** field. In order to verify that the variable has been set, a text widget below the field (C) displays the value of the variable.

Hit the **Continue** button to link to the first page with which the participant should interact. The following screenshot illustrates the interaction on this page:

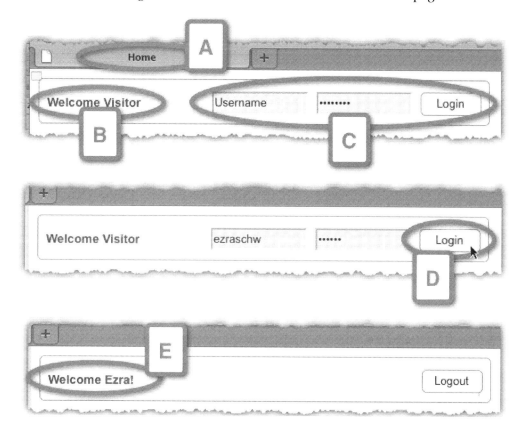

- The **Home** page (A) includes a generic **Welcome Visitor** label (B), standard **Username** and **Password** fields, and a **Login** button (C). Participants can enter anything they want in the field, or, you can instruct them to enter some specific values.

- When the participant hits the **Login** button (D), the variable that stores the participant's first name populates the **Welcome** label (E), changing the participant's experience of interacting with the prototype and making it more personal.

Variations on this basic concept can help you tailor the prototype for various testing situations, where such adaptability might add values to the testing.

Pros and cons of using variables

Be strategic! Always keep in mind the phrase "Just because I can, does not mean I should." In previous sections of this topic, we discussed many of the aspects involved in using variables and the value of integrating them into the prototype. If you plan to use variables extensively, it is important to understand how interactions in general, and variables in particular, will effect your work, and in a case of a team, everyone who is using the file.

Axure makes it fairly easy to figure out the construction of a prototype and the interactions involved. Events, cases, and conditions are presented in a natural language that shields you from the obscurities of programming the language code. As long as you label your widgets in a meaningful way, any Axure user should be able to open your file and understand how you wired it.

However, in reality, if you open a file after several weeks or months, you might need a few minutes to remind yourself what is going on in the file. It is not uncommon to forget which variable value meant to trigger which path and so on. Moreover, as Axure does not include yet a debugger, it can be difficult sometimes to identify a broken interaction. Thus, my advice is to document key interactions and variable assignments. Some techniques, to do this, include the use of dedicated documentation pages and add an "Other" action at the end of complex interactions.

The use of variables enables you to gain considerable construction efficiencies. Instead of redundant instances that show variations of a page, you may use just one page and manipulate its layout with variables. For someone who looks at the HTML version of the file, how you constructed the file may not make a difference. However, when you generate the Word specifications document, will the output make sense to developers and others who consume the specs?

Another specifications issue involves an option to include interactions. The question is: Is there a real value in including interactions details, or will they add bulk to the documentation while confusing the developers? The short answer: It will probably add no value.

There is a difference between the way we construct our prototype simulation and the way the actual application is coded. Many of the interactions we create in Axure are only meant to make the prototype work, but may not make sense from a developer's viewpoint.

Therefore, if you are expected to deliver development grade specifications, as well as a highly interactive prototype, you may need to consider having two files, one for each target delivery. Obviously, there is overhead in this approach, but it gets you the best deliverable for each medium. It is possible to find a middle ground, where the interactions are constructed such that the Word specifications still provide a meaningful output, but you will have to experiment with the output often, until you and the teams who consume the specifications are comfortable with the result.

Tips and techniques from the experts

It is a real pleasure to include in this book a few advanced techniques which were contributed by Jeff Harrison, Loren Baxter, and Fred Beecher—three of the most knowledgeable Axure wizards, who are also very generous with sharing their expertise with the community. RP files associated with these examples are posted on the book's website.

Hiding and showing list elements, by Jeff Harrison

This example shows you how to build a table with controls that give you different filtered views of the data. In earlier versions of Axure, you might have ended up creating a dynamic panel with as many states as you have views, and creating a different view of the table for each one. That works fine, but if the data changes it means you have to change it in multiple places. In addition, as tables frequently incorporate form controls, it means you need to have multiple copies of these too, requiring lots of logic to keep the hidden copies in sync with the visible ones.

Axure 6 makes it pretty easy to use a different approach: create each row just once, and hide, show, and rearrange them for each view.

The approach

My example, as illustrated in the following screenshot, will show a list of users of a system, and allow an administrator to select a user record for editing. It will also allow the administrator to filter the list of users by department:

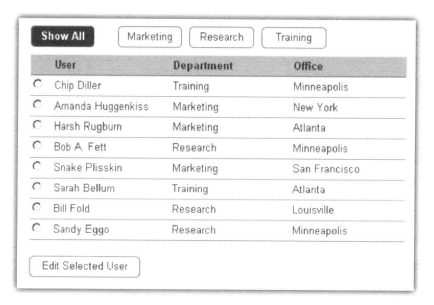

By default, it will display all the rows, but clicking on one of the three department buttons across the top will display only the associated user.

In the table, the buttons will define which rows are hidden and which are shown. The trick is to move the remaining ones around, so there are no gaps or overlapping rows. We will design each row, so that when it disappears, it will pull everything below it up, and when it appears, it will push lower rows down.

Step 1: Creating the row template

The first thing I will do is create a single data row.

I have already made a few decisions about my table. I know that the rows will be 25 pixels high, and separated by a rule. I know that it will display the users' names, departments, and locations. In addition, I know that I want to use radio buttons to let the administrator select a user, and an "edit selected user" button to go on to the next page.

As I want to hide, show, and move the rows around independently, each row will need to be in a dynamic panel.

I arrange my elements in the row, and add a radio button. I right-click on the radio button, select **Assign Radio Group**, and name the group **select user**. The prototype will allow only a radio button in a radio group to be selected at once, so doing this is important in order to get the radio buttons to work right. Of course, at the moment, the radio button is a group of one, which is not very impressive, but when I make copies of the row, the new radio buttons will be automatically assigned to the same group. (It pays to plan ahead with Axure.) I also put a horizontal line widget along the bottom edge of the row.

Now, we will define a little more behavior. Axure 6 gives dynamic panels a number of new events, including **OnShow** and **OnHide**. Thinking back to our approach, whenever this row is hidden, I want it to move up to make room for the ones below it to close the gap. Whenever it is shown, I want it to move down in order to move into the space below it. In each case, I am going to move it by its own height-see the following screenshot:

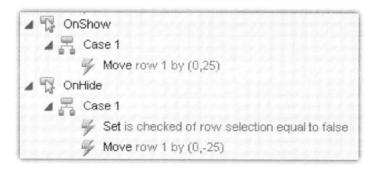

You will note that there is an extra action on the **OnHide** case. I have decided that if the selected row is hidden, it is going to become unselected. This is a simple way to prevent a situation in which the user has an option selected that is not displayed. It is not the only solution, but it is an easy one.

Okay, let's move on.

Step 2: Moving rows together

The next step is to make a copy of the row—just one—and put it below the first one. In the example, I am entering the row data as I create the rows, but you can wait until later if you want. However, at this point, you will want to give each row a label. Call the top row "row 1" and the other one "row 2".

In any case, I now have two rows, and it is time for me to insert the next bit of logic. Our approach says that when a row disappears, it should pull everything below it up, and when it appears, it will push everything below it down. Each of these rows will already move in the right direction when it is hidden and shown. The trick now is to get the rows below it to move with it.

It turns out that this is really easy by using the new **OnMove** event on the first row panel-see the following screenshot:

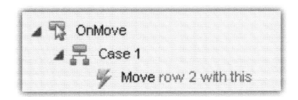

Now, whenever row 1 moves, row 2 will go with it.

Of course, there is nothing below row 2 yet, so we cannot do anything with it. This brings us to our next step.

Step 3: Repeating as desired

Now, select both rows, copy them, and paste a copy directly below them. Label these "row 3" and "row 4".

Note that the interaction you just created was copied along with the two rows. Moving row 1 will also move row 2, and moving row 3 will also move row 4. The only thing you need to do to string these together is to connect row 2 and row 3 with the same **OnMove** interaction. See the following screenshot:

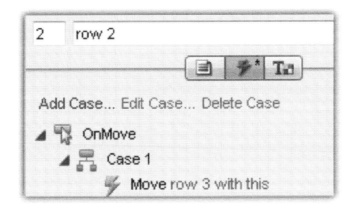

By copying and pasting the whole table, then stitching together the pieces, you can quickly build this into a very long list. For my example, I stopped at eight rows, but doing it again would give you 16, then 32, and so on. This is another great example of why it pays to plan ahead when working in Axure.

Once you have all the rows you want, create a header row. It does not need to be interactive, or in a panel; it is just there for clarity, as is illustrated in the following screenshot:

	User	Department	Office
○	Chip Diller	Training	Minneapolis
○	Amanda Huggenkiss	Marketing	New York
○	Harsh Rugburn	Marketing	Atlanta
○	Bob A. Fett	Research	Minneapolis
○	Snake Plisskin	Marketing	San Francisco
○	Sarah Bellum	Training	Atlanta
○	Bill Fold	Research	Louisville
○	Sandy Eggo	Research	Minneapolis

Step 4: Adding controls

You have done all the work. Now all you need to do is to create the filter controls, and have each one designate the rows to hide, and the ones to be shown-see the following screenshot:

Show All	Marketing	Research	Training

	User	Department	Office
○	Chip Diller	Training	Minneapolis
○	Amanda Huggenkiss	Marketing	New York
○	Harsh Rugburn	Marketing	Atlanta
○	Bob A. Fett	Research	Minneapolis
○	Snake Plisskin	Marketing	San Francisco
○	Sarah Bellum	Training	Atlanta
○	Bill Fold	Research	Louisville
○	Sandy Eggo	Research	Minneapolis

The **Show All** button shows all the rows, as illustrated in the following screenshot:

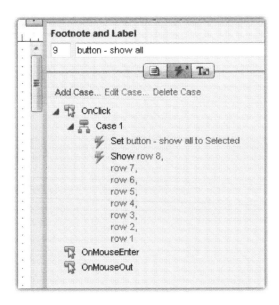

The other buttons show only the rows that correspond to the filter, and hide the rest, as shown in the following screenshot:

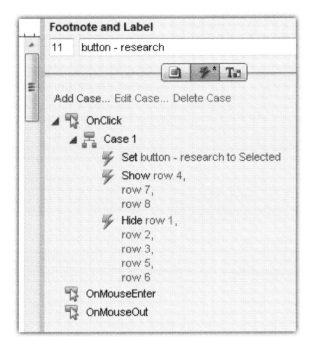

Creating new filters is that easy.

To finish off the example, I defined a "selected" style for each button (white on black) put all four filter buttons in a selection group (by selecting them all, right-clicking on them, and selecting **Edit Button Shape | Assign Selection Group**), and setting the **Show All** button to the selected state on page load, as shown in the following screenshot:

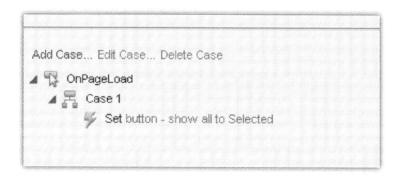

This general approach can be adapted for any set of items in which pieces of the set will appear and disappear—each item moves the one below it as it is shown or hidden, which in turn moves the one below it, and so on. The only other thing to keep in mind is that each thing has to move by its own height. In this example, all the rows are of the same height, but in a form with expanding sections, you will likely have to adjust the "move" interactions once the heights of the various sections have been defined.

Keyboard Shortcuts by Loren Baxter

You can simulate keyboard shortcuts in Axure. It is a great way to communicate and test the effectiveness of shortcuts for power users. See the simple example for switching tabs, and a complex example that simulates some of Gmail's keyboard shortcuts. (Example files are posted on the book's page on the publisher's website)

High-level Interaction

Fundamentally, you have a hidden input field that forces itself to maintain focus. Any characters entered on the keyboard will be read by this textfield and checked for matches to active characters. If a match is found, an interaction is performed. Finally, the textfield clears itself and resets the focus.

Detailed steps

I recommend creating a separate, duplicate page to communicate your keyboard shortcuts. The technique prevents any other text input on the page from being usable, so it should be quarantined.

1. Place all elements, dynamic panels, and unique states on your page that will change based on the keyboard input.

2. Create a small, hidden dynamic panel somewhere on the page.

3. Place a textfield named `_control` inside this textfield. This will perform all the interactions.

4. Create an `OnPageLoad` event that sets focus on `_control`.

5. Set the interactions on `_control` as follows:

   OnKeyUp

   - If text on widget "_control" = "a" or "A"   [check for character 1]
   - Then perform interaction 1   [if match, perform interaction 1]
   - If text on widget "_control" = "b" or "B"   [check for character 2]
   - Then perform interaction 2   [if match, perform interaction 2]
   - If true
   - Then set text on widget "_control" to ""   [always clear the textfield afterwards]
   - Set focus on widget "_control"   [reset focus on textfield]

   OnFocus

   - Set text on widget "_control" to ""   [redundant clearing of textfield, helps]

   OnLostFocus

   - Wait 100ms   [hack to make certain browsers work]
   - Wet focus on "_control"   [if lost focus, regain focus immediately]

6. Test it out! You should be good to go. You can go on from here and add new cases or make them more complex. Take a look at the Gmail example to see complexity in action.

Notes

- Only keystrokes that produce characters will work. To make the directional keys work, you have to try a different technique involving radio buttons or checkboxes.

- Remember, no other text inputs on the page will work while this technique is in use. Perhaps there is a scalable solution to this challenge, but no one has found it yet.

Axure tricks by Fred Beecher

As Fred jokingly mentioned:

> *Sadly, Axure keeps improving such that my best "tricks" become unnecessary. I guess that's a good problem to have, eh?*

Still, Fred has a number of tricks that are still relevant in Axure 6, and fortunately, Fred shared those with us:

Trick 1: Debugging your Logic

With the addition of math operations, Axure 6 allows for much more intricate interactive logic. Whereas, I normally only rely on variables to pass information between pages, I now use variables on pages themselves to keep track of how many items are listed, how many times someone has done something, and so on. When things don't work, it can be really frustrating to figure out why. I deal with this by creating a text panel that displays the variable's value at all times. I call it, cleverly, **Variable Value**. On every interaction on which I set the value of a variable, I also set the text on this text panel. When something is going wrong, I can usually figure out what it is by comparing what the value of the variable is *supposed* to be with what is actually displayed on the screen.

Trick 2: Passing variable values between pages

One of the main uses of variables is to pass values between pages. However, this commonly does not work. Why? The reason is that most people set up an interaction such that the Open Link interaction comes *before* the Set Variable interaction. Put Set Variable first and *then* Open Link and all your problems will go away (well, all your inscrutable variable-based problems anyway).

Trick 3: Hidden link to clear variables

When performing a lot of complex conditional logic, the variable situation can get pretty murky. Phantom values might be interfering with whatever it is you are doing after you have interacted with the prototype a whole bunch. The solution to this is to have a link somewhere on the page that clears all variables and reloads the page, to really make this effective though, this link needs to be on a master that is on *all* pages. As you add variables, you have to keep coming back to the interactions on this link to add them to the pile that is cleared. Then, you just have to do this once! A trick such as this is crucial for user testing, as it ensures that a previous user's session has been completely cleared out. In terms of formatting, I usually make my link a very light gray and place it to the right of the header. Users never see it. Moreover, when I am done testing, I just remove it from the master, so it does not show up in the functional spec or make the generated screenshots look weird.

Trick 4: Text fields masquerading as text panels

One tiny new feature in Axure 6 that has already had a huge impact on how I work is the new text field option to toggle borders on and off. One of the great things about Axure is that you can use an interaction to set the text of one widget equal to that of another widget, as long as that widget is a form widget of some type. However, that is *very* frustrating when you are trying to, for example, edit a selected item. However, now if you have the text in your editable items displayed in read-only text fields with the border turned off, you can do exactly that and, visually, the screens will work the same. The only drawback is that there *must* be a background color to the text fields. They cannot be transparent. Feature request? :)

Summary

In this chapter, we covered a set of Axure functionalities that are responsible for creating truly interactive prototypes. Conditions, raised events, and variables extend our ability to move beyond the basics of navigating from one wireframe to another. We can also create a relevant context in response to inputs.

The use of these capabilities, while not too complicated, does require a higher-level of discipline and focus. We are not engaged in coding, by far. However, conditional logic and variables involve formal evaluation of possibilities. As long as you document the values of variables, and the possible actions that should take place given each one, you should be able to reduce interactions that don't work and save time on debugging.

Finally, don't hesitate to experiment, to try interactions that may help you communicate to stakeholders and users, your vision for the user experience you plan for the application.

In the next chapter, we will cover change management. As the prototype stabilizes and the schedule tightens, there are often many dramatic modifications, requirement changes, and other situations that require changes to the prototype. We will look at the Axure functionality and best practices that help apply changes quickly, and efficiently.

6
Widget Libraries

Axure's widget libraries are all about efficiency, consistency, and sharing. They are about not having to re-invent the wheel each time we start a new UX project. They have the potential of saving needless work and they can help you in being more productive, faster. More importantly, they help maintain the consistency of design patterns across the entire prototype project. This chapter covers the basic concepts involved in the use, creation, and sharing of widget libraries.

An Axure widget library is basically a collection of custom widgets that are stored in a special file format named RPLIB. These collections greatly extend Axure's built-in widget libraries. You can create these collections yourself, or download a library made by others.

We are tasked with delivering a compelling user experience that meets business requirements, technical constraints, and user expectations. The process typically moves very quickly from high-level conceptual sketches to detailed design, and from static diagrams to clickable simulations of interaction flows. If there is one constant aspect to the work, it is *change*. For mid-to large-scale design projects the challenge is two-fold:

- Produce many wireframes, quickly. Using ready-made widgets saves the time of having to create those from scratch.

- Manage consistency of design patterns across existing and new wireframes: Wireframes are assembled from approved patterns stored in a project's widget library.

Before we dive deeper into widget libraries, it is important to have a brief discussion on design patterns because the concept of design patterns is a deeply grounded principle across disciplines, from arts to computer science. The use of patterns in UX design is commonplace and complements the paradigm of object-oriented programming and application development. Within the user experience context, a pattern is a template for an application-agnostic group of widgets, which solves a specific interaction requirement in a generalized way.

Patterns are considered to be a very good thing in principal, but can be difficult to apply in practice. Everyone seems to agree that the adoption of patterns within an application and cross-applications improves skill transference, reduces the learning curve, and yields a superior user experience overall. Yet, millions of users still have to put up with significant inconsistencies brought to bear by operating systems. To add to the decade-long battle between generations of Microsoft Windows and Apple OS, we now have to deal with inconsistencies among mobile platforms such as Google's Android, Apple's iOS, HP's webOS, Rim's BBX, and so on. To make things worse, the move to applications in a Cloud often translates to interaction patterns that are inconsistent with patterns of desktop applications. It is a mess, and we need to deal with it.

The following screenshot illustrates the differences in the implementation of a key Microsoft pattern named **the ribbon**, in the Mac and Windows versions of Microsoft Word, perhaps the most popular word processor in the world. Despite the fact that this is the same application, a user switching from one platform to another might easily get disoriented:

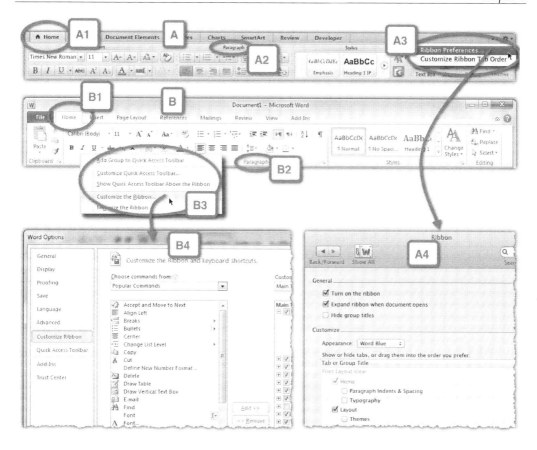

- A casual comparison between the Ribbon of Mac's (A) Word 2011 and the Ribbon of Window's (B) shows significant inconsistencies in the treatment of tabs (A1, B1), the location of section titles (A2, B2), and access to the customized Ribbon menu (A3, B3).

- The look and feel of the dialog box for customizing the ribbon (A4, B4) varies widely between the two versions.

There is little one can do about cross-platform consistencies; and one could argue that the impact of such inconsistencies is relatively minor, because few users switch regularly between operating systems. However, this is not the real issue. The example underscores the fundamental problem with trying to leverage too much on any particular set of design patterns, because the rate of change is too high.

While the effectiveness of patterns depends on uniformity and consistent application, it is important to preserve openness to constant refinement, adaptation, and new patterns, to avoid becoming dogmatic and enslaved to existing patterns.

Some examples of interaction categories where patterns play an important role include:

- Navigation
- Data entry
- Grids and lists
- Search
- Message and error handling
- Shopping
- Sign-in/out and authentication

[Don't enforce or lock into a pattern library too early in the design process. Remember that your ultimate goal is to design an application, not a pattern library.]

With Axure, you can approach the creation and management of patterns using the masters and/or widget library features.

Axure's built-in libraries

Widgets libraries are accessible from the **Widgets** pane. Axure includes two built-in libraries which provide the basic building blocks for developing an extended user experience vocabulary. The built-in libraries cannot be altered, which means that it is not possible to add or remove widgets from these collections. It is quite possible to prototype an entire application, even a complex one utilizing only a portion of these built-in widgets. The following screenshot illustrates the libraries and the way to switch between them:

- There are currently 22 widgets in the **Wireframe** library accessible from the **Widgets** pane (A), the default one being the Axure library. To switch a library, use the droplist (B) and select the **Flow** option (C).

- There are currently 15 flow widgets (D) which are meant to be used for diagram construction.

The mechanics of the Widget pane are described in more detail in *Chapter 2*.

Axure and community libraries

In addition to the built-in libraries, Axure's website provides links to a growing number of widget libraries (see the following screenshot). Most have been posted by UX practitioners for fellow UX practitioners (visit `http://www.axure.com/widgetlibraries`):

The generosity of people within the UX profession goes back to the days when Nick Finck, Henrik Olsen, Peter Van Dijck, and others offered free Visio stencils and Omnigraffle palettes. This culture of generosity also flourishes in Axure's active user community in the form of freely shared tips, techniques, and custom widget libraries.

The types of widgets that you will find in the community libraries include iPhone, iPad, the OS-X user interface components, Android, Windows 7, various icons and social media elements, and much more!

Most of these community libraries are free of charge, despite the substantial amount of thought and labor that was invested in creating them. One such example is the work by Loren Baxter, an accomplished user experience designer and top Axure expert. Loren authored the "Better Defaults Widget Library" (see the following screenshot, A), which has added 34 widgets to Axure's 22. His library includes elements such as an error popout, stylized popouts, date picker, and many other very useful items.

His other creation is the "Social Widgets" collection (see the following screenshot, B), which includes widgets such as a complete "Leave a comment" form, "Share This" popup, and animations for when you need to visualize a "Loading This" animation.

You can either use these libraries as provided or tweak the widgets you want to make them fit your particular need. Either way, you can save a lot of time by not having to make some of these widgets yourself:

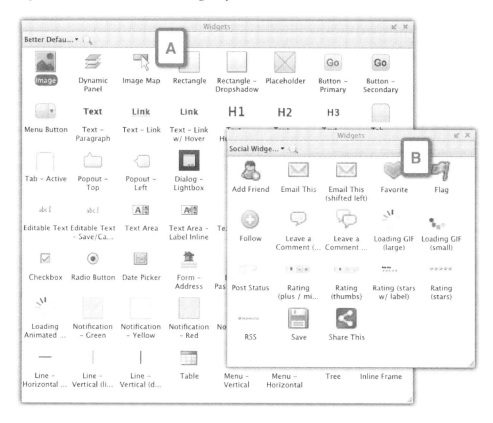

Of course, when you develop your own cool widget library, make sure that it is listed on the Axure site!

Your own widget library

Axure makes it very easy to create, manage, and distribute your own widget libraries, which is great because there are several circumstances for which extending Axure's built-in widgets is beneficial:

- When you find yourself spending too much time repurposing parts of existing wireframes in new wireframes
- When you design user interfaces for applications that are based on an interface framework used by development teams such as Google's GWT, the Dojo toolkit, Oracle's ADF, and so on
- When you want to share with the world, a set of widgets, which you think would benefit others in their prototyping projects

Guided example: Widget library to support prototype

In this example, we will establish a widget library for the purpose of supporting consistency of design patterns in a prototype, in this case, the books demonstration project, Alexandria.

Step 1: Create the library file

As mentioned earlier, a widget library is an independent Axure file that is managed separately from your project file. The following screenshot illustrates the process of creating the library from within the Alexandria project file:

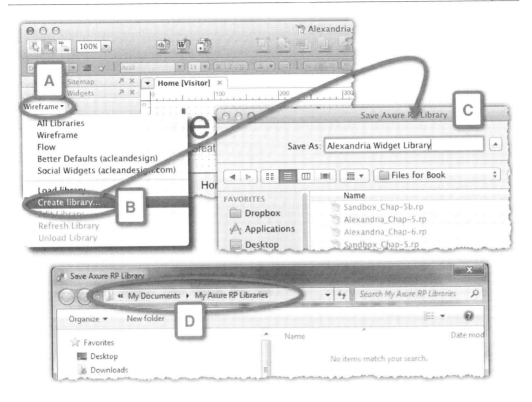

- From the droplist in the **Widgets** pane (A), select the **Create Library** option (B). This is the only place in Axure from where you can create a library.

- Save the library to any destination you want (C) or Axure's suggested defaults:
  - Windows: **My Documents** | **My Axure RP Libraries** (D)
  - Mac: **Documents** | **Axure** | **Libraries**

The new widget library file opens on top of the project file. Axure's RPLIB user interface is a little different from the RP interface, as illustrated in the following screenshot:

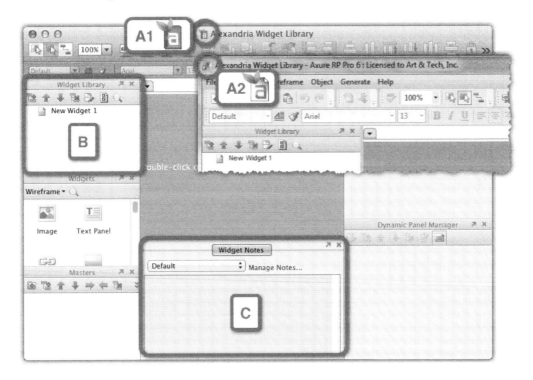

- On Mac, a widget library file sports the special library icon (A1), although the Windows version keeps the standard RP icon (A2).

- The **Widget Library** pane (B) replaces the **Sitemap** pane.

- The **Widget Notes** pane (C) replaces the **Page Notes** pane. Notice that the **Widget Notes** pane has only a single tab, for notes. **OnPageLoad** interactions and **Page Formatting** are not applicable here.

- Note that the share menu is a part of the RPLIB file format. This means that a widget library file cannot be converted into a shared project file. This poses some challenges for teams who share libraries.

With the widget library file ready, we can move on to creating some widgets.

Step 2: Creating a custom widget (lorem ipsum)

Let's begin with the lowly text placeholder. Lorem ipsum, the reliable pseudo Latin text filler has been used, according to some accounts, since the sixteenth century in publishing, and it is still going strong today.

The use of text placeholders in wireframes is common because often we do not have the actual text that should accompany the page. Some argue that the use of lorem ipsum in hyper-realistic prototypes is problematic because it confuses participants in usability tests. The critics may have a point. On the other hand, using inaccurate text can also lead to misunderstandings, especially if dealing with particularly literal stakeholders. Use this element with caution—make sure that the placeholder makes sense and its intended use is clearly understood.

The following screenshot illustrates the process of creating the widget:

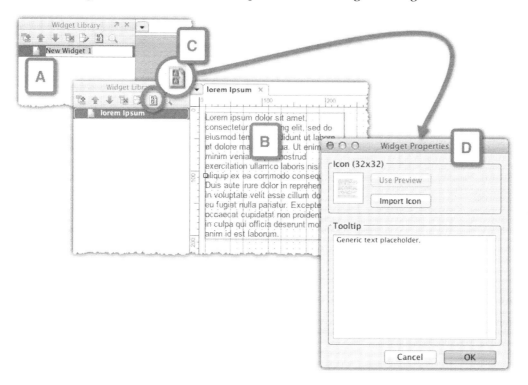

- In the **Widget Library** pane, rename the default New Widget 1 as **lorem Ipsum**.
- Drag over a **Text Panel** widget and paste the lorem ipsum text (B), which you can find in Wikipedia or on one of the 28,300,000 web pages Google identifies when you search the term.

- Adjust the width and length of the text block as you see fit. There is no need to make specific definitions here. However, since in the Alexandria project we applied the 16 column **960 Grid**, it makes sense to take advantage of the grid's proportions in the library as well.

- With the widget selected in the **Widget Library** pane click on the **Widget Properties** icon (C). In the **Widget Properties** pop up (D), define the icon and tooltip. For the widget icon, which is displayed when the library is loaded in the **Widgets** pane, the default **Use Preview** should work fine. For the **Tooltip**, add a brief description and click on **OK** to close the pop up.

The information you provide in the **Widget Properties** pop up will help you, or any user of the library, figure out what the widgets are, when the library is loaded into the project file.

Congratulations! You have just created your very first custom widget!

Step 3: Refresh the library in the project file

We will add a few more widgets to our new library shortly, but for now, save your work and close the widget library. The following screenshot illustrates the final steps involved in integrating the new library with the project file:

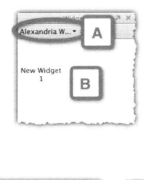
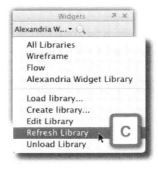

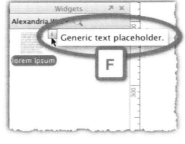

- Back in the project file, the widget library appears in the droplist (A), still displaying the default, blank **New Widget 1**. From the droplist (A), select the option **Refresh Library** (C), and the **lorem Ipsum** widget will appear (D).

- If you click on the widget, a little icon appears on the upper-right corner of the widget (E). Click on the icon and the description you wrote in the **Widget Properties** pops up (F).

- To switch to another widget library, use the droplist (D).

From now on, when making changes to the widget library file, we need to remember to refresh the library in the project file in order to reflect those changes.

Expanding the library—design patterns

The following are a couple of systematic examples for constructing useful widgets to add to any project library. The widgets are meant to enforce a design pattern that is specific to the application at hand. Granted, creating widgets in a widget library is not very different from creating such widgets in your project file. However, this is another opportunity to go over the construction process.

Example 1: A confirmation/alert box widget

This example will demonstrate a simple yet important aspect of widget libraries: A method for ensuring that the construction of widgets and interaction patterns is consistent throughout the prototype. The method is especially beneficial for a team of UX designers who collaborate on a project, and it can certainly benefit you as a single practitioner. You can find the widget in the sample file Alexandria Widget Library RPLIB.

Step 1: Defining the pattern

For many projects, and certainly, projects of a certain size and scope, creating and documenting a pattern library is highly recommended. However, it can be difficult to maintain the library, especially as work pressures mount. An Axure widget library makes it easier to manage and maintain the pattern since all of them are concentrated in the library file, and loaded into the project file.

In this example, we want to create a confirmation and alert box which will be used to prompt the users during various flows. The following screenshot illustrates the list of rules which help define and design this custom widget (A) in the library:

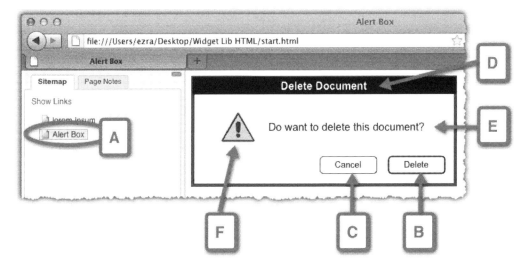

- Confirmation messages will have two action buttons: The primary confirmation action (B), and **Cancel**, a secondary action button (C)

- Alert messages will have a single action button, **OK**, styled as a primary action button

- The primary action button should be on the right

- The styling of primary and secondary action buttons should be visually clear

- There will be no "Close" icon on the upper right corner

- There will be a horizontal bar at the top of the dialog for the message header (D)

- There will be a brief text description of the message (E)

- There should be an appropriate icon to the left of the message description (F)

When you put pattern rules on paper, it becomes clear why it is so easy to break patterns and so difficult to maintain consistency. Even this simple dialog box has eight rules, excluding visual styling!

Documenting patterns is important, yet sometimes, it is not entirely clear whose responsibility it is to do the job. Is it the visual designer's role? The UX designer's role? Should this be a collaboration of both? The dynamics of each project determines the answer that is appropriate for it.

Step 2: Construction

Therefore, let's create this alert box. For now, avoid visual styling and stick to grayscale. There are, of course, a number of methods to construct this wireframe. The following screenshot illustrates the construction:

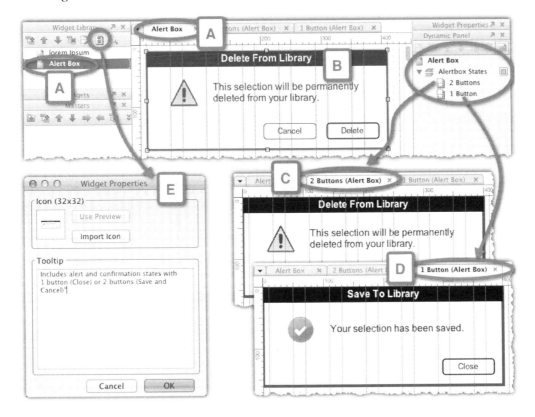

- Create a new widget in your widget library, label it **Alert Box**, and open the widget for editing in the **Wireframes** pane (A)

- Display the 16 column 960 grid, to ensure proportional compatibility with the main project file

- The widget should include two states, one with a wireframe for an alert box with two action buttons (C) and a single button (D)

- In the **Widget Properties** pop-up, add the **Tooltip** text, for example: **Includes alert and confirmation states with 1 button (Close) or 2 buttons (Save and Cancel)** (E)

- Save your work and remember to refresh the library in the project file when you get back to it

You may consider adding a couple more widgets to your library that are based on this dialog, for example, a pattern for a primary action button and the other for a secondary action button.

Our final example for the topic is a little more complicated, but it involves an extremely popular interaction pattern, the Incremental Search field.

Example 2: An incremental search widget

According to Wikipedia, the incremental search feature, also known as "search as you type", "type-ahead search", and so on, has been around since the late 1970s. It has been popularized on the Web by Google and has now become a standard requisite feature in modern applications, regardless of the device for which they were made.

There are two good reasons why this feature has earned such an overwhelming adoption. From a user experience perspective, this is a wonderful, easy-to-use, and time saving feature. As the user types into a searchable field, the system immediately provides the user with a list of potential matches. As a result, the user can select one of the suggested terms with high confidence of finding relevant data. The second reason, is that from a technical perspective it is possible to implement this capability on the Web with little impact on performance.

As the probability of using incremental search in a prototype is high, adding it to the library makes sense.

Step 1: Defining the pattern

The following screenshot illustrates the desired behavior of the type-ahead search widget (A). You can find the widget in the sample file Alexandria Widget Library RPLIB:

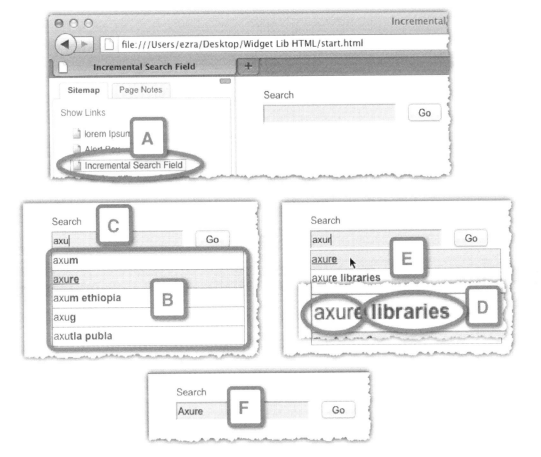

- Suggested words or terms will appear in a droplist (B) after the user has typed *three* characters into the search field (C).

- The style of the matching characters in the list will be *normal (D)*.

- The style of the characters that follow the matching characters in the list will be *bold (D)*.

- Each row in the list should respond to rollover by changing its appearance. The text will have an *underscore* styling, and its *background color* will change *(E)*.

- When the user clicks on a row, its content will populate the search field and the list will be dismissed (F).

- The user should be able to ignore the recommendations and keep typing in the search field. When no matches are available, the droplist will close automatically.

Step 2: Construction

In order to simplify the example, we will simulate a user typing in the word "Axure". When you create a list of recommended words and terms you can save time by using Google or Bing, instead of developing one on your own list of potential hits. The lists we create will have the following recommendations:

After three characters	After four characters
axum	axure
axure	axure libraries
axum ethiopia	axure tutorial
axug	axure widgets
axutla publa	axure review

The following screenshot illustrates key steps in the creation of this widget:

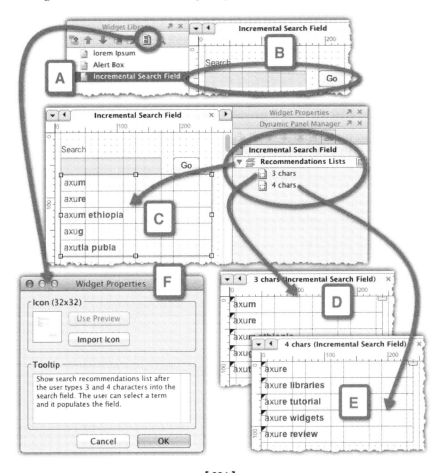

- Create a new widget in your widget library, label it **Incremental Search Field** and open the widget for editing in the **Wireframes** pane (A).

- Add the field and button widgets (B) and make sure to label widgets as you go.

- Add a dynamic panel widget (C) for the recommendations list. As discussed earlier, the two states correspond to a potential list of recommendations for three (D) and four characters (E).

- Finally, add a description to the **Widget Properties** pop up (F), for example: **Show search recommendations list after the user types 3 and 4 characters into the search field. The user can select a term and it populates the field.**

Step 3: Interactions

Finally, add an interaction that will trigger the display of the search recommendations droplist as per our requirements. The following screenshot illustrates this:

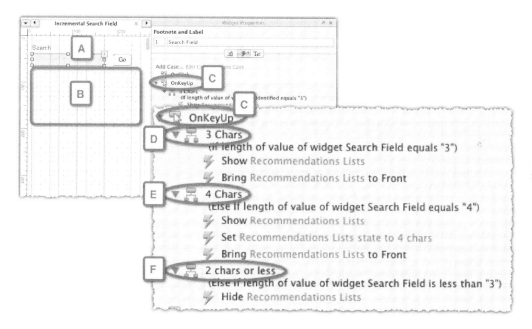

- The interaction is triggered by an **OnKeyUp** event in the search field (A). The idea is that the length of the string typed into the field will be evaluated after each keystroke.

- The recommendation list dynamic panel, by default, is set to be hidden (B) and should become visible if the length of the string in the search field is equal to, or greater than, three. There are three cases for the **OnKeyUp** event (C):
    - Case 1: Evaluates if there are three characters in the field, and if so makes the recommendation menu visible, sets the dynamic panel to its first state, and brings the panel to the front to ensure it is not partially blocked by other widgets (D).
    - Case 2: Evaluates if there are four characters in the field, and if so makes the recommendation menu visible, sets the dynamic panel to its second state, and brings the panel to the front to ensure it is not partially blocked by other widgets (E).
    - Case 3: Evaluates if there are less than three characters in the field, and if so hides the recommendation menu (F).

The combined effect of these cases helps create a recommendation droplist that simulates an immediate responsiveness to the number of characters the user has in the search field. Obviously, the search term itself is canned, which means that in usability testing you will have to script the task in such a way that it will prepare the participant, since the behavior of the widget is such that, it will respond to any text typed in.

Widget libraries with masters

The first time you drag over a widget that includes a master from a loaded widget library onto a wireframe page on your project file, the master will be imported automatically into your project file. Once a master exists in the project file, it *is not* replaced automatically when the library is refreshed or another instance of the widget is dragged over. The easiest way to update the master is to use the option **Import from RP File** from the **File** menu of your project file, which also works for importing from RPLIB files.

Managing widget libraries

You just created your first widget library. Perhaps you also downloaded a few community libraries. Now you are ready to use them in your prototype file. The **Widgets** pane is the hub for all activities related to widget libraries. Using the libraries' drop list in the **Widgets** pane, you can initiate the following tasks:

- Load library
- Create library
- Edit library
- Refresh library
- Unload library

When you want to use a custom widget from one of your loaded libraries, drag it over just as you would do with the built-in widgets. If the widget includes variables or a custom style, the **Import Wizard** dialog would flag such dependencies. If you want to create your own interactions, or avoid importing styles that are incompatible with your project, then use the **Cancel** button to import only the widgets, or click on the **Finish** button to import the entire package.

Once you create an instance of the widget in your wireframe, that instance is no longer associated with its originating widget library, a behavior that is similar to those of built-in widgets and flattened masters. Thus, modifications to a widget in the widget library are not applied to any of the instances of that widget in your project file even after you refresh the library.

Remember that the widget library is a discrete file, completely unaware of, and separated from, your project file. When you add more widgets to the library, make improvements and modifications to existing widgets, or download an updated version of a library you downloaded from the web, these changes are not automatically reflected in the **Widget Library** pane of your project file until you use the **Refresh** option. Moreover, I will repeat again: widgets that are already placed on wireframes will not be updated.

Local masters or external widget libraries?

Widget libraries are a great distribution vehicle for sharing your coolest widgets ever with the world. However, when it comes to managing a pattern library for a large project, or an entire application suite, we need to consider the following two options:

- Option A: Store the project's patterns in an external RPLIB widget library and load it into the project file
- Option B: Store the project's patterns as a collection of masters within the RP project file

There are pros and cons to both approaches and depending on the circumstances of your project, you should determine which type of widget collection is appropriate for your particular needs.

Using RPLIB

Here is a list of pros and cons for using a widget library file:

- **Pros**
    - The library can be used simultaneously in multiple projects. Updates to single library files will become available to all the projects upon refresh.
    - The library can become a company's standards and patterns file-of-record as it evolves and expands over time and projects.
    - For UX consultants, a personal library of often-used patterns, can become an invaluable time-saving tool.
    - In a team situation, easily distribute the library file to team members.

- **Cons**
    - In a team situation, need to notify team members that new updates are available, so that they know to refresh their link to the library.
    - In a team situation, owner of the library might make changes to widgets, without taking into account the impact such a change might have on the wireframes of another team member.
    - In a team situation, only a single user can make updates to the library at any given time. In large, high velocity projects, this may become a workflow bottleneck, because modifications to patterns are needed at a much faster rate than the serial.
    - Updates to widgets do not apply to widgets used in the project. Change management of the prototype may require a significant amount of rework if the wireframes are constructed from non-master custom widgets.

Using masters in a PR or RPPRJ file

Here is a list of pros and cons:

- **Pros**

  ○ Updates to pattern widgets are immediately applied across all wireframes where the masters are used.

  ○ In a team situation, a designer who is about to change a custom widget pattern can check first where the master is used and then discuss potential implications with team members who are using the master in their wireframes.

  ○ No need to deal with loading and refreshing an external widget library.

  ○ A smoother update workflow because the pattern library is built into the project file.

  ○ In shared project files, multiple designers can own and update their custom widget masters. This parallel workflow works well for large, high-velocity projects.

- **Cons**

  ○ Widget patterns tend to be project-specific, so it may be more challenging to consider a more generalized construction of patterns.

  ○ Sharing with other prototype files has potentially serious limitations: The project file has to be made available to the importing user, if that user is working in another

  ○ Difficult to evolve the patterns over time and across multiple projects, especially when the specific project file in which the masters were created is no longer in use.

Practitioner's corner

I have asked Pete Karabetis—an Information Designer at Vim Interactive—to share some tips based on his experience in creating widget libraries, such as the Social Media Icons Widget Library. So, here is Pete:

Why widgets?

A good widget library is great fun to make and always takes time and patience. The reason I made my first Axure widget library, Social Media Icons, is that I was tired of searching online for icons to use in my prototypes each time I needed one. I decided to make my own library to better my own workflow at first and then I polished it up and shared it with the Axure community to make life easier for fellow prototypers.

Not only should your widget libraries be easy to use, but also they should have a nice presentation. Here are three best practices to consider before you share yours with the world: Set an icon for each widget, give each icon a clear name, and add a tooltip for extra information.

Pixel-perfect icons

Be a perfectionist. Take the time to ensure all your widgets look sharp and noticed in the **Widgets** pane by setting a custom icon in their widget preferences. The following screenshot illustrates the simple process of replacing Axure's default preview icon with your own:

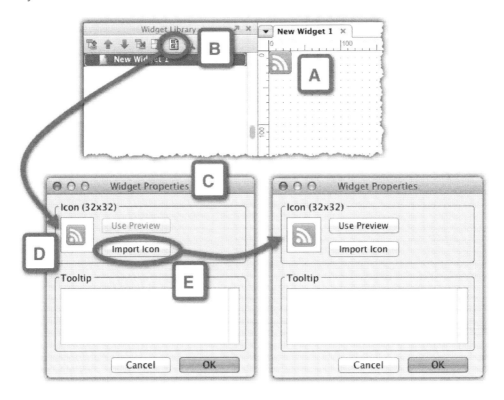

This is an example of an RSS icon widget (A). Click on the **Widget Properties** icon (B) to view the **Widget Properties** pop up (C). If you don't set your widget's icon, Axure will automatically create one for you by taking a snapshot of the widget and resizing it to fit inside the preset grid of the **Widgets** Pane (D). Instead, click on the **Import Icon** button (E) to import the icon you wish to use.

The widget's dimensions are only 32 x 32 pixels, which is small enough to set an icon of the same size to represent it in the **Widgets** pane. I used the same 32 x 32 pixel PNG image to make both the widget and its icon, but you can customize your icon in any way you like. Compare the preview icon created by Axure to the actual widget and you will notice that it is smaller and blurrier than the widget itself.

Clear widget label and tool tips for extra help

A clear widget label describes what your icon widget is, or what your widget does. Avoid obscure names or abbreviated shortcuts and try to be as informative as possible. For example, instead of labeling the widget obliquely as "RSS", label it "RSS (Color, 32x32)". The widget's **Tooltip** field in the **Widget Properties** pop-up (see the following screenshot, A) provides room for added information, such as the use of local variables which are used to support interactivity, the widget's behavior, color values, and so on. When the library gets loaded into a project file, the information is available through a pop up (B):

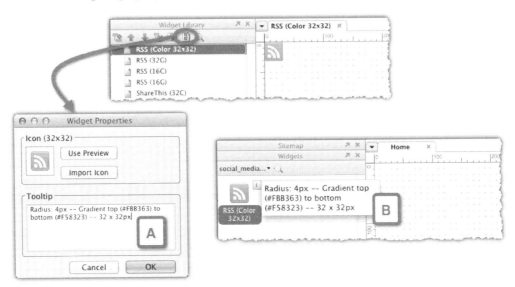

Summary

Widget libraries help extend Axure's built-in collection of widgets and share custom widgets with others, for free or for a fee. The libraries available for download on Axure's website, and elsewhere, save you significant time and effort if you need to prototype mobile devices of various flavors, social networks, and other commonly used elements. Additionally, widget libraries help develop, evolve, and enforce a global pattern library for projects or an entire suite of applications. In other words, they offer a strategy for managing prototype change, which is the topic of our next chapter.

7

Managing Prototype Change

Most UX projects are subject to two major drivers of change which often place the design effort at some risk, due to conflicting objectives. On one hand, good UX places a premium on as many iteration cycles of design, review, user validation and revision as possible, which are likely to yield successful results. The process is inherently slow, can be costly, and involves constant change to the prototype. On the other hand, there are business realities of ambitious plans coupled with aggressive schedules and limited budgets. The mix often inflicts on the project shifting priorities and scope—another source of constant change, but one that is typically not aligned, and often contrasts with, changes called for by UX.

Additionally, there is the sort of change that is tied to our design tool. As we shift from sketches and high-level wireframes to detailed design and interactivity, we are constantly evolving the Axure file. New pages, masters, and dynamic panels are added rapidly and wired with new interactions. It is tempting to use timesaving shortcuts, such as copy-and-paste, to quickly create alternative paths and possible states, instead of taking a longer path of thinking about construction of masters and their re-use. It is also normal to keep previous versions of wireframes, if we need to use or repurpose them at a later point. Before you know it, you will be looking at a fairly bloated Axure file. It may take longer to generate the HTML prototype, not to mention, finding the latest version of wireframes.

In this chapter, we look at Axure features and construction strategies for dealing with prototype changes in a productive and efficient manner.

From vision to reality

UX projects tend to follow an unfortunate, predictable path. We begin with a project launch fuelled by excitement, high aspirations, and a bucket full of ambitious strategic goals. We follow with an intense, stimulating, high-level conceptual explorations phase, in search for a "killer" user experience. The outcome—a polished, high-fidelity vision is presented to decision makers, who are justifiably impressed and excited, bless the ambitious project with the "Green" light. They allocate a meager budget and issue a directive for delivery yesterday. The organization immediately shifts into a scramble mode, and your polished hi-fidelity prototype now needs to address the details of low-level requirements, technical constraints, and pragmatic compromises that need to be made in order to meet the timeline and the budget.

Perhaps this description is bleaker than what you have personally experienced so far in your projects, I truly hope so. However, the numbers talk for themselves: According to the **2010 IT Project Success Rates** survey by *Scott W. Ambler*, Chief Methodologist for Agile and Lean for IBM Rational:

- Less than 55% of IT projects, on average, are successful
- About 32% of IT projects, on average, are challenged
- The rest, about 13%, on average are failures

Hopefully, we all get to work on the 55% of the projects that are successful. However, there is a high probability that constant requests for changes in scope and direction will compromise for the UX to some degree, require re-thinking of the design, and refactoring of the prototype. Our goal is to balance such changes in order to maintain the integrity and cohesiveness of the original UX vision that got the project approved in the first place.

 Visit the following URL for more information:
`http://drdobbs.com/architecture-and-design/226500046`

Aligning expectations

What *exactly* are you expected to deliver, and what is the impact, from an Axure construction perspective? These are tricky but tightly-coupled questions, especially for medium and large projects. The answers to the first question underscore the relationships and agreements between you and the project's stakeholders. The answers to the second question affect your ability to deliver successfully on the agreements made.

A shared understanding of, and agreement about, the level of work and granularity of details expected from UX deliverables is critical. Mismatched expectations are likely to result in a blunder.

Before you can come to an agreement, however, you need to estimate the requested work, in order to develop a reasonable estimate of time and budget. There is a tendency to come up with overly optimistic estimates. The reasons might be competitive—you are bidding on the project and want to come ahead in the competition. It might be a lack of previous experience in developing an application for a specific domain, or lack of experience due to distortion of scale: Something that worked in a small startup project may not work for a large enterprise project. Regardless, bad estimates will put the entire project at risk.

Not to be under-estimated, is also the impact on your well-being. There is a high probability that you might find yourself working impossible, crazy hours, just to keep up with an endless stream of demands and changes that you did not estimate for, but stakeholders expect you should deliver. This situation is not uncommon, but it can be avoided, or at least minimized.

There are three major elements that influence the ability to estimate the UX effort, from an Axure perspective:

- The software development model of the project
- The expected granularity level of the prototype
- The expected detail level of the UI specifications document(s)

Implications of these elements on your ability to manage the budget, schedule, and the quality of deliverables such that they are always in alignment with the project, is critical.

UX and software development models

We are working on software, and traditionally, UX has been weak on integration with development organizations and methodologies. In many projects, UX is being recruited by the business side and is imposed on the development organization, which may be concerned that UX will not be aligned with internal methodologies and processes. Therefore, it is important for UX to:

- Get familiarized with prevalent development methods in general, and the development flavor of your projects, in particular
- Seek alignment of UX and development around process and methods

The following is a very brief description of the most common methodologies, a flavor of which can be found in most organizations. In larger organizations with multiple development groups, it is not uncommon to find misalignment among the groups. Things can get complex for UX, so map out your eco-system early on.

Waterfall

Just a few years ago, an acceptable practice was to estimate the UX effort based on the number of wireframes needed to visualize an agreed-upon set of screens and user flows. The common development model followed a fairly linear path, known as "Waterfall", in which requirements were developed first, followed by software and interface design activities, software build, testing, and release. After its first release, the software would continue to evolve through cycles of incremental enhancements until the end of its life cycle.

The traditional waterfall model did not require much collaboration or iteration and contributed greatly to the creation of a "siloing" culture, in which business and development teams worked in relative isolation from, and hostility towards, each other. The process called for each group to focus on its part of the project, and hand off its deliverables to the next team.

It looked roughly something like this: The business team would spend a year on developing the complete business requirements for the product and hand the document over to the development team. That team would then spend another year on coding the software and present the complete new product to the business team when finished. The gaps between the expectations of the business, and what has been developed, would often be substantial, although on paper, all or most requirements were being fulfilled. So basically, the organization would spend two or more years of substantial investment in the product and end up with a flop. Each group would blame each other, due to lack of shared accountability and ownership of the entire process.

UX often had little or no input in the planning phase. With little understanding of the UX process, business and development stakeholders would make assumptions around how the interface should be designed, based on their understanding of what users want. Little was done to validate these assumptions with real users.

A minor benefit to UX was the relative ease of planning and estimating of the user interface effort, because so much of the planning was done up-front. Of course, once the UI work actually started, the actual deliverables almost always deviated from the original estimate. However, keeping track of changes was relatively easy, as long as you and the stakeholders on the project established a clear change control process.

Agile

These days, Agile development is all the rage. The Agile model shares fundamental values and principals with the well-established UX approach to User Centered Design. In fact, the first value listed on the "Agile Manifesto" is: "Individual and interactions over processes and tool" (see `http://agilemanifesto.org/` for more information). Although the individual referred to here is a member of the project team, and not the end user UX has in mind, this is a value to which any UX practitioner would subscribe.

The Agile software development model is highly collaborative, iterative, and follows four key phases: Requirements, architecture and design, development, and finally testing and feedback. Without iteration and emphasis on delivering working software, these phases may remind you of the Waterfall model. However, instead of establishing both high and low-level requirements before the development begins, as is the case with traditional Waterfall model, Agile starts with high-level requirements as input for immediate coding. Agile also considers requirements in a flexible way, which supports rapid adaptations and change as the iterative process unfolds.

Jargon

However, from a UX perspective there are some pitfalls to keep in mind. To start with, Agile is fraught with technical jargon and terminology such as Scrum, Sprint, Timebox, Backlog, Burn Down, Team Velocity, Planning Poker, DoD, and on and on. Fortunately, there are also plenty of good resources online that can help you sort things out.

Jargon heavy practices are always problematic, because there is an increased risk of communication failures due to misinterpretations of key terminology. Always remember not to take anything for granted, and make sure that you, and those in charge of the Agile process, are on the same page regarding the definition of various Agile terms. This can reduce the risk of problems down the road, due to inconsistent application of the same term, by yourself and other team members.

If you are not familiar with the meaning of a term, don't hesitate to ask. If you are embarrassed to ask, or worried that not being familiar with terminology will have a negative impact on how others in the team perceive your competence, research the term first, and then discuss.

Agile flavors

There are several Agile methodologies that share the basic principals of the Agile model, but differ on implementation and sometimes also terminology and practice. These methodologies include Scrum, Extreme Programming (XP), Crystal, Dynamic Systems Development Method (DSDM), Feature-Driven Development (FDD), and Lean Software Development.

The profusion of methodologies can be daunting for UX professionals, who in general, tend not to be well versed in the arcana of developers. Agile is practiced in many flavors, and differences between implementation nuances of the model at various organizations can be substantial. Make sure to get a solid understanding of the particular Agile process that is planned, or is being practiced on your project, as early as possible. Your previous experience with Agile may lead you to make assumptions about the process that may be irrelevant. So remember: When you are part of a larger interdisciplinary team, don't make assumptions and don't be shy about asking for clarifications.

Sometimes, the project plan has been outlined by the development team well before the UX resources join the project, especially when the UX effort is outsourced. This plan may not take the full impact of specialized UX tasks into consideration. For example, the usability testing activity may be included, but none or few of the activities that support the effort are accounted for, such as allowing enough time for recruitment, creating the scripts, and preparing the Axure file to match tested scenarios. Reviewing the plan and ensuring that you are comfortable with the plan is important.

Estimating Axure work

It can be difficult to estimate the amount of Axure work that will be involved in an Agile or Waterfall-flavored projects. A few years ago, agreements could be easily made around the number of wireframes and the number of revisions—estimates that formed the basis for acceptance of work. If an interactive prototype was commissioned, it was a separate deliverable, typically coded by a frontend developer. However, with Axure, the boundaries are blurred, and consequently, the most fundamental of questions need to be considered in order to avoid costly misunderstandings.

For example, *what is a wireframe?* Suppose we agree that the home page is an example of a wireframe. Before Rich Internet Applications (RIAs), back in the days of static wireframes produced with a tool such as Visio, the home page wireframe would be considered a single wireframe, for the purpose of estimating and delivery. Today, we still have a home page, but when it is constructed for an RIA, in a tool such as Axure, it is a composite of widgets, masters, and dynamic panels. Each master is an independent wireframe, made of widgets, dynamic panels, and perhaps other masters. Each dynamic panel may be a set of unique states sometimes composed of other dynamic panels and masters. Moreover, the wireframes also include interactions.

Therefore, a single Axure wireframe can translate to a lot more work as compared to what a traditional wireframe used to require. This is not because Axure is inefficient. On the contrary, it is because:

- Axure enables UX designers to visualize rich Internet applications, at a level of fidelity that is generally on par with developer-produced prototypes.
- Modern applications are asynchronous, which means that data can be sent to and from a single page without having to reload the page. This means that modern pages are a composite of widgets that can operate independently from other sections on the same page, while maintaining a contact with the entire page. A page in an Axure prototype can model personalization, context, and local. The level detail and complexity that UX designers can visualize has increased tremendously, but not the allocated schedule and budget of the typical project plan.

When it comes to the Agile model, UX can become tricky. In each sprint, developers produce code that supports the work in the upcoming sprints. Similarly, the Axure file gets more and more detailed, as the prototype elaborates flows and interactions that were developed in earlier sprints. However, the efficiencies that come from writing code do not translate efficiencies in your Axure file.

Instead, the file grows as more pages, masters, and dynamic panels are added and old drafts are mixed in with new proposals. Interactions, variables, and raised events increase the complexity of the file. In an environment that requires rapid iteration, estimation, and change, constructing your Axure file in a disciplined way is paramount. What appears as a minor requirement change might cascade to you having to modify any number of widgets and interactions. This can affect your ability to keep up with the pace of the project.

Calculating your time

Schedules of many projects include a built-in fallacy of equating a day's eight hours block, to eight hours of productive work. Many UX practitioners, from inexperience, optimism or a desire to be good team players, tend to gloss over this detail when reviewing the schedule. The following are some of the key culprits that require time which is typically not accounted for in the plan:

- **Analysis and synthesis**: UX is about creative problem solving and coming up with good UX, especially for complex task flows. You need time to digest the information that you collect during discovery and requirement development, and time to analyze and synthesize the material and emerge with a concept or an approach. In short, you need time to think, and thinking takes time. Most project plans don't include thinking time, unfortunately.

- **Exploration and iteration take time**: It is rare to hit the appropriate solution on the first draft. Often, several options need to be developed and explored, and the wining solution will emerge through discussions. This is a time consuming process, which is also not accounted for in plans.

- **Meetings**: UX is face-time heavy, meaning that face-to-face meetings with stakeholders and team members will consume a significant portion of your day. At some points in the project, meetings can account for over 50% of your weekly schedule, for example, during the development and review of business requirements.

- **Elaboration**: Despite Axure's efficiencies and ease of use, wireframing and interactions take time, especially if you are modeling multiple use cases, conditional flows, and exceptions. You will be generating the HTML prototype frequently, reworking masters and states, and so on. This is all time-consuming.

- **Snags**: Sometimes, you will get unexpectedly stuck on a wireframe or interaction. You may have to reconstruct a wireframe previously considered as finished, as a result of a required change. Don't assume that each Axure session will go absolutely smooth and fast.

- **Communication**: Phone calls and conference calls, responding to and writing e-mails, creating presentations, reading and creating support documentation. These activities will quickly add up to a substantial amount of time spent daily on project-related work which you cannot postpone much.

- **Downtime**: We are not machines yet, although in some projects you may feel the expectation to act like one. Taking food, coffee, snack, and washroom breaks are fortunately still allowed, and should be encouraged, because productivity, creativity, and motivation suffer as a result of work pressures. Taking a break every 50 minutes or so is also encouraged, in order to rest your eyes, stretch and improve your circulation. Finally, even if you are in a progressive environment, a quick visit to the washroom turns into half an hour spent listening to a colleague's stories.

- **Health issues and personal emergencies**: We all get ill at some point or another. Flu, allergies, and other normal, seasonal maladies will require us to take a few days off from work in order to recover, not to mention avoiding getting the entire office catching your bugs.

There are no absolute answers to estimating both the amount of the Axure work needed, such as wireframing and interaction, or the amount of real time it will take to produce. However, you can apply common sense and experience to any of the following formulas:

- **The optimist**: 8 hours minus (25% meetings and communications + 15% other project-related work + 10% downtime) = 50%. In other words, plan to be productive, work of about 4 prototyping hours.

- **The realist**: 8 hours minus (40% meetings and communications + 20% other project-related work + 10% downtime + 10% buffer) = 80%. In other words, plan to be productive, work of about 2 prototyping hours.

And that is why, dear reader, you most likely will find yourself, at some point, working well over eight hour days, including weekends, and sometimes through holidays. If your experience does not agree with my description here, please let me know! Sometimes, software projects, including those that started with the best of intentions, but a weak project plan, degrade into a dreaded "death march" in which the entire project team is made to follow an impossible schedule in order to meet an unrealistic goal.

Expectation alignment

You may not be able to affect the entire project plan of a large project, or even a small project, but you should align stakeholders with UX methods and processes. Keep in mind that generally people have only a vague idea about the work UX designers perform. Stakeholders and team members from other disciplines consume our deliverables and work products, but often underestimate the amount of effort that was invested into producing them, which is a problem for UX.

Make sure that you explain the UX work-process to stakeholders on your project (from top executives, if you have access to them) to key members of the business and development teams. You will gain substantial cooperation and understanding after you explain the work process, the value of using Axure, and the amount of work you need to do in order to create those great interactions and contextual flows. Most people get that, and will begin taking into account the leg-time that UX requires. The following are a couple of examples:

- Prototype granularity: The prototype will be consumed by everyone involved in the project. You will use it throughout the project to demonstrate to stakeholders how the requirements and flows are fulfilled in the design, and in usability validation and testing activities. What level of granularity is expected from the prototype? Stakeholders may not realize that the more granular the prototype, the more effort has to be invested in managing it through iterations.

- Specifications: The primary audience for UI specifications is the development team. Don't assume that your understanding of what a UI spec is, matches that of the development team. Stakeholders might incorrectly focus on the ease with which it is possible to generate specs in Axure with a click of a button and forget about the tedious effort of writing the content that goes into the annotation fields, and the manual cleanup process that might be needed after the raw specification document has been generated.

Transitioning from concept to detailed design

The first phase of most UX projects can be considered as the "honeymoon" phase. The period is characterized by the following attributes:

- **Excitement**: It is a period of exploration during which you have an opportunity to understand the goals of the project, develop, and validate a concept with stakeholders and end users.

- **Team building and familiarization**: Like the honeymoon of a newly-married couple, everyone is on their best behavior, but some cracks may open here and there. If you are a consultant, you may also start getting a sense of internal politics. If you are an internal resource, you may already know many team members and be familiar with internal politics, which in turn might help you make fast assessments about the level of collaboration you can expect from others.

- **High-level requirements**: People often travel for their honeymoon to some remote, romantic destination such Paris, for example, or some tropical island. It is an opportunity to be away from the grind of daily routine. Similarly, the vision prototype is a high-level concept built to address strategic, high-level goals. You can explore and propose fascinating user-interactions, highly efficient contextual presentation of information and user flows, and so on. Your work is unencumbered by the constraints of low-level business and technical requirements.

Typically, your transition from concepts to detailed design will be affected by the work products and deliverables you created, and the expectations around the level of detail and elaboration in the following phases.

From vision mode

In the vision prototype, you articulated a high-level UI framework, navigation, and layouts of the application. You demonstrated key interaction flows and interactivity features. Using Axure to wireframe and build the concept file, your progress rate was probably high, and so was your ability to respond to feedback and requests for modifications. Stakeholders and management embrace the concept, and you are good to go and to move on to the detailed design phase.

- Are you expected to continue and deliver such a level of detail in interactivity during the detailed design phase? If the answer is yes, then, is the intent to generate specifications out of it?

- Do you have the time and/or UX resources needed to sustain a fully-fledged, high-fidelity prototype throughout the detailed design phase?

From sketch mode

If you were using the sketch mode for initial explorations of the user experience, there is a point in the process when the "sketchy" styling becomes extraneous. At the conceptualization phase, the sketch effect can help communicate to a stakeholder and reviewers the rawness of what they are looking at. This is important, because most people tend to respond to what they see and the sketchy look helps mitigate the risk of taking early drafts as actual designs.

There is a potential for an opposite situation to occur in which stakeholders and participants in early validation sessions might assume that the sketchy design **is** the intended design. After all, it is subject to the same potential tendency to consider a visual presentation as a finished, or a close-to-finished approach. The viewer may not realize that the sketch effect is meant to communicate a draft. Sketch effects are new to Axure, and it is not yet clear how useful it will be. In any case, if you find that it creates confusion instead of helping out, cancel the effect.

Foundations and scaffoldings

The following section covers basic wireframing construction principles, including concepts which were introduced in previous chapters, such as guides and grids. While useful, you might wonder what these have to do with managing change. The answer is simple—*modularity*. The ability to quickly and efficiently make modifications to the prototype is directly associated with how wireframes are constructed.

Determining the Wireframe width

The width of Axure wireframes is always fixed, which means that the wireframe will not resize dynamically to fit the available screen width, when the prototype is generated. In other words, you cannot simulate the layout elasticity.

In order to determine the maximum width of wireframes, you need to consider:

- The target device
- The screen's resolution

While the evolution of display resolution for desktop and laptop computers has evolved in standard leaps, inching its way from 320 x 200 pixels or less, to today's HD screens, tablets, and other mobile devices which are all over the map when it comes to screen size and resolution. Unless you are designing an application for a specific device, it is impractical to create a wireframe layout for each possible target display. However, there are some practical approaches to consider.

If you are developing a web application which will be viewed on a computer screen, it is advised to select a lower common denominator, such as 1024 pixels. This number increases every few years, as the quality and screen resolution improves. Many UX designers work with very large screens, because the larger the screen, the more productive you can be. It is common to use multiple displays to further increase the productivity. However, it is important to remember the target audience for the application we are designing. Many users may be restricted by much smaller screens, for example, sales people, whose primary monitor is a small laptop.

Another benefit of designing with 1024 pixels in mind is that a number of tablets, including the iPad and the Samsung Galaxy, use a screen resolution of 1024 pixels horizontally. In order to make life interesting, however, a tablet screen can be viewed as a landscape (horizontally) and as portrait (vertically) as the user rotates the device. This often means the app needs two sets of wireframes to accommodate each viewing option.

The actual width of page wireframes should be less than 1024 pixels for a number of reasons, as illustrated in the following screenshot:

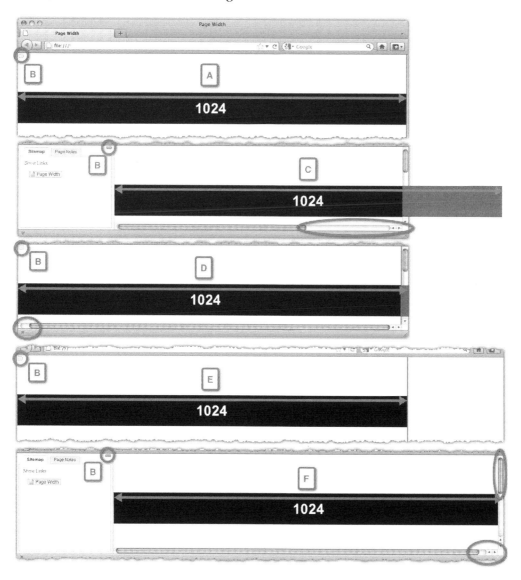

- If you present the prototype on a screen with a resolution of 1024 (A), a projector for example, the wireframe will extend the entire width of the browser. Note that the **Sitemap** pane has collapsed.

- When you click on a button to show the **Sitemap** pane (B), you will no longer be able to show the entire screen and have to scroll horizontally (C).

- With the **Sitemap** pane collapsed, but the vertical scroll bar on (D), about 20 pixels on the right will be lost, which may be a problem in a presentation.

- At higher horizontal resolution settings, for example, 1280 pixels (E), an entire wireframe set to 1024 pixels will fit, leaving a wide margin on the right.

- This margin will be eliminated when you turn on the **Sitemap** pane (F), and moreover, a vertical scroll will cause a loss of about 20 pixels on the right, requiring use of the horizontal scroll bar.

Guides

The idea that the contents of a fixed-width page can be organized in a flexible, yet proportional arrangement of columns is ancient. The overall effect helps to create good page layouts that are pleasing to the eye, because the width of all columns is based on the same ratio. If you consider the guide early in the design process, you are likely to gain efficiencies of construction, because the width of widgets will be set to a standard ratio, allowing you the flexibility to mix and match widgets across pages.

The most common use of guides, however, is casual. Typically, the guide is needed to align objects across a horizontal or vertical line. Most users of drawing and painting applications are familiar with the convention of creating guides by dragging them over from the vertical or horizontal rulers. Guides are a welcome addition to Axure 6, and the same convention applies, as illustrated in the following screenshot:

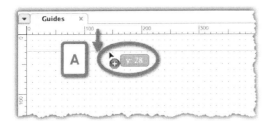 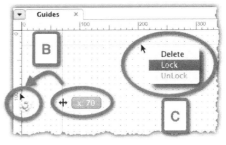

- In order to add a horizontal guide to the page, click on the horizontal ruler and drag down to the page area. A thin green line will appear. The Y coordinates will be displayed to assist with exact positioning (A).

- In order to remove a guide, you can either click and drag it out of the page (B), or right-click on it and use the **Delete** option from the context menu.

- In order to lock a guide to the page, right-click and select the **Lock** option from the context menu (C).

With Axure, it is possible to move beyond the casual use of guides as a temporary alignment aid. You can also take advantage of guides as scaffoldings that support the consistency of layouts and patterns across multiple pages of your prototype. Axure supports both page level and file level (global) guides.

Global guides

Think of global guides as an extension to the concept of a master—both maintain their physical properties across pages. Need to make a modification—do it only once, and all the instances will be updated.

Axure comes loaded with two global guides based on the 960 grid-system that was created by Nathan Smith. (See `http://960.gs`). His idea was to streamline web development by providing commonly used dimensions, based on the width of 960 pixels. Note the terminology mix-up here—Axure has decided to keep the term 'grid', which is used by the 960 system, despite the fact that in Axure, the term grid is used elsewhere. However, the global guide functionality is basically about applying a guide-set master. The application of guides is discussed in detail in *Chapter 3*.

Page guides

Guides are also available on a page level. This means that each page, or a set of pages, can conform to the alignment and spacing governed by guides that you dragged over from the horizontal and vertical rulers. Page guides are typically the casual guides mentioned earlier. Perhaps your design does not conform to the 960 grid, or you cannot use a global design because your application contains a variation of layouts. The ability to control guides per page provides flexibility for page-level design.

I mentioned that page-level guides can be applied to a set of pages because you can copy and paste the guides from page to page. Unfortunately, you cannot save local guides for reuse on other pages, but it is likely that such functionality will be added at some point.

The grid

A grid is a visual tool that helps in organizing wireframe layouts and is common to most drawing and illustration software. The grid is an infinite pattern of horizontal and vertical lines that are set to a pre-defined interval, and are part of the page background in editing mode, but not visible in the generated prototype or Word specifications screenshots.

The grid is perhaps a trivial, little noticed feature of Axure, and many users don't bother to display it, or ever to change the default 'out-of-the-box' settings. However, you can improve the construction quality of your wireframes by taking advantage of the grid to align widgets across a horizontal or vertical axis.

Customizing the grid

You can customize the Axure grid by using the **Grid Settings** dialog, which you can access from the **Grid and Guides** option in the **Wireframe** menu. Alternatively, you can right-click anywhere within an empty space in the **Wireframe** area. You can toggle the visibility of the grid. Axure also lets you toggle the **snap** feature, which makes grid lines function like a magnet; as you drag a widgets across a wireframe, it "snaps" to the closest grid line. The following screenshot illustrates the process of customizing the grid:

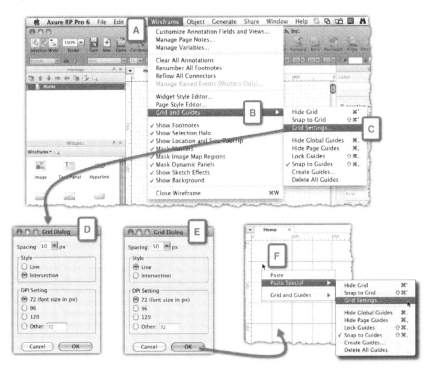

- From the **Wireframe** menu (A), select the **Grid and Guide** option (B), and from there continue to select the **Grid Setting...** option (C).

- **Grid Dialog** (D) opens. The default Axure grid is set to 10 pixel spacing **Intersection** style. If you are using Mac, the default DPI setting is set to 72, which is the Mac standard. If you are using the PC version, it is defaulted to 96 DPI.

- You can modify any of the settings (E), although changing the DPI is typically not required.

- If you switch the grid style to **Line**, keep in mind that it might be difficult to distinguish between grid lines and guide lines. Note that in the screen capture, the lines are red (F), but this was done only to make it easier to see the otherwise faint-blue grid lines.

Page templates

Visual consistency is a fundamental principal of good software design and an attribute that can significantly help with managing change. Of course, not all screens in a given software have the same layout. Rather, a level of visual coherence can guarantee a consistent experience across the application.

It is a common practice to develop pages as templates, for the following reasons:

- Advantage for you as a UX designer: Leverage design patterns across instances of the same screen, to simplify construction of your Axure prototype and specifications, since we often need to create multiple versions of the same page in order to visualize variations.

- Advantage for the development team: Developers typically think about templates and code reuse, efficiency and reuse being native to programming. Developers will instantly understand and appreciate your approach of templates in the design. Discuss the structure of templates with the developers to align your modular approach to the coded modular approach.

The concept of page templates is very similar to that of masters, except that templates are not a built-in Axure feature. They are a choice of a construction method you choose to use. In this section, we discuss several Axure features that lend themselves to the creation, use, and modification of Axure templates.

Page style editor

With the page style editor, a new feature is introduced in this version, where you can create custom page-level styles, which you can apply to specific pages in your prototype. Key benefits of this feature are as follows:

- Consistency across all pages that share similar properties
- Ability to change wireframes quickly and efficiently during the detailed design phase: when changes to any of the page style properties are called for, you only need to make the modification once to the custom page style

We touched on the page style editor earlier in the book, in the context of the **Sketch Effect** feature. However, there are additional properties you can control, which—similar to the properties listed in the widget style editor—map to cascading style sheet (CSS) properties. Axure shields you from having to know CSS, its terminology, and syntax. However, understanding the mapping can be useful when you discuss visual design with developers and designers.

Axure Page Style Editor	**CSS**
Page Align	Margin and Padding
Back Color	background-color
Back Image	background-image
Back Image-Import	background-attachment
Horz Align	background-position
Vert Align	background-position
Repeat	background-repeat

To further explore the template concepts, several pages of the Alexandria demonstration project come to mind. For example, the Home, Media Category, and Item Detail pages:

Home page template

You might wonder why the home page is considered as a page template, as there is only a single home page in the application. As you think about your Axure prototype file, you realize that in fact, you use several variations of the home page. The following screenshot illustrates the structural similarities between the three variations of the home page in the Alexandria demonstration project:

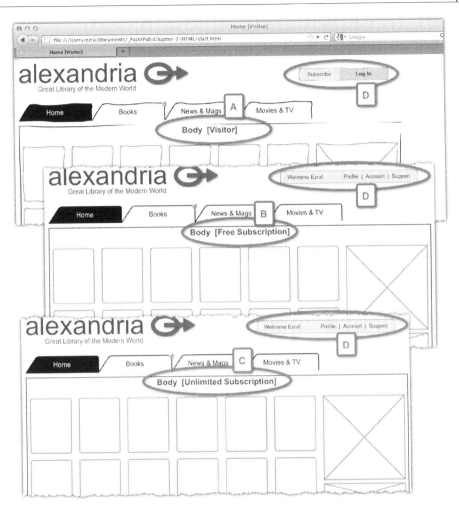

The three flavors of the home page are **Visitor** (A), **Free Subscription** (B), and
Unlimited Subscription (C). In the RP file, there are only two unique pages, one for
visitors, and the other for the masters. When you compare the initial sketch (A) to the
iterated version (B), you note the change in the body area. The rest of the framework
evolves as well, of course, but the use of masters help maintain the over all trajectory.
The intent is to try and keep the same home page structure consistent throughout
the interaction flow for all from a visiting user to a paying subscriber. The content
and messaging will change, of course, but the underlying construction can be reused
across all variations.

Category page template

Although the site offers various kinds of media, it is desirable to present them using the same layout. This enables efficiencies of code, and from the user's perspective, a consistent experience when browsing for items, regardless of their category. This is typical to experience in popular applications such as iTunes and Spotify. The following screenshot illustrates the structural cohesiveness across the three types of media offered by the application:

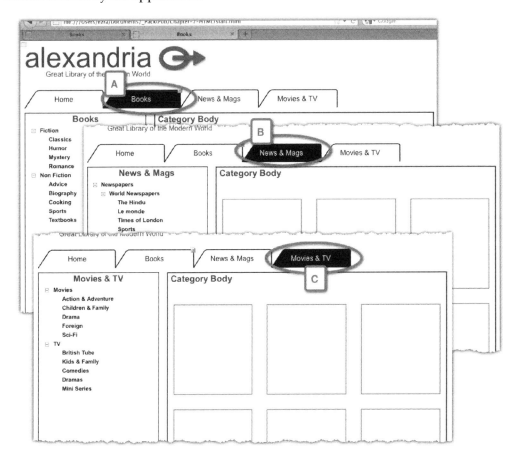

- As long as the underlying concept calls for consistency of the design pattern across all types of media, the use of masters and dynamic panel can greatly reduce the speed and flexibility with which we can model context, on top of a uniform template.

- Each of the categories, **Books** (A), **Newspapers** (B), and **Movies** (C) is made of the exact same masters. Each category has a wireframe page in the sitemap in order to reduce the overall complexity of the construction and support the documentation and specifications generation.

Detail page template

For the page detail, we are also incorporating an example of design for multiple devices, in this case, the web-based layout (A), and an iPad layout (B). While the presentation is different, both item details are essentially constructed of the same masters:

 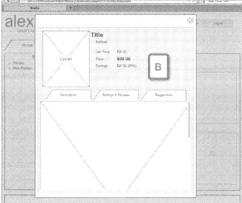

Widget style editor

The widget style editor affords a *global* control over the visual properties of a widget type. In other words, it is the Axure's user-friendly way to apply Cascading Style Sheet (CSS) properties to widgets, with the exception of widget height and width.

Note that:

- Not all the widgets that appear in the **Widget** pane are listed in the style editor. This is because some widgets, such as the dynamic panel or iFrame, don't really have independent visual properties of their own.

- The **Rectangle**, **Placeholder**, and **Button Shape** widgets are referenced as **Button Shape** widget in the style editor, so changes to the default of that style apply to these three widgets as well:

Widget	Style properties													
	Font	Font Size	Bold	Italic	Underline	Alignment	Vert Align	Padding	Line Spacing	Font Color	Fill Color	Line Color	Line Width	Tree Node
Image Box	Y	Y	Y	Y	Y	Y	Y	Y		Y				
Text Panel	Y	Y	Y	Y	Y	Y			Y	Y				
Hyperlink	Y	Y	Y	Y	Y	Y			Y	Y				
Button Shape	Y	Y	Y	Y	Y	Y	Y	Y	Y	Y	Y	Y	Y	Y
Button	Y	Y	Y	Y	Y	Y				Y				
Text Field	Y	Y	Y	Y	Y	Y				Y	Y			
Text Area	Y	Y	Y	Y	Y	Y				Y	Y			
Droplist	Y	Y	Y	Y	Y					Y	Y			
List Box	Y	Y	Y	Y	Y					Y	Y			
Check box	Y	Y	Y	Y	Y	Y	Y			Y				
Radio Button	Y	Y	Y	Y	Y	Y	Y			Y				
Flow Shape	Y	Y	Y	Y	Y	Y	Y	Y	Y	Y	Y	Y	Y	Y
Tree Node	Y	Y	Y	Y	Y					Y	Y	Y	Y	Y

Default widget styles

When you start a fresh Axure file, all the widgets have an 'out-of-the-box' default. By tweaking the default style of the widgets in your project file, you can save time and enforce consistency across all your wireframes. The changes you make will be immediately applied to all widgets for which you modified the default style, across the entire file, with the exception of widgets to which you assigned a custom style.

The following screenshot illustrates an example:

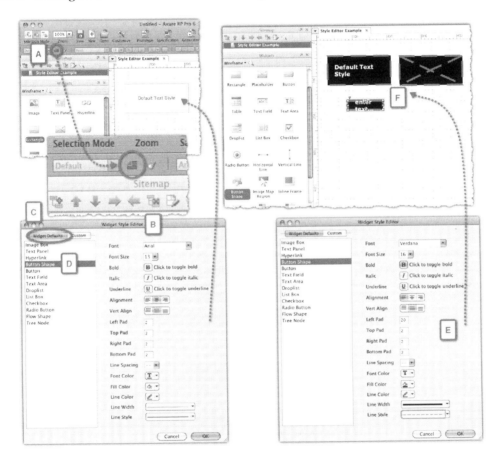

- Each time you drag a **Rectangle** widget onto the **Wireframes** pane, its visual properties will be pre-set to the default setting. These include:
    - Black line and white fill
    - Arial font, size 13, and so on

- In the toolbar, click on the widget style editor icon (A), to launch the **Widget Style Editor** dialog (B).

- Widgets that can be controlled by the editor are listed on the left-hand column, under the **Widget Defaults** column (C).

- When you click on any of the widgets on the list, you can see its visual properties.

- Modifications that you make to these properties (E) will be applied to all the widgets of this type *across the entire prototype*. For example, if you change the font, font size, background, and fill colors of a **Rectangle** widget, the new settings will apply to *all* the **Rectangle**, **Placeholder**, and **Bottom Shape**-based widgets (F) across all your wireframes in this file.

If you change the font family of one widget, for example, from Ariel to Verdana, make sure to apply the same properties to all widgets listed in the editor, unless the font variation is called for by the design. Also, make sure to review all your wireframes — some fonts are wider than others, so text wrapping may occur.

Style painter

The style painter is a welcome new addition to Axure 6, and a common feature of a drawing and painting application. It allows you to apply visual properties from one widget to other widgets.

The following screenshot illustrates a practical example: Suppose you have a dialog box with a primary-action button, and four secondary-action buttons. Initially, all the buttons, made of **Rounded Rectangle** widgets share the default style for that widget, and all of them look the same. You want to style the action buttons in a way that distinguishes the primary button from the secondary button:

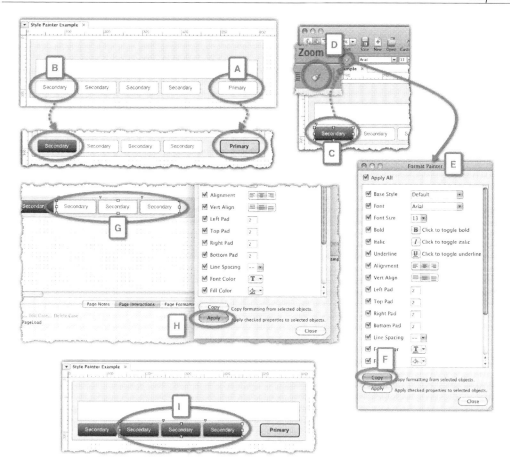

- You start by applying the visual properties for the **Primary** button (A), and the secondary-action buttons (B).

- You want to apply the styling of the first secondary button, to the other three instances. With the newly styled button selected (C), click on the **Style Painter** icon on the toolbar (D), or on the **Formatting** tab in the **Widget Properties** pane, under the **Style** section.

- The **Format Painter** dialog (E) appears. Click on the **Copy** button (F). Don't close the dialog yet. It will float above the work area, but you will be able to make selections on the wireframe.

- Select the three unformatted secondary buttons (G), and then click on the **Apply** button (H) in the **Format Painter** dialog. The desired style will be applied to the selected buttons.

Easy and fast, the style painter helps you maintain visual consistency across widgets. It is a real time-saver when you have to apply a set of visual properties that includes gradients, from widget on one page to widgets on other pages. This is especially convenient in cases where using copy-and-paste to replace unformatted widgets with formatted ones is not a productive option.

There are a number of drawbacks for using the style painter as a systematic method for implementing style changes:

- You must apply the desired style to all like-widgets across all wireframes, which can be time consuming, especially if the style needs to be changed as a result of feedback.

- Even when minor style changes are required, for example, changing one of the gradient values used for the fill of primary action-buttons, the task of change is still time-consuming because you have to go through the entire file and then make the changes.

- It can be difficult to differentiate between widgets that have been updated and those that have not been updated. Pressing the **Apply** button will be fast, but the rest will not be.

- If you started to apply the change to some widgets and had to stop due to some reason you may have a hard time figuring out which widgets have already been modified, and you may have to go through the entire file again and make sure that all widgets were updated.

Additionally, you cannot apply the painter styles to other button states such as rollover, selected, and so on. The style painter is a welcome addition to Axure's widget-editing capabilities. It is great when creating quick drafts because it greatly reduces tedious repetitive formatting steps. However, when it comes to maintaining the consistency of an application's style guide, consider the approach I propose in the following section.

Integrating with the project style guide and CSS

The following technique promises to provide substantial efficiencies and speed in our ability to adjust wireframes and prototypes to the visual design. Axure still does not support explicit integration of CSS files, but hopefully we will see this in coming versions.

The style guide

A style guide is an extensive document that is typically produced by the visual designer on the project. A typical guide should cover the following aspects of the visual design:

- **Branding**:
  - ° The color palette: Listing the HEX values of all the major colors, including gradients
  - ° Application logo: Including all the allowed instances and sizes of the logo on various pages and display rules
  - ° A template anatomy: Labeling of all the layout elements that make up the structure of each major page template of the application

- **Design elements**:
  - ° Typography: The fonts and the styling of fonts across the applications
  - ° Graphics: The rules and styling for buttons and icons, including size, order, margin, and padding

- **Structural elements**:
  - ° Covers the styling and sizing rules for data grid tables, windows, light boxes, alert, message and error boxes, and finally, forms.

The visual design guide should be the document of records for anything related to visual design. The style guide is accompanied with a CSS style sheet which translates many of the properties sheets listed in the guide into CSS classes and IDs.

Some elements that are listed in the style guide, such as the details of the page anatomy, may also be covered in your UX documentation. Make sure to synchronize with the visual designer about the names and labels of various elements to avoid conflicting references.

Currently, Axure does not support explicit CSS integration either in the form of linking with external CSS files, or by creating the CSS internally. However, it is getting close. We have covered a number of methods that are available to quickly modify the visual style of widgets. We found that using the **Style Painter** or default widget styles have their limitations when you have to reflect the latest visual design in your prototype.

Axure custom styles, however, get as close as ever before, to emulating the usage and behavior of CSS. While the implementation is not perfect, you can still gain substantial efficiencies in the change process and maintenance of the widget's styles, and the ability to conform with the project's style guide and some of its CSS.

The following diagram illustrates the use of custom styles to apply primary and secondary look and feels to buttons:

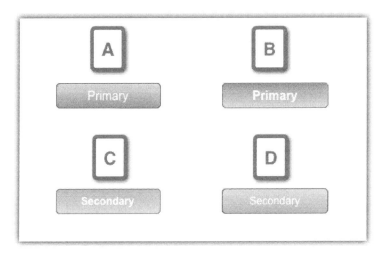

The following table is a section of the style guide, as it would pertain to the buttons in the preceding diagram. It looks very different from a CSS file which will be handed over to the developers.

Widget	State	Style guide	In the preceding diagram
Primary Button	Default	Fill Gradation: Hex#: FF6600 bottom, to Hex#: FFCC00 top Border-Width: 1px Border-Color: 99000 Font-Family: Ariel Font-Style: Normal Font-Weight: Normal Font-Size: 16px Color: Hex#: FFFFFF Text-Align: Center Padding-Left, Right: 12 px Padding Top, Bottom: 6 px	A
Primary Button	Rollover	Fill Gradation: Hex#: FFCC00 bottom, to Hex#: FF6600 top Border Width: 1px Border-Color: FF0000 Font-Family: Ariel Font-Style: Normal Font-Weight: Bold Font-Size: 16px Color: FFFFFF Text-Align: Center Padding-Left, Right: 12 px Padding Top, Bottom: 6 px	B
Secondary Button	Default	Height = 32 px Fill Gradation: Hex#: FF9900 bottom, to Hex#: FFCC99 top Border Width: 1px Border-Color: 99000 Font-Family: Ariel Font-Style: Normal Font-Weight: Normal Font-Size: 14px Color: FFFFFF Text-Align: Center Padding-Left, Right: 12 px Padding Top, Bottom: 6 px	C

Widget	State	Style guide	In the preceding diagram
Secondary Button	Rollover	Fill Gradation: Hex#: FF6600 bottom, to Hex#: FFCC00 top. Border Width: 1px Border-Color: FF0000 Font-Family: Ariel Font-Style: Normal Font-Weight: Bold Font-Size: 14px Color: FFFFFF Text-Align: Center Padding-Left, Right: 12 px Padding Top, Bottom: 6 px	D

The benefits of a style-guide, as a communication method, over a CSS document are as follows:

- Style guides are a lot easier for non-developers to read, in comparison. Reading a CSS document is like reading a code. Not a complicated code, but still, class and ID names can be very obscure, and there may be other properties and writing conventions that typical UX designers may not be familiar with.

- Often the CSS document will not be available for quite some time. While the style guide is created and handed over by the visual designer, converting it into a working CSS is typically performed by a developer. This activity may take place later in the development process.

Up to Version 6, there were two methods to implement visual design in Axure, without custom styles. In context to the buttons in the preceding example:

- **Method A**: Create the buttons to the project's widget library. Whenever a primary or secondary instance of a button is needed, drag it over to a wireframe.

- **Method B**: Construct each button as a master within your prototype file. To use, drag the master over to a wireframe, and flatten it in order to modify the text or size.

When it comes to managing changes of the visual design in your prototype, the major drawback of both these approaches is that once applied to a wireframe, you can no longer make a global change in any of the button's visual properties. You will need to go over each wireframe and apply the changes manually, which is a tedious and time-consuming process.

With Axure's **Custom Style** feature, it is possible to capture the visual properties of all elements listed in the project's style guide, as custom styles, and from then on, use only these styles, most importantly, in masters—flattening masters will not remove the widget's link to the custom style. Consequently, updating the custom style will instantly update the master, its instances, and its flattened instances.

The following screenshot illustrates a simple example of the application of a custom style to a master, in this case, a button widget:

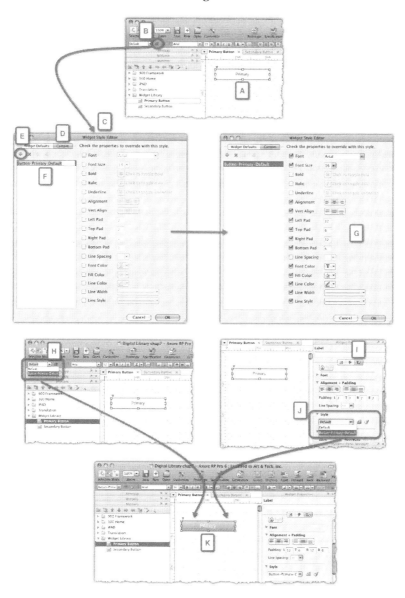

- In the **Masters** pane, create a folder and label it **Widget Library**.

- Create two masters. Label the first **Primary Button** and the other **Secondary Button**.

- Open the **Primary Button** for editing. Use a **Rounded Rectangle** to create a button with a height of 32 pixels, according to the style guide. Type the label **Primary** on the button. (A).

- That is it for now, as far as styling the master goes!

- Click on the **Widget Style Editor** icon on the toolbar (B) to open the **Widget Style Editor** dialog (C), and switch to the **Custom** tab on the left-hand pane (D). Initially, this column will be empty.

- Click on the **Add** icon (E) to create your first custom style and label it **Button-Primary-Default** (F). You can use spaces and other characters to separate the words in the name of a custom style, I recommend getting used to maintaining compatibility with CSS guidelines.

If you have, and understand, the project's CSS document, you can use the class name used there. Otherwise, keep in mind the W3C's CSS 2.1 guidelines:

"In CSS, identifiers (including element names, classes, and IDs in selectors) can contain only the characters [a-zA-Z0-9] and ISO 10646 characters U+00A0 and higher, plus the hyphen (-) and the underscore (_); they cannot start with a digit, two hyphens, or a hyphen followed by a digit."

Visit http://www.w3.org/TR/CSS21/syndata.html for more information.

- The style properties listed in the **Widget Style Editor** match the properties in your style guide, as well as the standard CSS syntax:

Axure Widget Style Editor	Style Guide/CSS Syntax
Font	Font-Family
Font Size	Font-Size
Bold	Font-Weight
Italic	Font-Style
Underline	Text-Decoration
Alignment	Text-Align
Vert Align	Vertical-Align
Left Pad	Padding-Left
Top Pad	Padding-Top
Right Pad	Padding-Right
Bottom Pad	Padding-Bottom
Line Spacing	Line-Height
Font Color	Color
Fill Color	Background-Color
Line Color	Border-Color
Line Width	Border-Width
Line Style	Border-Style

- Define the relevant properties for the button widget, for example:
    - Font-Family: Ariel
    - Font-Size: 16px
    - Font-Weight: Normal
    - Font-Style: Normal
    - Text-Align: Center
    - Padding-Left, Right: 12 px
    - Padding Top, Bottom: 6 px
    - Color: Hex#: FFFFFF
    - Fill Gradation: Hex#: FF6600 bottom, to Hex#: FFCC00 top
    - Border –Color HEX#: 99000
    - Border-Width: 1px

- After you capture all the properties for the style (G), click on the **OK** button to dismiss **Widget Style Editor**. Remember to save the file, as a habit.

Back on the **Primary Button** master comes the real fascinating part with two options to apply the custom style to the widget:

- Option A: Click to select the widget from the droplist (H) to the left of the **Widget Style Editor** icon. This droplist now lists the new style you just added: **Button-Primary-Default**. Select this value, and see your widget change to that style! (K).
- Option B: In the **Widgets Properties** pane, switch to the **Formatting** tab (I). The style droplist also appears in the **Style** section there (J). The button will change to match the selected custom style (K).

This, in a nutshell, is the method. Continue to add the other styles and expand the custom styles library. As long as you style your widget using custom styles, you will be able to respond to changes in the style guide very quickly.

In fact, you can start your custom style library fairly early in the design process. Suppose you want to start, as many practitioners do, with a grayscale palette. You can still define custom styles. When the actual style guide is provided, all you need to do is update the custom styles. This can save days of tedious manual updates, as illustrated in the following screenshot:

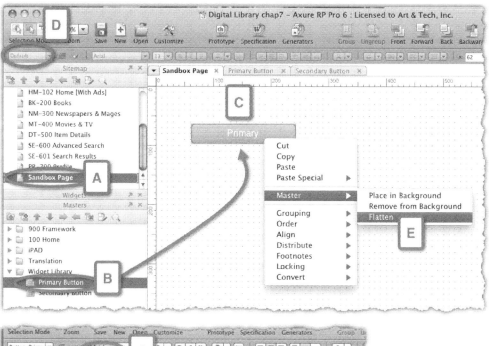

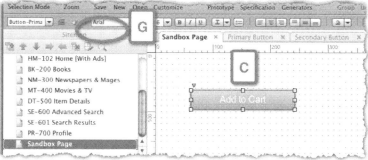

- Create a new page in your file, and label it **Sandbox Page** (A). I find that, in addition to using Axure sandbox files to quickly test ideas in isolation from the entire project file, it is convenient to have a sandbox page in the file, for some quick tests and explorations.

- Drag over the **Primary Button** master (B) and place it on the page (C). Notice that the **Widget Style** droplist on the toolbar (D) is disabled. This is because changes to the styles are at the master level, not the page on which the master instance is placed.

- As you need to change the button's label from "Primary" to "Move to Cart", you need to flatten the master. Right-click on the widget and select the **Flatten** option (E) from the Master's menu.

- The link that the master instance had to the master "mother ship" has been severed. The button is no longer a master, and so you can edit the button's label. Flattening a master is similar to how Axure handles widgets that are dragged over from a custom widget library.

- Most importantly, and a significant benefit over widget libraries, is that although the master has been flattened, the widget is still associated with the custom style: Notice that the **Widget Style** droplist on the toolbar (G) is now enabled. Changes you make to the custom style when you *update the master* will *also update the widget* that was based on the master, well after the tie had been broken.

To sync or not to sync?

Should the prototype be aligned with the application's visual design? The benefits are substantial:

- Stakeholders and participants in usability testing can provide a valuable response to the overall look and feel of the proposed user experience. Response to a change is inherent in user experience prototyping projects.

- Less confusion during development. The developers can easily see, both in the HTML prototype and the Word specifications, what it is that they are supposed to code.

The second item is actually very important. When the prototype is kept at its basic grayscale, low fidelity design, there is a need to manage two different types of wireframes:

- The wireframes of record, which are wireframes created in our Axure prototype.

- The visual design wireframes, which are delivered by the visual designer. These typically reflect an older version of the wireframes, the actual wireframes, of course, are not being updated to reflect the latest version of the prototype.

The problem is that it is very confusing, especially to developers, who need to figure out how to deal with those two different sets of wireframes. Fundamentally, the project is driven by business drivers, such as response to competitive pressures and changing needs, dissatisfied customers and sales force, high support costs, or a window of opportunity to increase the market share with innovation. The UX project is typically accompanied by a major branding or styling effort. Company and product logos, new or extended color palette, new visuals, including photos and icons are all part of what should become a master style guide for the project.

The desire to incorporate the new visual design is compelling, but it is only through the use of techniques such as custom styles and masters that the effort can be manageable from a prototyping perspective.

Integrating the visual design into a prototype poses some challenges for us. It is a common best practice to begin the prototype with rough grayscale wireframes. Axure 6 allows you to present initial concepts in a sketchy style, further reinforcing the tentativeness of the design.

The goal in the early stages is to get the "important" things right: the information architecture of the application, global and intra-page navigation, high-level functionality, critical task flows, and so forth. The assumption is that the visual design is premature in the early stages of the project and can often unnecessarily shift discussions from matters of substance to more superficial topics of colors and graphics.

This approach is becoming quickly outdated. User interfaces are becoming the forefront of innovation as they provide immersive environments that engage the user in the most trivial of data entry and data consumption tasks. The boundaries between gaming and serious applications are also blurring as direct manipulation capabilities on all computing platforms, and especially on handheld devices such as smartphones and tablets, transform interactions with data into a seriously engaging activity. Prototyping a rich user experience that involves data visualization and manipulation is becoming as much about visual design as it is about the data.

Regardless of the approach you favor, it is important to remember a fundamental principle: data and the presentation of data should be separate. It is the only way to create device-agnostic interfaces, facilitate easy integration of data, and share it with other applications. This principle should be reflected in the user experience design, which falls under your domain, just as it should be clear in the application's technical design, which falls under the developer's domain.

Prototype with existing visual design

There are situations in which you are restricted to an established design pattern. This happens when an application has to comply with the look and feel of other applications produced by the company, be consistent with the branding guidelines of a corporation, and also in other similar situations. The application you are asked to design can be new, or perhaps you are asked to extend the functionality of an existing application. The user experience you develop may represent a departure from the company's existing or legacy assets, but the visual design must match.

You may have access to the master files of the visual assets in the form of Photoshop, Illustrator or PNG files. However, often all you have to work with are the graphics that are used on an existing site or application. These you can extract and modify for use in your own prototype.

Axure provides an exceptionally fast method to create, extend, and manage interactive prototypes that are based on an existing application. The following example demonstrates how to use screen captures of an existing site to create a custom widget library that becomes the source of building blocks required to design an extension to an existing application.

The following screenshot illustrates an example, which is based on the home page of `packtpub.com`:

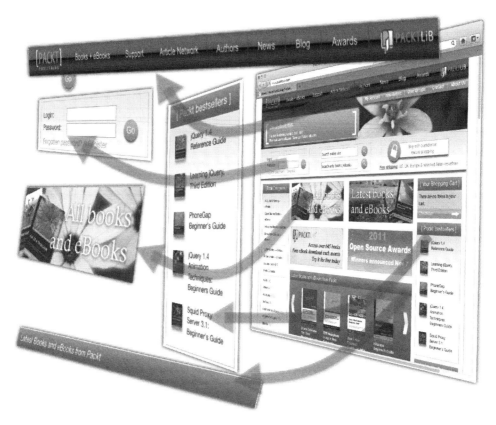

- Take screen captures of the page. PNG Format is best.

- In Axure, use the **Slice Image** option to carve out repeating visual patterns.

- You can also refine the various widgets in an image-editing tool such as Fireworks or Photoshop, or a screen capture tool such as Snagit.

- Create a widget library and add all the graphic assets.

Further, refine the widget library by remaking the widgets in Axure. In other words, replace the sliced images with actual Axure widgets to which you will apply a matching custom style.

Summary

In this chapter, we discussed the challenges that most UX practitioners face, when it comes to managing changes to the prototype. Many of these challenges have nothing to do with Axure. They are associated with the larger domain of software development and the evolving integration of UX into various development methodologies. Of course, change is inherent to UX. Consequently, it is in our best interest to figure out how to avoid the most tedious, time-consuming chores that typically involve tweaks of layout and visual design.

Axure provides a number of features that support change on a global level. Some are common to many applications, such as **Find** and **Replace** for modifying text strings in the prototype. The powerful and still-evolving **Custom Styles** feature provides dramatic time and effort savings in maintaining the consistency of visual design patterns across the prototype.

The key to successful change, however, is *managed expectations*. Assume that the stakeholders you work with have no idea about what is involved in UX work. Your ability to estimate the level of wireframing, prototyping, refactoring, and specifications effort, should be combined with your ability to educate and articulate what is involved in your work.

In the next chapter, we discuss the workflows involved in the creation of the UX functional specifications document. As mentioned here, the process will begin with the alignment of expectations of what information should be specified and the output format of the document.

8

Functional Specifications

The UX functional specifications document is a communications tool: It is written in a formal way by which the interaction designer prescribes to the developers the desired behavior of the user interface. If you need to deliver such a document, your takeaways from this chapter should be the following:

- Seek the development team's input and approval on the format and scope of the specifications, as early in the project as possible

- Estimate early, and correctly, the effort involved in creating and generating the specifications

- Start planning and testing the specifications output when you start your Axure file and continue testing and tweaking the output throughout the project

The tendency to postpone dealing with the specifications until later in the project is natural. After all, the document is typically due at the conclusion of UX activities for the project, and other more pressing tasks on the UX plate take priority. Consequently, the UI specifications document is a bit like the iceberg that sunk the Titanic: It is big, mostly hidden, and if you don't watch for it, it will hit you when you think all is going great.

Axure provides an integrated specification creation and output environment. This feature addresses the iceberg nature of specifications heads-on, in that it significantly reduces the labor and time involved in updating and producing the UI functional specifications deliverable. In other words, it translates to real value for UX practitioners who use the tool. This capability has been prominent on Axure's long list of groundbreaking features since the product's release back in 2004, and helped propel the tool's popularity within the UX industry.

To understand why, it is important to compare it to a non-integrated workflow, which was the de-facto practice just a few years ago. Visio is used in the following example, but you could easily substitute it with any of the other graphics tools, such as Adobe Fireworks:

1. Create the first draft of the specifications:

    ○   Create a wireframe in Visio.

    ○   Add annotation footnotes to the wireframe, which is a manual process: a footnote shape needs to be created, sized and formatted, then duplicated and renumbered, for each annotation footnote on the wireframe.

    ○   Create the UI specification document in MS Word.

    ○   Take a screen-capture of the wireframe.

    ○   Label the captured wireframe such that you can recall later where it belongs in the specifications document.

    ○   Save the captured wireframe in the appropriate directory.

    ○   Import the captured wireframe into the Word document.

    ○   Write the annotations for the captured wireframe in the Word document, typically, in a table above or below the image.

2. Update and maintain the specifications:

    ○   In Visio, reorder and renumber annotation footnotes: This is often required due to iterations and updates applied to the wireframe since the first draft has been captured. Consequently, new annotation footnotes are added, and depending on their position, renumbering of existing footnotes is needed to maintain orderly sequence of top left to bottom right. This is a manual process.

    ○   Take a screen capture of the updated wireframe.

    ○   Label the capture: If you wish to maintain a new version of the previous capture for that wireframe (wise tactic), your naming convention for screen captures should also consider a serial version id, or date.

    ○   Save the capture in the appropriate directory.

    ○   Open the specifications Word document.

    ○   Find the appropriate section in the Word document.

    ○   Replace the previous capture with the updated capture.

       ◦   Update the annotation table. You have to make sure that the footnote numbers in the wireframe match the sequence and numbers of table rows.

Each step listed in the preceding production workflow is manual, and often painstakingly so. Each step translates to seconds and minutes, which add up to hours and days, since the entire process needs to be repeated for each wireframe included in the specifications. For medium and large projects, we may be looking at tens of screenshots.

Set aside the time needed to create or update each wireframe or the time needed to write or update its related annotation. In addition, time yourself using a sample wireframe: Add up the minutes needed for going through the workflow of updating it in the spec—from Visio to Word. Multiply the result by the number of wireframes and you will get a rough estimate of the time it will take to revise the spec for each new iteration.

If the average time per wireframe is about 10 minutes for the entire manual process, the manual process of updating just 10 wireframes will take close to two hours. Now, to make things even more complicated, think about a team project and the effort required to coordinate the specification work among a team of UX designers. This is a real challenge.

Axure removes a great deal of the manual labor out of the workflow involved in the production of the specifications document, which translates to a saving of significant time and effort. In recent years, the landscape of UX prototyping tools has flourished with abundance of new products, and many offer-integrated specification environments. However, as you will see, while most of the manual work has been removed, generating meaningful, comprehensive specifications is still time consuming, and is not a trivial effort.

In this chapter, we cover the details of specifications' creation and output process, and review best practices that will help you streamline the production of this deliverable into the complete, high-value deliverable.

Collaboration with the development team

Let's face it. Much of the UX work on the project is often throwaway. For a brief moment in the development life cycle, UX is bathing in the limelight: the creativity invested into conceptualizing the new user experience, the intensity of joint iteration and change cycles, and the excitement of validating the interactive prototype with decision-makers, stakeholders, and end users. At the end of the day, however, developers need to translate the prototype into a fully-functional application. The UI functional specification is the document that binds the visualization we have created throughout the project—the wireframes and prototype—with the technical details of the user interface.

There are a couple of well-worn truisms that illustrate why the interactive prototype and the functional specifications document complement each other so well:

The first is that "no one reads anymore". In software, this is expressed pointedly by the famous abbreviation **RTDM (Read the Damn Manual)**, which nobody ever does. This is true not only to consumers of software, but also to those who make it. Typical software projects generate an obscene amount of internal documents. Many of the documents that you are not responsible for authoring, you are expected to review and comment on. When a crunch time sets in, even the best-intentioned team member will find it impossible to read carefully AND to do their work.

When it comes to UX generated documents, the specifications document can be a substantial tome. This is where the adage "A picture is worth a thousand words" comes to play: Visualizing the intended interaction of a rich Internet application is a significant time saver. The UX designer is spared having to write long descriptive verbiage, annotate multiple screenshots, and manage the updates. The developer can see the intended experience in an unambiguous way instead of following text, aided only with static wireframe screenshots.

In *Chapter 7*, we reviewed various development methodologies and their impact on the user experience track. Typically, UX has a little influence over the choice and practice of the particular development methodology on the project, but we do have the ability to influence and understand how UX will integrate into the project. For this reason, I emphasize the importance of communicating early with the development team and stakeholders, so that you and your team can align the UX work with the larger application road map.

Very broadly speaking, UX practitioners, regardless of their employment model, whether consultants or in-house resources, find themselves in favor of one of the following situations:

- Business 'owns' UX: In this setup, the UX team is most likely to be external to the firm, parachuted in to solve a particular need and dismissed at the end of the engagement. The drivers for engagement are almost always strategic: Response competitive pressure, desire for market leadership, new product initiative, and so on. There is some risk of possible friction with the development team over methodologies, approach, and deliverables, but also an opportunity to influence a real change.

- Development 'owns' UX: In this setup, the UX team is part of the technology group. The UX team is more likely to be made of internal resources that are in better sync with the group's goals and methodologies. The risk here, however, is that UX may be less inclined to propose bold, new ideas that conflict with the goals and constraints of the development team, and resist change demanded by the business.

Both scenarios are not ideal for UX because the reposting structure places UX under the umbrella of one side of the organization, business, or technology, and potentially in a built-in conflict with the other side. We know that UX is the glue that unifies a project's wants, needs, vision, and constraints. Ideally, UX would enjoy a reporting structure that would effectively provide it with both influence and independence across the entire business.

However, this situation may be too rare, and until then, remember that one of the most important factors for UX success involves building solid relationships with all stakeholders on the project. A spirit of collaboration and communication leads to trust, and helps avoid problems down the road. As the development team is the primary consumer of the functional specifications, achieving an agreement on the format and scope of the document has an impact on how you will construct your Axure file.

Aligning expectations

The development team is typically the primary target audience for the UI functional specifications document. In order to be successful with this deliverable, you need to apply the same approach as you would to voting in Chicago ("Vote early and vote often"). Meet with the development team early and often to determine the format and scope of the document. It will be a big mistake to wait with the specifications just because the delivery comes much later in the project plan. At that point, your Axure file has matured, evolved, and is practically complete from a construction perspective. Adjustments may be difficult to make.

The following are some concrete steps that can pave the road for a successful partnership. These steps are important if you have never worked with the team before:

- Meet with the development team very early on in the project to explicitly discuss the specifications document.

- Ask to see examples of specifications which the development team has been using for other projects. Don't be surprised if you don't get much in the way of examples, however.

- Demo Axure's specifications features to the development team. There is a high probability that the tool will be exotic and unknown to the team, which may lead to initial resistance to Axure, if the team is used to looking at Visio/ Word documents.

- Whatever hesitations the developers may originally have, it is likely that education and review of various possibilities for the generation specification will help you build a compelling case.

- Discuss with the team the attributes and level of detail they would like to see. Schedule a follow-up meeting in which you will present a draft of the specifications that includes the agreed upon fields. Tweak as needed.

At the end of this process, you will have established a good working relationship with the development team and have their buy-in for the specifications deliverable. While they may not be the only consumers of the document, this will be the group that will sign off on this deliverable. You will find that in general, developers are very open to changes, especially when it means helping them with the chore of reading massive documents. As mentioned earlier, people don't like reading big documents. Less is best.

Capturing UI specifications

As mentioned at the start of this chapter, Axure provides an integrated, configurable, specification capture and output environment. However, by no means should you assume that the process of creating the specs involves filling in the annotation fields and hitting the 'Generate' button. You will get a document, for sure, but it may not be something you want to hand over to your development partners.

A good specifications document should provide a high-level description of the user experience across the entire application, continue to cover the structure and behavior of the application's various screens, and conclude with the behavior of various widgets down to button-level elements. In other words, the document's underlying structure should be composed of the following:

- Global aspects of applications, using the Word template that is part of the spec generator
- Page level description, using page notes
- Widget level descriptions, using field annotations

The following sections will describe in detail how to customize the various elements to best fit the document you want to generate for your project.

Global specifications

There is a great deal of information about the user experience that applies to the application at its entirety, and the first part of the specifications should cover the principals, considerations, and activities that led to the application prescribed in the specs. Also, keep in mind that readers of the specifications may not be well versed in the details of UX concepts and terminology. Not all the items listed below may be relevant to any given project, but in some configuration or another, these apply to any UX project:

- Introduction: The purpose and target audience: What is this document, and who is it written for?
- Guidelines and principles:
    - Screen resolution
    - Devices support
    - Handling the date and time
    - Browser support
    - Performance: The acceptable response time for various interactions from a UX perspective

- Messaging display:
  - User and system errors
  - Confirmations
  - Alerts
- User assistance and guidance (help)
- Handling user access, permissions, and security.
- User customization features
- Localization features
- ADA compliance

- Interface layouts
- Key patterns (samples):
  - Windows and dialogs
  - Notifications:
    - Error messages
    - Warning message
    - Confirmation message
    - Informational messages
  - Miscellaneous:
    - Calendars
    - Button patterns
    - Icon patterns
    - Sign In

- The naming convention
- Abbreviated glossary of Axure terminology, where you define in simple terms what are masters, dynamic panels, and widgets
- Document control:
  - Document versioning
  - Related documents (such as the visual design guide)
  - Reviewers list
  - Approvers list

It may be tempting to consider composing this section in Axure. However, remember that the output will be an image. This is because the content of Axure's pages, master, and states, which you edit in the Wireframe pane, will be generated as screen captures of the application in the Word output file. While this is an option for some type of information that you may want to keep within Axure, you really need a word processor to author and format this section effectively.

Generators and outputs: Specifications and prototypes

Before we dive into the details of capturing the project's global specifications, let's clarify the relationship between Axure's generators, specifications, and the prototype. The following screenshot illustrates the concepts:

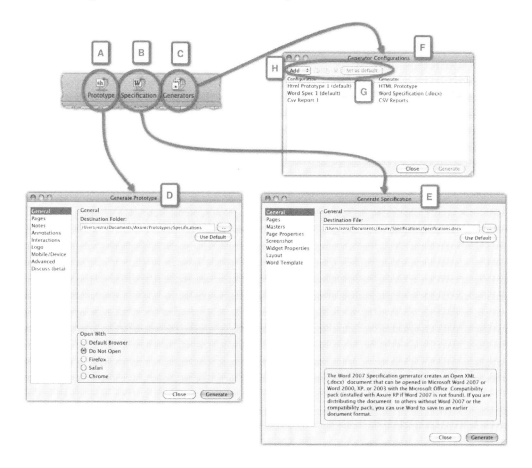

- Prototype: This always refers to an *HTML output* of your Axure file. Whenever you click on the **Prototype** button (A) on the toolbar, you are presented with the **Generate Prototype** dialog (D). Under this dialog, you can specify various options of the *default HTML output generator*. You *can* create multiple HTML outputs, which are useful for breaking apart a large project into sections that generate faster.

- The HTML prototype generates the contents of the pages in your sitemap in the web browser of your choice.

- Specification: This always refers to a formatted *Word output* of the Axure file. Whenever you click on the **Specification** button (B) on the toolbar, you are presented with the **Generate Specification** dialog (E). In this dialog, you determine the format and output options of the *default Word output generator*. Similar to the HTML output, you can create multiple Word generators. For example, you can divide a large project into smaller specifications chapters that correspond to application modules.

- As opposed to the HTML output, for the specifications to be meaningful, you need to annotate the wireframes: Pages, masters, dynamic panels, and widgets. This means that the effort involved in generating specifications extends well beyond the configuration of a generator.

- Generators: Axure provides three output options: HTML, Word, and CSV. Out-of-the-box, Axure comes with one generator of each type. When you click on the **Generators** button (C) on the toolbar, you are presented with the **Generator Configurations** dialog (F) which lists all the generators you currently have in your project file (G). Under this dialog, you can manage your generator collection (H):

    ◦ Creating new generators in one of the output formats
    ◦ Editing a generator
    ◦ Duplicating an existing generator
    ◦ Deleting generators
    ◦ Setting the default generator for the HTML and Word outputs

Why would you need multiple generators? Consider the following examples:

- You may want to generate an HTML version with the footnotes visible, and another one with the footnotes hidden. When you meet with stakeholders, you can have both versions available allowing you to easily switch between one that is visually clean, and the other, which provides descriptive details about various elements of the interface.

- For large projects, you may want to generate the HTML of only a subset of pages, the ones you are currently working on, in order to speed up the HTML generation.

- For large projects, you may want to divide the Word output into chapters, each corresponding to a workstream, or an application module. This works well when there are different stakeholders and development teams for each module or workstream. Each can review and respond to the relevant portion of the specs.

Customizing the Word specifications generator

Let's start with the first Word generator for the project. Although you can use the provided generator, I would recommend creating a dedicated generator, and leaving this one for experimentations. See the following illustration in order to follow the flow below:

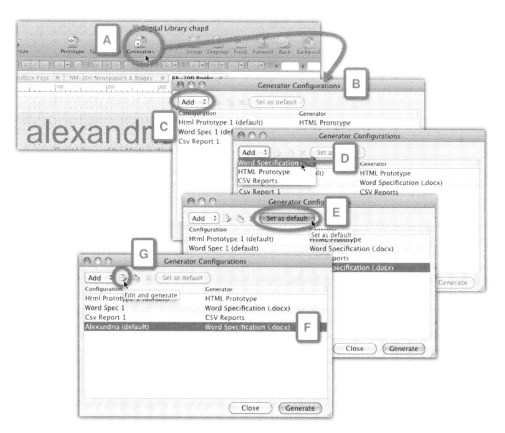

- Click on the **Generators** icon (A) on the toolbar. Alternatively, select **Specifications...** from the **Generate** menu.

- In the **Generator Configuration** dialog (B), select the **Word Specification** option (D) from the **Add** droplist (C).

- Rename the new generator as relevant.

- Click on the **Set as default** button (E). The default generator is the one that is launched when you press the **Generator** icon on the toolbar.

- Now you can click on the **Edit and generate** icon (G), which will launch the **Generate Prototype** dialog. There, you will set the various properties that determine the final output of the Word specification. We will cover this dialog in detail later in this chapter.

Now that you understand the relationship between generators and specifications, and have a Word generator waiting to be configured, it is time to dive into the mechanics of capturing specifications.

Page notes

Axure's Page notes provide the mechanics for capturing the page-level description and other specifications. This is the place to provide:

- High-level overview of the page
- Page entry points
- Tasks that the user can accomplish on this page (actionable items)
- Important user experience principles
- Key interface components

Out-of-the-box, Axure provides a single page notes field named **Default**, which you probably should rename. You can add additional note fields, which will help you to provide an organizational structure to the page note section in the specification. For example, you can consider adding notes for discussing key business requirements that are addressed by this page, functional specifications, localization and personalization notes, and so on.

 Although the section is named page notes, you can use it for pages *and* masters

The page note categories you create in the file are available to all pages, although this does not mean that you have to fill all the notes sections on all pages. The following screenshot illustrates the required flow to customize the notes section:

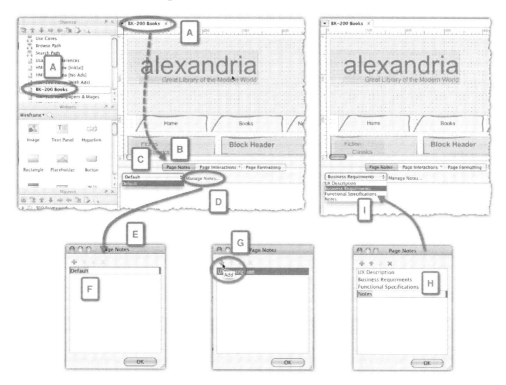

- Open the page for editing (A) on the **Wireframes** pane.

- Click on the **Page Notes** tab (B) in the **Page Properties** pane.

- You will see the **Default** note field (C) listed in the droplist.

- A good reason to rename this field is that you will have an option to use the note name as a header in the specification document. Obviously, to the reader the word 'Default' will be somewhat vague.

- In order to rename the note field, click on the **Manage Notes...** link (D).

- In the **Page Notes** dialog (E) that appears, click on the first item (F) and type the new note field name, for example, **UX Description**.

- In order to add additional note fields, click on the **Add** icon (G). Consider carefully the note fields you are adding:

  ○ Is the section going to be applicable to the majority of pages?

  ○ Who is the audience for this note? Developers or business people?

- It is a good idea to add a note field for your personal use (H)—a place to capture issues, ideas, questions for stakeholders, and so on. You can generate a version of the specification that has only this field, which will provide you with a good issue management system.

- Close the **Page Notes** dialog when you are done adding the fields you need. You can always tweak this section, although, once you have started to capture information, be careful about deleting note fields.

- From this point on, the renamed and new fields are listed in the droplist (I). Switch between fields using the droplist.

One note section versus many

While discussing this topic with colleagues, there seems to be an agreement that a lot depends on the nature of the project. As a result, there is no right or wrong answer here. However, evaluate your needs and your approach in light of the following:

- Some developers are interested in very detailed specifications, while others want to focus only on the absolutely necessary details.

- The specifications may be consumed by a remote team, often overseas, and developers will interpret your words verbatim, while in an Agile environment, developers might barely read anything.

- In a few projects, the specifications are also going to be consumed and signed-off by business analysts, business stakeholders, and other non-developers. Understand what they are looking to get from the documentation and tailor the note field content for such an audience. This will help in getting their approval.

- With multiple note fields, it is easy to make mistakes! Most commonly, forgetting to switch note fields will result in typing notes in the wrong note field.

Annotation fields

Think about a snapshot you take with your camera. The lens picks an incredible amount of detail in addition to whatever was your intended subject and focus for the shot. Now compare this to a sketch you draw on a sheet of paper. Every single mark on that page is there because you placed it there. The analogy to a wireframe is that every element on a wireframe was placed there for some reason—you started with a blank after all. Someone, a developer, will need to translate the wireframe to live code.

In the UI functional specifications document, you are expected to provide both descriptive and prescriptive information about any widget in a wireframe. We have discussed earlier in the chapter, the level of effort involved in manually creating the specifications. Axure takes care of many of the most labor-intensive tasks and delivers profound time savings. Still, you must expect to spend a significant amount of time on the specifications.

After establishing your page notes, it is time to configure the annotation fields. Across the UX industry, there is no standard for the UI specifications document. The deliverable's format and depth of coverage depends on the UX practitioner, the tools used to generate the document, and what has been requested by the development team.

Axure comes with a set of nine annotation fields. Some of these fields you will want to rename, or remove. You can easily add your own fields, and customize both their label and type. Annotation field types are:

- Text
- Select list
- Number
- Date

Each UX project may be vastly different, but one can argue that across the board, there are generalized properties that can be, and are, applicable to any interface project. Naturally, UX, as a discipline, is rapidly evolving and we need to address new interaction methods such as gestures, haptic feedback, and other factors.

This evolution is likely to expand the type of information that has to be captured in the specifications, and consequently, the annotation fields needed to capture and communicate such information to developers.

The following table shows a listing of annotation fields. Those that come out-of-the-box, and ideas for fields you could use in practice:

#	Out-of-the-box	Possible	Minimal set of fields
1	Label (Text)	Label and Widget ID (Text)	Label and Widget ID (Text)
2	Description (Text)	UX Description	UX Description
3	Status (Select List)	Widget Type	Widget Type
4	Benefit (Select List)	Behavior & Display Rules	Behavior & Display Rules
5	Effort (Text)	Required	Validation & Errors
6	Risk (Select List)	Exceptions	Defaults
7	Stability (Text)	Defaults	
8	Target Release (Text)	BRD Reference	
9	Assigned To (Text)	Validation & Errors	
10		Sort Order	
11		Dependencies	
12		Persistence	
13		Content source	
14		Release or Phase	

Is it possible to have a widely-accepted 'minimal' set of fields that would work across most UX projects? It is a compelling possibility that could help achieve some level of standardization for the UX specifications delivery. Luke Perman pointed me to the AXLIB open source library that includes an annotation set of 10 fields, many of which include droplist values to speed up the entry and help standardize the input.

It is highly recommended that you firm up the list of annotation fields before you actually begin writing your annotations. The following screenshot illustrates the process of customizing the collection of annotation fields:

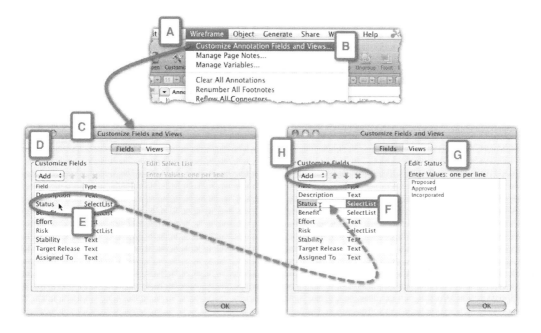

- From the **Wireframe** menu (A), select the **Customize Annotations Fields and Views...** option (B).

- The **Customize Fields and Views** window (C) will appear, listing Axure's out-of-the-box fields in the **Customize Fields** column (D).

- In order to rename a field (E), click on it and type the new label. While you can change the label of the annotation field, you will not be able to change its **Type** (F).

- If the field happens to be a **Select List** type field, the current values are listed in the **Edit: 'Field Name'** column (G). You can easily modify, add, and remove values by typing in that area.

- In order to add new annotation fields of various types, reorder them in the list and delete fields, use the controls above the list of fields (H). I highly recommend that you delete fields that you don't plan to use in order to avoid confusion, such as entering content in such fields by mistake. Regardless, in the process of customizing the Word generator, you can control the fields to include or exclude from the output.

The following screenshot illustrates an alternative way to access the customization feature of your collection of annotation fields:

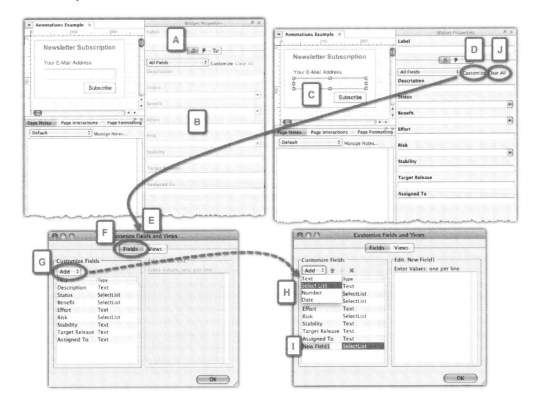

- Switch to the **Annotations** tab (A) in the **Annotation Properties** pane.
- Axure's out-of-the-box list of fields (B) is displayed in the pane, initially disabled. Once you select a widget (C) in your **Wireframe** pane, the annotation fields become active and you can type your annotations or select a value from a list.

- In order to customize the list of fields, click on the **Customize** link (D) to open up the **Customize Fields and Views** dialog (E). The dialog will be set to the **Fields** tab (F).

- In order to add a new field to the list, click on the **Add** droplist (G). You will have to decide the type of the field from the list of options (H). You will not be able to change the field type once the field is created. If you select the wrong type, delete the field and create a new one of the type you need.

- The new field will be added at the bottom of the list (I). Make sure to rename all your fields in a meaningful way, so that the reader understands what to expect there. Try to keep the labels concise—ideally, a single word: The output of the annotation fields is in tables, where each field label is a column header.

- The **Clear All** function (J) is very handy for copy-paste situations. This is a common scenario: Well after you start annotating your widgets, you are likely to copy widgets either for use in the same wireframe, or on other areas of the prototype. As the pasted widget inherits the contents of the annotations field, make sure to clear them if the information is not relevant for the pasted widget. Do this immediately after pasting, to avoid problems later in the project, when irrelevant information will appear all over the specification, potentially confusing reviewers and developers who consume the document.

Annotation views

Annotation view is a feature that allows you to group your annotation fields. This is useful if you have a long list of fields, and want to organize them in smaller groups. For example, you may decide, together with your development team stakeholders, on a subset of fields that are mandatory, and the rest are optional. By setting the **Annotation** tab to the **Mandatory** view, the much shorter list of fields will be easier to scan as you go over your widgets and ensure that all mandatory information has been captured.

The following screenshot illustrates the flow for setting up your views:

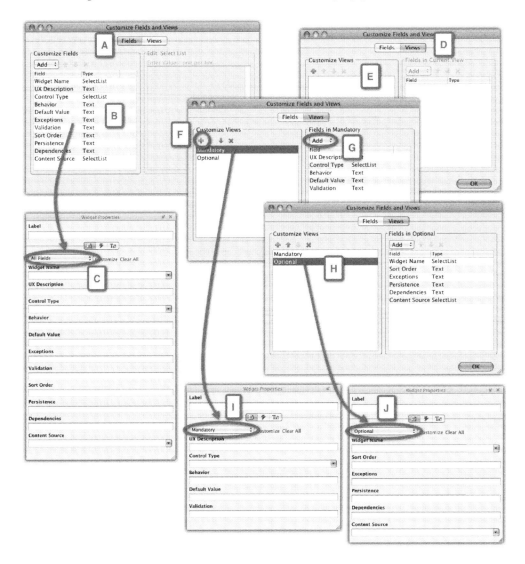

- When you open the **Customize Fields and Views** window, the **Fields** tab (A) is selected by default and all the fields in your file are listed (B) in the **Customize Fields** column. All these fields appear when you switch to the **Annotations** tab in the **Widget Properties** pane (C).

- When you initially switch to the **Views** tab (D), the **Customize Views** column (E) will be empty, because you still do not have any custom views.

- Click on the **Add** icon (F) to add the first view and label it. For example, **Mandatory**.

- In the **Fields in Mandatory** column, Axure will make this a contextual label, once you reopen the dialog or add another view, so it always references the selected view you have on the **Customize Views** column.

- Use the droplist **Add** (G) to select the fields that will be part of the **Mandatory** view.

- Repeat this process whenever you want to manage your views. Close the window when you are finished.

- Now, the view droplist in the **Widget Properties** pane shows your new views. Now, only the fields you need are displayed (I and J, in our example). You always have the option to view all fields.

Generating specifications

As mentioned throughout this chapter, it is important to experiment and test the output of the specifications early and often.

You control all the output properties of the specification document in the **Generate Specifications** window. The window is divided into eight sections. When you are done tweaking them and press the **Generate** button, Axure will launch Microsoft Word which will open with the specification document ready to be reviewed and edited by you.

The General section

The following screenshot illustrates the first section in the spec configuration window (A):

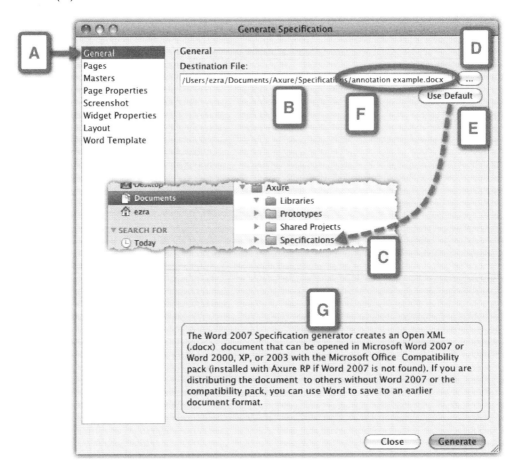

Under this window, you instruct Axure about the following two things:

- The location where you want to create the generated specifications: By default, the path (B) leads to the **Specifications** directory (C) that is created when you install Axure. For Windows users, the directory name is **My Axure RP specifications** and it is located under the **My Documents** folder, or in the **Documents** folder on Mac. Click on the ellipsis button (D) to change the path to your own destination, for example, if you want to store the document in a special folder you have for all your project's files. You can always use the default by clicking on the **Use Default** button (E).

- The name of the specifications document: By default, it is the name of your Axure prototype file. You can modify the last segment of the path (F) as needed.

The Pages section

Under this section (A), you select the pages from the prototype's sitemap which will appear in the specifications, as illustrated in the following screenshot:

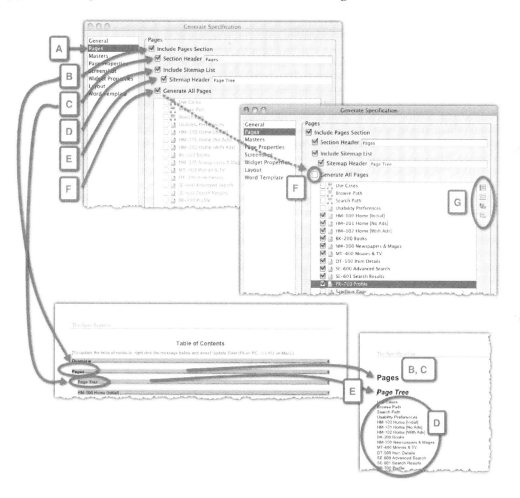

Option	Description
Include Pages Section (B)	This option supersedes the rest of the items below. If you uncheck this option, *none* of the pages in the sitemap will be generated.
Section Header (C)	It lets you customize the name of the Pages section. For example, instead of Pages, you may want to rename it to "Screens". If you check this option, don't leave it blank. This label will appear in the Table of Contents of the generated specifications.
Include Sitemap List (D)	If you check this option, Axure will include a list of all the pages in your project's sitemap. Keep in mind, however, that if you choose to generate some of the pages, the list will still show all of them, which may be confusing to the reader.
Sitemap Header (E)	Using this option, you can re-label the default sitemap header from Page Tree to Application Screens, for example. If you check this option, don't leave it blank. Your custom label, or the default, will appear in the generated Word document.
Generate All Pages (F)	By default, this option is checked. However, as mentioned earlier, it is most likely that you will want to uncheck it. The ability to segment pages is extremely useful. Not only can you have precision and select just the relevant screen you want to include in the spec, it also opens up the possibilities to generate chapters and sections that are tailored for specific audiences. In large projects, each workstream can generate its own set of specifications.
	Useful in large projects with many pages and subpages, where Axure controls **Check All**, **Uncheck All**, **Check All Children** and **Uncheck All Children** (G).

The Masters section

Under this section (A), you select the masters from the prototype's sitemap that will appear in the specifications and the way they will appear, as illustrated in the following screenshot:

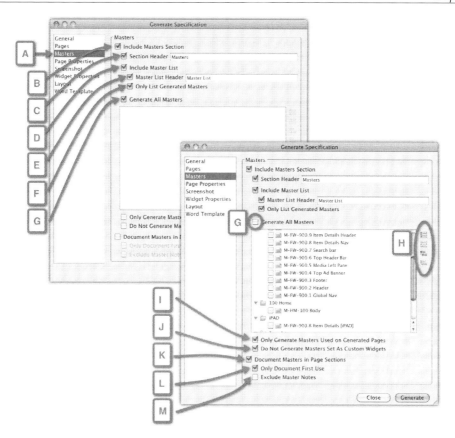

Option	Description
Include Masters Section (B)	This option supersedes the rest of the items below. If you uncheck this option, *none* of the masters in the prototype will be generated. To clarify, the masters will still appear in wireframes, but there will not be a special section for them in the specifications document. This can be useful if you want to create, for example, a PowerPoint presentation showing only key screens of the applications. Instead of manually taking screen captures of each from the HTML prototype, you can generate a specification of only the pages you need, and exclude the masters. All the screenshots you need for the presentation will be automatically generated, faster.
Section Header (C)	It lets you customize the name of the **Masters** section. For example, instead of the default 'Masters', a term which might be foreign to readers not familiar with Axure's terminology, you may want to call the label 'Reusable UI elements'. Moreover, even if you stay with 'Masters', don't leave it blank, since the label will appear in the Table of Contents of the generated specifications.

Option	Description
Include Master List (D)	If you check this option, Axure will include a list of all the masters in your project.
Master List Header (E)	You can re-label the default master list header from Page Tree to 'List of Reusable Components', for example. If you check this option, don't leave it blank. Your custom label, or the default, will appear in the generated Word document.
Only List Generated Masters (F)	By default, this option is checked, and I recommend leaving it checked — there is little value in listing items that do not appear in the document.
	Useful in large projects with many masters, is Axure's control to **Check All**, **Uncheck All**, **Check All Children**, and **Uncheck All Children** (H)
Generate All Masters (G)	By default, this option is checked. If this option is kept checked, it will generate all the masters in your file. You should consider unchecking it, especially if you are tweaking the pages that will be generated. Typically, your file may include an old version of pages and masters, various design candidates, and even work in progress — there can actually be quite a bit of stuff you want to keep out of the specs.
Only Generate Masters Used on Generated Pages (I)	By default, this option is not selected, but I recommend you consider checking it, especially if you are generating only a subset of pages. Remember, masters are not independent elements; they are reused in one or more pages. If a master does not appear in the pages that are generated in the spec, it will make little sense.
Do Not Generate Masters Set As Custom Widgets (J)	Masters that are set as custom widgets are typically intended to be modified once they are placed on the page. This means that a master set as a custom widget will actually not be easily recognizable as such on the page. As a result, it will not be very valuable to developers and most likely create some confusion.

Option	Description
Document Masters in Page Sections (K)	By default, Axure generates the **Masters** section after the **Pages** section. The table of content looks like this:

Page section

> Page 1
> Page 2
> Page n

Masters section

> Master 1
> Master 2
> Master n

This means that a developer working on a particular page needs to jump from the page to the masters section and locate a master mentioned in the page section, which can be inconvenient and sometimes confusing, as not all the elements associated with a single page are in one place.

By checking this option, Axure will generate the page with its associated masters.

The table of content looks like this:

Page section

> Page 1
>> Master 1
>> Master 2
> Page 2
>> Master 1
>> Master n
>
> Page n
>> Master 1
>
> Master 2
>> Master n

This organization packages all the information about a screen in one section.

Option	Description
Only Document First Use (L)	If you checked the previous option, one immediate downside will be a redundancy of masters. Basically, each master will repeat on each page where it is used. Depending on the size, the project, and the construction of your prototype, this redundancy may translate to hundreds of additional pages in your specification document—I am not exaggerating here.
	Therefore, the option to generate only the first instance of a master—under the first page it is used on—can be a tremendous space saver. However, it does end up intensifying the original problem of spreading masters in the document, because this arrangement forces the reader to potentially hunt for masters all over the document.
Exclude Master Notes (M)	Similar to pages, you can also add notes to masters. This is a very useful feature, especially if the master is a large, composite component that can benefit from its own set of notes. However, you can use this option to exclude those notes.

The Page Properties section

Axure 6 has significantly improved controls over the organization and content of the functional specifications document. In the **Pages** section, you selected which pages from the sitemap will be generated in the specifications, and in the **Page Properties** section (A), you are offered a wealth of 14 options to configure the page information. These options will apply to all the pages in the sitemap, as illustrated in the following screenshot:

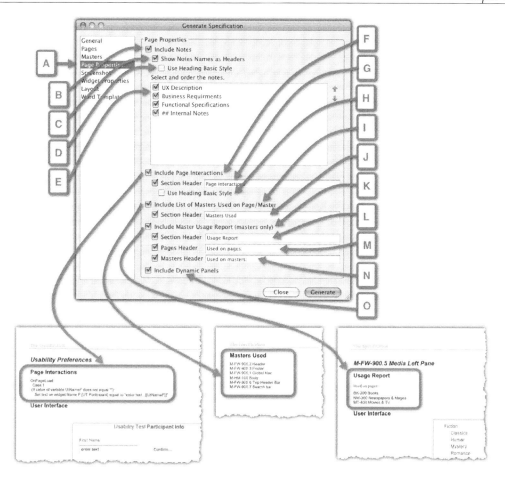

Option	Description
Include Notes (B)	With this option selected, page notes will be generated for each of the pages.
Show Notes Names as Headers (C)	As discussed earlier in the chapter, you can create multiple note fields. With this option selected, these note names will appear as headers and the content of the notes below.
Use Heading Basic Style(D)	If you checked the previous option, this option will become active. It is unchecked and the style Heading 3 will be applied, giving page notes a significant prominence. If you check the box, the basic heading will be Heading 5, which is gray, with a smaller font, making notes less prominent.
Select and order the notes (E)	This option lets you govern the order in which the page notes will be generated within each page.

Option	Description
Include Page Interactions (F)	With this option selected, `OnPageLoad` interactions will be generated. Whether or not Axure's interactions provide any value to developers; it should be discussed with the development team.
Section Header (G)	If you choose to include page interactions, you can use the default Section Header or re-label it.
Use Heading Basic Style (H)	Similar to D, using this gives you the option of making the interaction section more or less prominent.
Include List of Masters Used on Page/Master (I)	As it is impossible to visually distinguish masters by looking at the wireframe on a page (unless you take special effort to identify them manually), developers will appreciate the listing of all the masters, which make it easier to locate them in the masters section.
Section Header (J)	If you choose the option above, which is highly recommended, you can modify the default label—given that you may choose to reference masters using a different term, this is a good option.
Include Master Usage Report (masters only) (K)	This too, is a very useful feature. Each master will have a listing of all its instances across the entire prototype. This is incredibly helpful.
Section Header (L)	This is similar to J.
Pages Header (M)	This is similar to J.
Masters Header (N)	This is similar to J.
Include Dynamic Panels (O)	If you are using dynamic panel in your prototype, you are likely to have this option checked in order to expose the various states associated with those dynamic panels.

The Screenshot section

One of the great timesaving features involved in producing the functional specifications document—automatic generation of all wireframe screenshots. This means that each time you generate a fresh version of specifications your screen captures are up-to-date! Not only that, but the annotation footnotes will be created as well. The **Screenshot** section (A) in Axure 6 provides a wealth of screenshot customization options, as illustrated in the following screenshot:

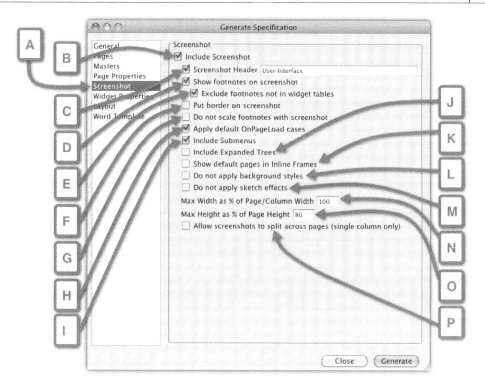

Option	Description
Include Screenshot (B)	This option supersedes the rest of the items below. If you uncheck this option, *none* of the screenshots in the prototype will be generated. It is difficult to think about a situation in which you might not want to include screenshots, however.
Screenshot Header (C)	You can modify the label of this section; for example, change the default "Screenshot", to "Wireframe", or "User Interface".
Show footnotes on screenshot (D)	With this option selected, the screenshots will include a little yellow-numbered footnote that references annotated elements on the wireframe. You will probably want to have this option selected for the specifications document. However, if you need to generate a set of wireframes to include in a PowerPoint presentation, the footnotes option can be skipped.

Option	Description
Exclude footnotes not in widget tables (E)	We discuss widget tables in the **Widget Properties** section, which comes up next. Basically, the idea is that you may have more annotation fields in your Axure file, fields that you want to output. You organize the fields in the widget table(s). With this option checked, footnotes that are associated with fields that are not part of the widget tables will not be generated. For example, you may have a field to capture internal issues, questions, and other miscellaneous details. Typing content in this field will create a footnote on the wireframe. However, since you are not going to include this field in the widget table(s) you don't want the footnote to appear. This option takes care of this situation.
Put border on screenshot (F)	This option does exactly what it claims. However, you may want to consider it if you want to use it. It might confuse the developer to think that perhaps the border is part of the wireframe, as visually it might be difficult to distinguish the Axure added border from a frame around the widget. Something to be kept in mind!
Do not scale footnotes with screenshot (G)	With this option, the size of the yellow footnotes stay constant.
Apply default OnPageLoad cases (H)	This may be an important option to check. There are many circumstances where rendering of the page depends on the execution of the OnPageLoad event. This works well in an interactive prototype, but also — as importantly — happens when the specification is being generated.
Include Submenus (I)	This option will generate screenshots of expanded menus, if you use Axure's menu widgets in your prototype.
Include Expand Trees (J)	This option will generate screenshots of expanded trees, if you use Axure's tree widgets in your prototype.
Show default pages in Inline Frames (K)	This is an incredibly important option to check if you load pages inside iFrames or other pages. It will ensure that the entire wireframe — the parent page as well as the page that is targeted for the iFrame — will be generated.
Do not apply background styles (L)	If you use a background effect for the prototype (for example, applying background colors), you can have these removed from the screenshot output.
Do not apply sketch effects (M)	It lets you maintain the option of sketch effects on your prototype, and also lets you remove them from the output.

Option	Description
Max Width as %of Page/ColumnWidth (N)	This option provides a measure of control over the width of the screenshot, in relation to the output page. For example, for 60 percent of 7.5" width for a Letter size page set to Portrait (with half an inch margin to the left and right), we generate a screenshot which is 4.5" wide, leaving a 3" space for annotation information. However, keep in mind that in a typical project, the variation between wireframes is significant, and you will want to experiment and ensure the quality of the output.
Max Heightas % of PageHeight (O)	This option is similar to the preceding section, but it controls the max height of the screenshot. This is useful for big, scrolling screens. However, keep in mind that in a typical project, the variation between wireframes is significant and you will want to experiment and ensure the quality of the output.
Allowscreenshotsto split acrosspages (singlecolumn only)(P)	This option is useful for very big screenshots. If you limit the height of the image, so that it fits onto the page you will, by default, also reduce its width, potentially making it difficult to identify details. However, splitting the screen capture across screens, you can keep the maximum width for best quality, without worrying about the height.

The Widget Properties section

We discussed in the first part of this chapter about the macro and micro means to capture annotation in Axure. The **Page Note** fields are the macro option, a configurable space that allows you to discuss an entire page and provide the UX overview and context. The **Widget Annotation** fields are the micro option, allowing you to capture UX properties of widget level controls.

The **Widget Properties** section (A) provides you with a number of controls that help you organize the presentation of widget annotations in the specifications document, as illustrated in the following screenshot:

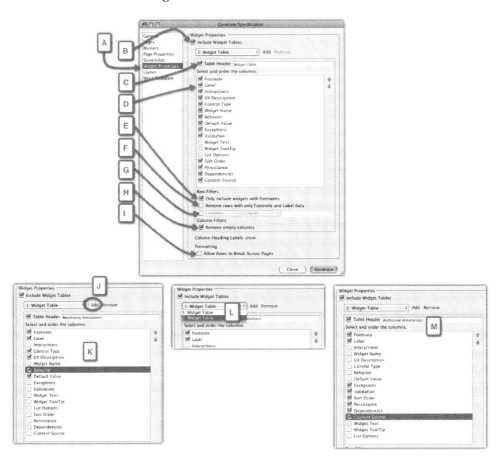

Option	Description
Include Widget Tables (B)	This option supersedes the rest of the items below. If unchecked, none of the widget annotations will be generated. Axure lets you create any number of widget tables. Click on the **Add** link (K).
Table Header (C)	You can change the label of this section. For example, if you add an additional table, the first can be labeled **Mandatory Annotations** (L) and the second table **Additional Annotations** (M). You can switch between tables by using the widget table droplist (N).

Option	Description
Select and order the columns (D)	All the widget annotation fields in your file are listed here. As each annotation field is a column in the annotations table in the Word output, the more fields you want to output, the narrower each table column will be in the Word output. At some point, the tables become unusable. Axure provides an easy and powerful method to avoid the problem by allowing you to associate fields with multiple tables. As a result, each table has fewer, wider columns, and the result is readable and clear. Within each table, you can control the order of the column, which will be their order in the widget tables.
Only include widgets with footnotes (E)	This option will reduce the unnecessary clutter from the specification, listing only widgets that actually have footnotes.
Remove rows with only Footnotes and Label data (F)	This is an excellent space-saving option that will filter out widgets that have footnotes, but have no actual annotations.
Filter droplists (G)	This is a useful option for controlling annotations which should be included in the output. For example, you have an annotation field named 'Release Version', where, for each widget, you note the intended version number. With the filter on, such as Release Version = 1.0, the generated spec will include the annotations of only those widgets for which the value of the Release Version field is 1.0. On the screenshots, footnotes will appear only next to the items that match the filter criteria.
Remove empty columns (H)	This is another useful space saver.
Column Heading Labels (I)	This is another space saver which will eliminate empty columns from tables, and by that increase the width of the columns with data.
Allow Rows to Break Across Pages (J)	This is a self-explanatory option. However, you my want to discuss this with developers. They may prefer to see the entire row in one place and avoid a potential error.

The Layout section

The **Layout** section (A) provides additional controls over the page layout of the specifications document, as illustrated in the following screenshot:

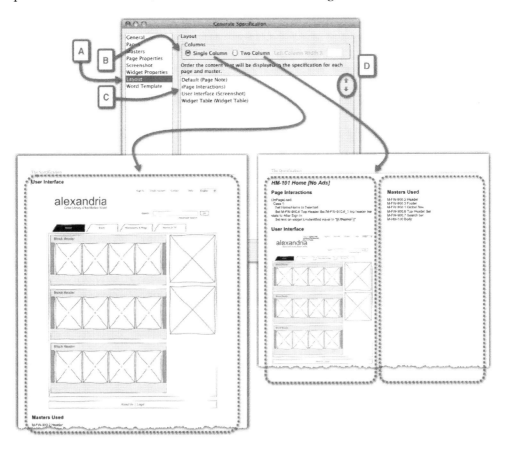

Option	Description
Columns (B)	You have a choice to keep a single column or two columns layout. Keep in mind that in a two columns layout, the screenshots may be too small for an application page. However, if these are specifications for an iPhone app, for example, this may be a perfect, compact format.
Order the content (C)	You can set the order of appearance of major content sections in the specification. Use the up and down arrows (D) to organize the sections.

The Word Template section

Finally, the **Word Template** section (A) is the last section under the **Generate Specification** dialog. When you click on the **Generate** button on this dialog, Axure opens up a Word template with all the content organized, based on your selection in the previous sections. This panel allows you to edit the Word template, import a template, or create your own, as illustrated in the following screenshot:

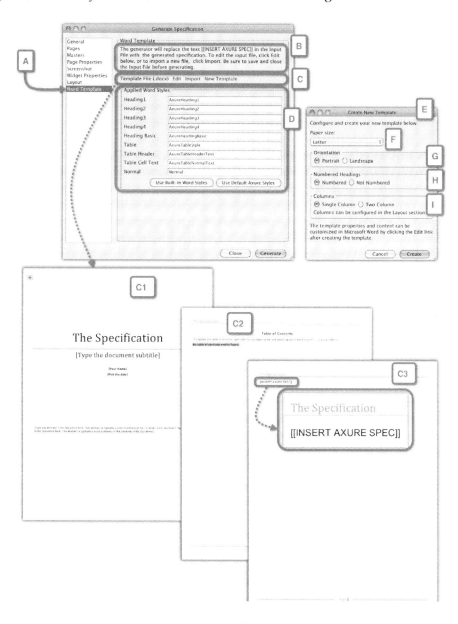

Option	Description
Edit, Import, New Template (C)	These links allow you to edit the provided Word template, import a new template, or create your own.
Applied Word Styles (D)	It lets you modify the default style names, if you want. You also have the option to use Word's built-in styles instead. You will have to experiment and determine which you like better.
Create New Template (E)	If you click on the link **New Template** (C), a pop-up window with the same title will appear, with options to customize the template.
Paper Size (F)	It lets you choose between US formats such as Legal, Letter, Ledger, and the International A4 format.
Orientation (G)	It lets you choose between **Portrait** and **Landscape** orientation.
Numbered Headings (H)	It lets you choose to have numbered or non-numbered headings. Here we encounter an interesting challenge: While it can be difficult, or nearly impossible, to reference sections in the specifications document without numbered headings, these headings will most likely change between drafts of the document. This is because you may tweak the output, add or remove the content, and so on. This is why it is impossible to rely on page numbers, because each generated spec might have a different page count, and elements may appear on different pages. Only a consistent and comprehensive naming convention scheme can help to maintain a reference mechanism that is reliable (see *Chapter 5*).
Columns (I)	Choose between one or two columns page layout.

Summary

Regardless of the tool you use, generating UI-functional specifications is a complicated affair. Think about model toys: despite the fact that each piece is labeled or numbered, it can be difficult to figure out what the complete model will look like once it is assembled. Similarly, the organization, context, and associations between various user interface elements on a screen and across screens can be easily ascertained when looking at the HTML prototype. However, delivering a document that maintains these relationships is not trivial.

Most dedicated prototyping tools currently available in the market offer some form of integrated specifications. Following the evolution of this Axure feature over the years, and recognizing the increasing complexity of user interface projects, the non-triviality of the effort is clear.

Finally, I feel that it is really important to conclude this chapter with three key takeaways which started this chapter:

- Seek the development team's input and approval on the format and scope of the specifications as early in the project as possible

- Estimate early and correctly the effort involved in creating and generating the specifications

- Start planning and testing the specifications when you start your Axure file and continue testing and tweaking the output throughout the project

The next, and final, chapter in this book deals with Axure's collaboration capabilities. Even if you are a 'lone wolf'—an independent UX practitioner, your Axure skills are quickly becoming valuable as Axure establishes itself as the de-facto prototyping tool in the market. Familiarity with Axure's shared project features will help you to quickly join larger enterprise projects.

9
Collaboration

Henry Ford once said "Coming together is the beginning, staying together is progress, and working together is success". If you have some experience with UX projects that includes working with a team of UX designers, you can appreciate the challenge of "staying together", or in modern terms, "staying in sync". This has been, and continues to be, an acute pain point for UX teams.

There are many good reasons for these difficulties. To begin with, a project has to be of a certain size and complexity to warrant the extended investment an organization will have to make in a UX team. Each UX designer is usually assigned to one or several workstreams or modules, each with its dedicated business and, sometimes, technology stakeholders. Add the constraints of a tight schedule and budget, and you will end up in a fast-paced environment with many asynchronously moving parts. You may be in one of those right now.

For a UX team that is using a traditional file-centric tool such as Visio, an immediate concern is keeping wireframes in sync, because:

- Only one person can edit a Visio file at any given time, which means that each designer works on a separate file

- In order to get a sense of the entire application, constant consolidation of the individual files is needed

- The larger the team, the more accelerated the project velocity and the harder it is to manage the consistency of interaction patterns and widgets across the files each designer is working on

The UX team faces a similar challenge of collecting feedback from stakeholders. A common practice is to have each UX workstream create PowerPoint presentations of the latest wireframes, add some verbiage describing the interactions, and send it out to stakeholders for written feedback. There are several drawbacks here:

- Stakeholders need to respond to a static presentation of a dynamic interface
- Redundant, extra effort for the team creating the presentations
- A challenge to consolidate feedback from multiple stakeholders
- A challenge to share feedback with the other UX workstreams on a timely and on-going basis

Axure 6 supports the following two forms of collaboration that help address major difficulties on both fronts mentioned earlier:

1. The **Shared Project format** enables a team of UX designers and others (BAs, for example) to collaborate on the same project in real-time.

2. The **Discussion** tab in the HTML prototype facilitates review by stakeholders, by enabling viewers of the HTML prototype to add comments for each page on the sitemap.

Like other important Axure features, these capabilities translate to real time and effort savings for the UX team. For a UX team that is considering a prototyping tool that supports a collaborative environment, there are few other 'industrial strength' options at the price point and maturity offered by Axure. The Shared Project feature has been around since Version 4.5, back in 2008. It is stable, reliable, and is being continuously refined.

The Discussion feature is new to Axure 6. It is an option integrated into the HTML prototype, where the entire team and stakeholders can share feedback and responses to wireframes.

Collaboration still continues to pose significant challenges, because it is the nature of the beast: any project with many simultaneously-asynchronously moving parts is inherently a complex process to manage. This chapter focuses on Axure's collaboration features and the methods which will help you keep the UX team, stakeholders, and prototype in sync.

Shared projects

When you launch Axure, it always starts a new project, following the pattern of, say, Microsoft Word. When you save the file, it will always be saved in the RP file format, Axure's standalone format, which means that only one person can access and work on it at any given time, similar to a Word or Visio document. In order to collaborate with one or more UX designers, save the project as a shared project, and you are good to go!

If you are a single practitioner, you might find it beneficial to use shared projects instead of the default standalone option. You will be able to work from your desktop and laptop computers, enjoying the peace of mind that comes from knowing the fact that you can always revert to a previous version of your work.

The environment

The Axure Shared Project environment is straightforward. The following diagram illustrates a typical setup:

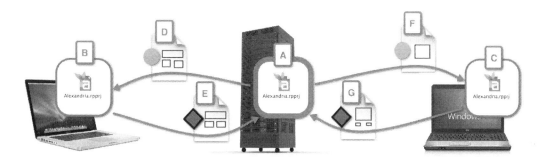

- The project file is created on a server or shared directory (A). This is done once by using the **Create Shared Project from Current File...** option. What is on that central location is, in essence, a repository of all the elements that make up the project—a very large collection of folders and files that are managed by the repository. It is highly advisable not to touch, manually, any of the files on the central repository or on your local copy of the project.

- When a team member accesses the file for the first time by using the **Get and Open Shared Project...** option, a local copy of the repository is created on that person's computer (B) and (C). Each team member may use a Mac or Windows machine, with the corresponding version of Axure. The only restriction is that all users must use Axure 6.

- Each team member can check out any element of the prototype, including elements that are checked out to other team members. Elements subjected to check out and check in are:

  ○ Pages

  ○ Masters

  ○ Annotation fields

  ○ Global variables

  ○ Page style sheets

  ○ Widget styles

  ○ Generators

- An important fact to remember is that team members work on their own local copy, and not directly off the server. In order to edit files that are on the shared repository, team members check out a desired element (D) or (F). The icon for that element, on each person's local copy, will display a green circle. If other users attempt to check out the same item, Axure prompts them that the file is already checked out; later in the chapter, we discuss such situations. Once the editing is done, team members check in the element (E or G), and it clears for editing by others.

Check out/in status

The following table shows the various statuses along with their description:

Status	Description	Icon
Checked in	The element is available for check out to all team members. However, the status indicates only what the local copy 'knows'. When you actually try to check out the file, Axure will let you know whether it is available or not.	A blue diamond.
Checked out	The element is checked out to you. The local copy of other team members will still display the file as checked in.	A green circle. The person who has the element checked out will see an indicator in the form of an icon or a label and marks its status. Local copies of the other team members will show that the element is checked in, until they attempt to check the item out.

Status	Description	Icon
New	When you add a new element, it is first created in your local Axure project file. Once you check it in, other members of the team will be able to see or use it.	A green plus sign. The icon is applicable to pages and masters, and appears only on the local copy of the person who created it. Other elements may not have an indicator.
Conflict	The element on your local Axure project file conflicts with a version of the same element on the master project file on the server or shared directory.	A red rectangle.
Unsafely checked out	You checked out an element despite being warned that it has been checked out by another team member. You or the other person will lose the work you did, once you attempt to check in the file to the repository.	An orange triangle.

Setting up a shared repository

The process of setting up a shared project is not unlike following a recipe. You need to prepare some ingredients in advance, so that you don't get stuck halfway through. In this case, you need to have the location of the repository.

As mentioned earlier, the repository can be stored on a shared network drive or on a dedicated SVN server, hosted on the company's server, or hosted by an SVN hosting service. Either way, you will have an address that points to that location, and with the location available, you are ready to proceed.

Hosting Service versus Internal Hosting

Organizations will be extremely cautious about putting anything outside of their secured environment. Whether your team's plan calls for using a third-party SVN hosting service, the organization's own dedicated SVN server, or space on a shared directory, make sure to get clearance from the appropriate department, as well as a clear understanding of the support that will be provided, such as regular backups of the shared directory, emergency backup restore, and so on.

The following screenshot illustrates the process of setting up a shared repository, which starts with a standard standalone Axure file (A). It can be a completely blank file or one that you have started as a preliminary sandbox:

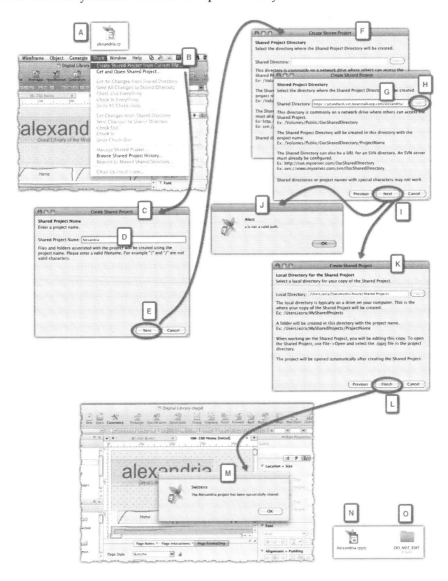

- With the file open in Axure, select the **Create Shared Project from Current File...** option (B) from the **Share** menu.

- The **Create Shared Project** window (C) will open, offering a wizard-type flow that will walk you through the steps of creating the shared repository.

- The first step is to name the project in the **Shared Project Name** field (D). Pay attention to the disclaimer: **Files and folders associated with the project will be created using the project name. Please enter a valid filename. For example "\" and "/" are not valid characters**. My recommendation is to keep the project name short and to use a hyphen to separate several words, for example, `My-Great-Project`. Click on the **Next** button (E) to continue.

- The **Shared Project Directory** step (F) is where you need to point Axure to the location of the shared repository. This screen includes the following instructions:

  This directory is commonly on a network drive where others can access the Shared Project.

  Example: /Volumes/Public/OurSharedDirectory

  The Shared Project Directory will be created on this directory with the project name.
  Ex: /Volumes/Public/OurSharedDirectory/ProjectName

  The Shared Directory can also be a URL for an SVN directory. An SVN server must already be configured.
  Example: http://svn.myserver.com/OurSharedDirectory/
  Example: svn://www.myserver.com/OurSharedDirectory/

  Shared directories or project names with special characters may not work.

- You can either paste the address you prepared into the **Shared Directory** field (G), or use the ellipsis button (H) to navigate to the shared directory on the organization's network.

- Before you click on the **Next** button (I) to move to the next step, make sure that you have spelled the project name correctly, because the typos will stay with the file throughout the life of the project. You can return to the previous screen and make the correction, if needed.

- After you click on the **Next** button, Axure will prompt you if there is a problem with the information you provide (J). You will have to validate that the path you have is correct. If you are dependent on someone else for validating the information, it is a good idea to do this setup during the time at which the person is available.

- In the following screen, Axure asks you to point to the **Local Directory for the Shared Project...** (K). This is where the local copy of the repository will be created on your hard drive. By default, Axure offers to store it in the directory labeled **Shared Projects**, in the Axure Directory; but, if you prefer to keep all your project work in a dedicated project directory, you can certainly do that.

- You are ready for the final step. Click on the **Finish** button (L), and within a short time, Axure will prompt you with a **Success** confirmation (M).

- When you look in the local directory, you will find that Axure has created two items. In order to use the example of our demo file, the first item is a file **Alexandria.rpprj** (N) and the second item is a directory labeled **DO_NOT_ EDIT** (O), which, as mentioned earlier, you really should not mess with.

Congratulations—you are good to go—the local copy of your shared project is ready for you to use. However, you are not done yet! Make sure to distribute the link to the shared directory to all your team members. It is also not a bad idea to keep this link readily available, if you need it in the future. For an SVN setup, you will also need to include the username and password that will enable your team to access the server the first time they attempt to load the file.

If you have been using a standalone version of the project, you will find the most prominent visual differences on the **Sitemap** pane and the **Masters** pane (A), as shown in the following screenshot:

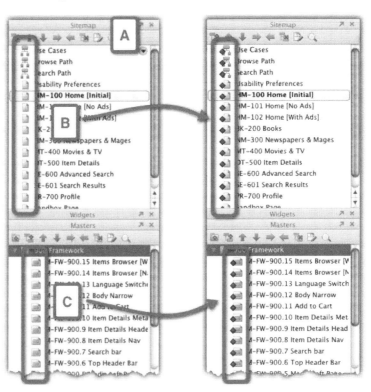

In the shared project .rpprj file, the icons for pages (B) and masters (C) include a status indicator. This indicator reflects the state of the element on *your* local copy of the project, not its status on the server.

Another difference between a standalone RP file and a shared project file is the directories and files that make up a shared project. Like the quintessential forbidden castle door in a fairy tale, the mysteriously labeled folder **DO_NOT_EDIT** might attract your attention. It is actually not a bad idea to take a quick glance to satisfy natural curiosity.

The following screenshot illustrates the local copy of the repository, which has been created in the **Shared Projects** directory—a subdirectory located inside Axure's main directory:

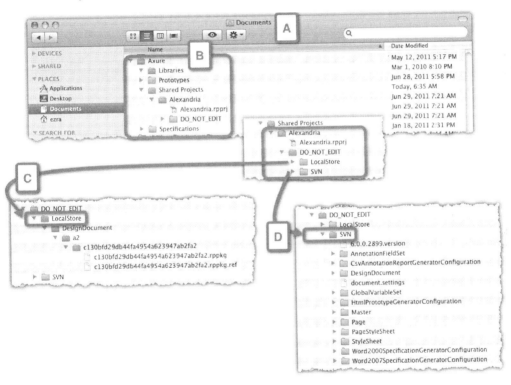

- This main directory (B) is created when you first install Axure. On Mac, it is located in the **Documents** folder (A), and on Windows, it is located in the **My Documents** folder.

- Your project has a dedicated folder within the **Shared Projects** directory, and as mentioned earlier, there are two items in its root level: the **Alexandria. rpprj** file, and the **DO_NOT_EDIT** folder.

- The **DO_NOT_EDIT** directory has the following two folders:

  ○ **LocalStore** (C): This folder contains a small set of files.

  ○ **SVN** (D): This folder contains all the project files. The size of this directory will grow as the project advances.

If you did not set up the shared project or, for some reason, you need to recreate the local copy of the project, you will need to create your local copy of the project by accessing the shared repository, which we'll discuss next.

Loading from a shared repository

The first item you will need is the path to the shared repository on the server. You will also need a username and password, if the file is hosted on an SVN server. It is highly recommended that the person responsible for setting the shared repository makes this information readily available to the team and is also available to help with the setup, if needed. On your part, make sure to store this information for future use!

You should have either a path to a network directory or a URL to an SVN server, that looks something similar to the following:

```
https://company.svn.beanstalkapp.com/alexandria/Alexandria
```

The following screenshot illustrates the process:

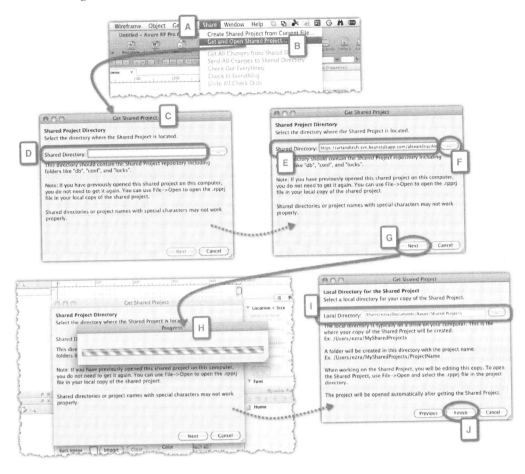

- From the **Share** menu (A), select the **Get and Open Shared Project...** option (B).
- Axure will present the **Get Shared Project** dialog box (C). This dialog has the following instructional text, which it is useful to keep in mind:

This directory should contain the Shared Project repository including folders like "db", "conf", and "locks".

Note: If you have previously opened this shared project on this computer, you do not need to get it again. You can use File->Open to open the .rpprj file in your local copy of the shared project.

Shared directories or project names with special characters may not work properly.

- The **Shared Directory** field (D) is where you either paste the URL or path that we discussed earlier (E) or use the ellipsis (F) button to navigate within the network to the destination, if you are familiar with it. Use the **Next** button (G) to continue.

- A **Progress** bar (H) will appear as Axure will attempt to connect to the shared repository. You will be prompted with an error if the path is incorrect. If all is well, Axure will move you to the next step.

- The **Local Directory** field (I) is where you instruct Axure to create a local copy of the repository. By default, Axure offers to store it in the directory labeled **Shared Projects**, in the Axure Directory; but, if you prefer to keep all your project work in a dedicated project directory, you can certainly do that using the ellipsis button.

- Click on the **Finish** button (J), and Axure will download all the necessary files from the server or network directory to the destination folder you indicated earlier. Depending on your network connection speed and the size of the file, this might take a few minutes.

The shared file will open and you can start working. Remember, in order to access the file on a day-to-day basis, you can use the **Open Recent** option from the **File** menu. If, for some reason, you forget where the file is located, use the file search to look for the `.rpprj` string in the filename.

The Share menu

Once you have the local copy of the project loaded, you will be using the **Share** menu constantly. It is highly recommended that you and the entire team have a strong understanding of the various menu options.

Creating and loading

You typically have to use these options only once per project.

Menu item	Description
Create Shared Project from Current file...	Use this option if you want to create a shared project file out of the current file. This menu item is active only when you have an open file.
Get and Open Shared Project...	Use this option to create a local copy of a shared project file. If you are also the person responsible for creating the shared project, you can skip this step, because a local copy will be created for you when you create the shared file.

Updating the entire file

This set of options applies batch-like functionality to updates, check out, and check ins. They are listed in the following table with their descriptions:

Menu item	Description
Get All Changes from Shared Directory	This option mass-updates your local copy of the project file with all of the changes that were made by other team members. Make a habit of getting all changes as the first thing you do each time you start working on the file; repeat it a few times during the day.
Send All Changes to Shared Directory	This option will update the shared repository with all the changes you have made since the last time you sent your changes. Consider this option as a form of saving your work. Although you can and should use the **Save** option to save your work to the local copy of the project, sending your updates will ensure that if something happens to the local copy, most of your work will be on the server. Note that the files you are working on are still checked out to you. The trade-off is that, when you send your changes to the shared directory, you can no longer undo them by undoing the check out.
Check Out Everything	This option will check the entire project out to you, a highly unadvisable action. Fortunately, Axure will prompt you with a warning, as shown in the following screenshot: If you do manage to somehow check the entire project out, check it back in as soon as possible, because the rest of the team obviously will not be able to safely check out any of the assets.
Check In Everything	This option will check in everything you have checked out. Develop the habit of using this option at the end of the day, which will insure that you have nothing checked out and that other team members can check out files, if you are out of the office.

Menu item	Description
Undo All Check Outs	This is a great option to help you undo undesirable work and revert the affected items back to the state they were in before you checked them out. It can happen to anyone: You check out a page and a few masters, with the intention of further developing the prototype. Things fall apart and you realize that the best bet is to start over. Now, in the meantime, you were saving your work, so you cannot undo the local copy. However, if you did not send changes, you can undo the check out.

Updating a single page or master

This set of options allows you to deal with a single element at a time. These options are listed in the following table along with their description:

Menu item	Description
Get Changes from Shared Directory	This option applies only to a selected page or master.
Send Changes to Shared Directory	This option applies only to a selected page or master.
Check Out	This option applies only to a selected page or master.
Check In	This option applies only to a selected page or master.
Undo Check Out	This option applies only to a selected page or master.

Manage Shared Project...

In a shared project environment, each team member has a copy of the project on his or her computer. During the course of a day's work, each team member will create new elements, check out files, and generally modify the project. These changes will not be reflected in the shared repository until the team member sends all changes to the server or checks in all their check out elements.

While you can tell if a page is checked out to you, you cannot tell, from looking at the sitemap, whether a page that is checked in is actually available for check out or has perhaps been checked out by another team member. This applies not only to pages, but also to all the elements that are controlled by the shared repository.

The **Manage Shared Projects** console provides any team member with a real-time view into all the elements that are managed by the shared project. In essence, you get a peek into the project's record files. The other information that you get is the status of each individual element on the project. This view can spare you from the hassle of attempting to check out an element that is checked out to another team member.

The following screenshot takes you through a normal use scenario:

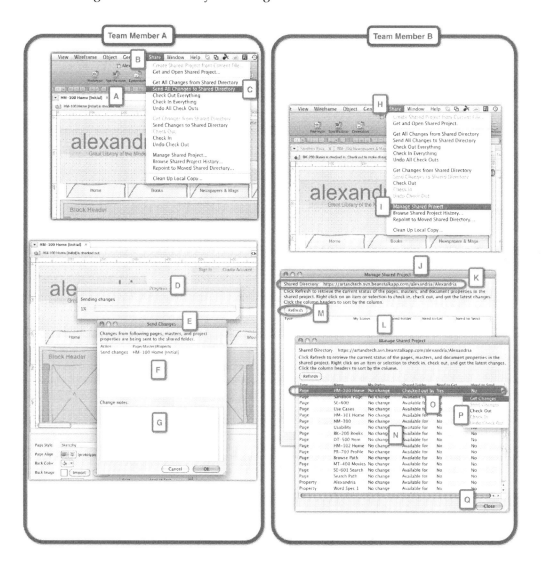

- Team member A has the page **HM-100 Home [Initial]** (A) checked out. After performing some work on the page and associated masters, which are also checked out to this user, it is time to send all changes to the shared repository using the **Send All Changes to shared Directory** option (C) from the **Share** menu (B).

- After a few seconds, during which the **Progress** pop-up (D) is displayed, team member A is presented with the **Send Changes** dialog (E), listing the elements that are going to be updated on the server in the top pane (F), and a field to enter what these changes were on the **Change notes** pane (G). Upon clicking on **OK**, the updates will be sent to the shared repository.

- Switching to team member B, who also wants to check out the same page **HM-100 Home [Initial]**. To this user, the page appears available for check out, on the **Sitemap** pane. However, the user chooses to use the **Manage Shared Project...** option (I), from the **Share** menu (H).

- The **Manage Shared Project** dialog (J) is presented. The top section of the dialog indicates the path to the shared directory (K) and also includes the following instructions: **Click Refresh to retrieve the current status of the pages, masters, and document properties in the shared project. Right click on an item or selection to check in, check out, and get the latest changes. Click the column headers to sort by the column.** Indeed, notice that the main table area (L) is initially empty.

- Upon clicking on the **Refresh** button (M), the table area (N) is populated with the list of all pages, masters, and design documents in real time.

- The user can see that the page **HM-100 Home [Initial]** (O) is checked out and can see which team member has the file checked out. Now, team member B can contact team member A and coordinate the check out. In the mean time, right-clicking on the row will present a contextual menu that will list available actions.

- Note that one of the available options is **Check Out** (P). While it is possible to do so, it is *critical* to make sure that all team members understand that this option is a last resort.

- Dismiss this dialog by clicking on the **Close** button (Q). It is a good idea to get into the habit of using the **Manage Shared Projects** before trying to check out pages that are the responsibility of other team members.

Browse Shared Project History...

In addition to Axure Shared Projects, provide your team with a couple of invaluable features:

- The risks of lost work are substantially reduced. As long as the SVN server, or shared network directory where you host your project, are reliably backed up, you can restore any previous version of the project, from day one. It is not possible to exaggerate the importance of this capacity and the peace of mind that comes with it.

- The team gains the precious ability to step back in time and access earlier iterations of the prototype. When you consider the realities of a large, fast-paced project, you realize that the need to revert to an earlier version of some pattern is likely to happen. One of the most challenging aspects of iterative design is having an effective way to revert to, or compare to, an earlier version of the application.

The value to the UX is real and measurable. The system maintains complete version control throughout the file's life cycle. Each time a team member sends changes or checks in their work, a new version is added to the log. Each version, precisely identified with a unique revision number and the date of its capture, can be transformed back into a fully functional RP file that reflects its condition at the moment the version was created.

Barring a catastrophic failure of the SVN server or a shared directory that has not been backed up properly, as long as the shared repository is available, you can access practically any restore point in the project, as illustrated by the following screenshot:

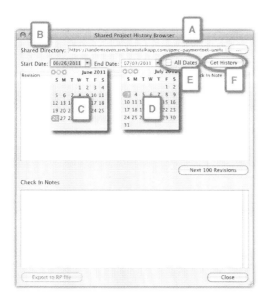
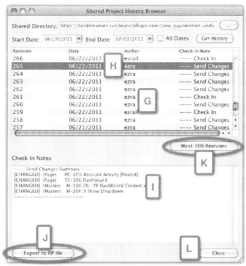

- From the **Share** menu, select the **Browse Shared Project History...** option.

- The **Shared Project History Browser** dialog (A) will appear. The top field points to the shared repository—you don't want to change this.

- Depending on the size of the team and the point in time that you want to recover, relative to the start date of the file, the list of all versions can be overwhelmingly long. In order to narrow down the list to the set of potential versions that correspond to the date and time you are looking for, use the **Start** and **End** calendar droplists (C and D). By default, the start and end dates are set to capture the last seven days' worth of work.

- If you want to override the calendar pickers, you have an option to retrieve the list of all versions by checking the **All Dates** checkbox (E). Click on the **Get History** button (F) to continue.

- Within seconds, the table area (G) will be populated by a list of versions, with each row representing a fully functional restore point of the Axure file. Each row can be sorted by one of the version's attributes, including **Revision**, **Date**, **Author**, and **Check-in Note**.

- Identify, in the list, the version that is most likely to contain the last good version of the item or items you are looking to restore. Normally, you will see several versions for each day. As the revision number is serial, the highest revision number corresponds to the last update for that date.

- When you click on a row (H), all the activity that has been automatically recorded by Axure will be displayed in the **Check-in Notes** pane (I), and additionally, so will any notes added by the team member who uploaded the changes. This information is incredibly valuable, because typically, you will be looking to restore a particular page or master.

- Now comes the truly fantastic part. I have to admit that I am still excited by it each time I get to use it. If you identified the revision, use the **Export to RP file** button (J). Axure will prompt you to save the file on your drive, and within a few seconds, you will be able to open a fully functional, standalone Axure file corresponding to the time and date of that revision. Now you can find the element you were looking for and import it into the current shared project file, if you want.

- However, if this ends up not being the snapshot you need, continue exploring until you find it. If more versions are available, the **Next 100 Revisions** button (K) will be active. Use the **Close** button (L) to dismiss this window when you are done.

A side benefit of the history browser is that there is no need to keep old versions of pages and masters in the active **Sitemap** and **Master** pane, especially as the constant additions and updates by multiple team members tend to greatly bloat the working environment. As the project moves deeper into detailed design, it is beneficial to perform regular audits with team members and discard pages that are no longer relevant, and masters that are not used on any pages. The result will be a leaner file that generates faster as both an HTML prototype and Word specifications document and, as we discussed, all previous work can be easily resorted, if needed.

Repoint to Moved Shared directory...

Occasionally, there is a need to move the shared directory from its location on the network drive. As long as the repository has been moved in its entirety, this is a safe operation. All team members can continue to use their local copy of the file but point towards the new location of the shared repository.

If there is a need to move the shared repository, as illustrated in the following screenshot, follow the ensuing steps:

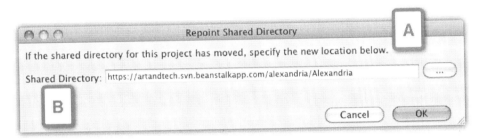

1. Coordinate the move with the entire team. Ideally, pick a date and time that will minimize the impact to the team's schedule. Try to avoid proximity to major deadlines.

2. Make sure that team members are aware of the planned move. Communicate to all clearly that the shared repository will not be available at the set timeframe.

3. At a set time before the move, all team members should use the **Check In Everything** option.

4. After the move, provide all team members with the updated path.

5. Each team member will repoint to the new location by using the **Repoint Shared Directory** option (A), and entering the provided URL into the **Shared Directory** field (B).

Clean Up Local Copy...

Sometimes, for some unknown reasons, bad stuff happens. With Axure, such events are extremely rare. However, suppose you are attempting to check in your work and get the error message `Working Copy Locked`. As explained by Axure, `A variety of things can cause Working Copy Locked errors. These include virus scanners and losing connection to the server or a computer failure during a previous operation.`

Carry out the the process illustrated in the following screenshot:

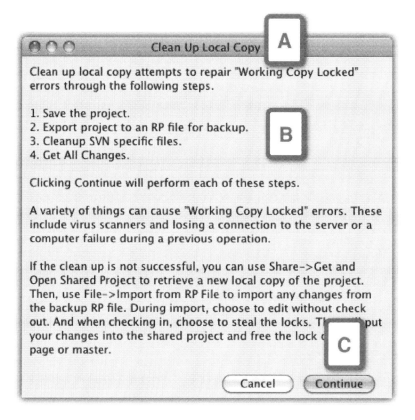

In the event of a `Working Copy Locked` error, typically, when you try to check in something, do the following:

1. Select the **Clean Up Local Copy...** from the **Share** menu.

2. Axure will attempt to repair the problem, as described in the **Clean Up Local Copy** dialog (A), a process which includes the following steps (B):

   ° Save the project (You do that)

   ° Export the project to an RP file for backup (You do that)

   ° Cleanup SVN specific files (Axure does that)

   ° Get all changes (Axure does that)

From my personal experience, and that of some of my colleagues, I can attest to the fact that this feature seems to work just fine and you are able to send your work to the server.

Best practices for UX Axure teamwork

Teams are complicated. The number of variables that determine a team's makeup and workings can be widely different, making meaningful comparisons difficult. However, as the famous proverb goes, *for every problem there is an opportunity*; in this section, I am not attempting to resolve this challenge but rather to isolate the most fundamental team attributes:

Attributes of the UX team

The following are the attributes of the UX team:

- **Team size**: How big is the UX team? Obviously, two people are a team, but the larger the number of UX designers involved in a project, the harder it is to keep everyone on the same page. Larger teams are likely to break into multiple workstreams, so there is also the challenge of cross-workstream communications.

- **Location**: Are all team members sharing the same physical office space? Is everyone on the same floor and in close proximity? Are people spread across the corporate campus, or across multiple cities? Are some team members working remotely from their home-offices? Are team members spread across the globe?

- **Knowledge of project's domain**: Some team members may have previous project experience with, and exposure to, the application's domain. Other team members are new to the domain and its nuances. This can be an issue with expert systems.

- **UX experience and expertise**: Some team members may be UX veterans, with established track records, but also with a set preference for how they are used to getting things done. Other team members may have a different take. Junior members may have significantly less experience with UX work and lack the ability to foresee potential problems, estimate workload, and display confidence when presenting to stakeholders.

- **Axure expertise**: Veteran team members are likely to have years of power-use skills with tools such as Visio, but little Axure knowledge, perhaps even some resistance. Some team members will be completely new to the tools, while a few may have significant Axure experience.

- **Individual personalities**: This section is impossible to cover in a few sentences, of course. However, the normal mix of extroverts, introverts, the assertive, the shy, the outgoing, the reserved, the blunt, self-starters, those with strong work ethics, the lazy, the overly polite, the alpha and beta types, and so on, can turn a team dynamic into a soap opera.

- **Cultural influences**: In some cultures, it is not polite to behave in an assertive way around team members of higher seniority. This might be mistakenly interpreted by one from an all-are-equal culture as timidity, hesitation, and lack of confidence. Team members might find the attitude and manners of others to be rude and inappropriate, leading to tension and hostile relations. The combinations are as diverse as the globe we live in.

Regular and effective communication is the fundamental ingredient for successful teamwork, yet it is easier said than done. This is especially true with virtual teams of individuals that work remotely from their homes and with on-site teams spread across several geographical locations. That said, all too often, colleagues who share a cubicle fail to exchange meaningful information despite their physical proximity. The following are a few practices to consider for your team:

- As far as possible, it is important to allocate time for staff development. Ensure that all team members possess a level of Axure proficiency that would not only make them productive, but would also avoid loss of work due to errors caused by an unknowledgeable team member messing up the shared file. As we know, such calamities tend to happen just before a major deadline.

- Team members should understand how to work with shared projects. All should be comfortable with the various options under the **Share** menu and the difference between options such as **Get all changes**... and **Get Changes**..., for example.

- New team members should have an on-board DeepDive session with a knowledgeable team member to cover the structure of the sites. In large, intense projects, new members are often thrown into the cold waters of a shared project file, to sink or to swim, because the team is at the height of some crunch. Disoriented and under pressure to get up to speed as soon as possible, the incoming member can be easily lost in the intricacies and work-around.

- All team members should participate in a weekly status meeting that covers the structure of the sitemap, variables (since those are global and limited), and other important changes. Use web sharing to view the file, and make sure that team members understand how other members constructed their wireframes.

- Despite looming deadlines, it is important to be careful and pay attention before checking in and out. A few seconds of concentration can save hours of lost work.

- Team members should avoid unsafe check outs — this is critical. There are a few and clear reasons for breaking this rule, say when the person that has the elements checked out is going to be away for some time.

- Before you begin work on a page, make sure to get all changes from the shared directory — this will insure that you have the latest copy.

- Start your work session by getting all changes. Continue to update your file frequently throughout the day.

- When done editing a page or master that you checked out, check it in so that it will be available for other team members.

- Check out only what is needed for your design work; check in as soon as you are done and check out the next chunk you are going to work on: Avoid hogging files by checking out any that you are not working on.

- If possible, structure the sitemap and masters in sections, such that team members can work on chunks of the file in parallel. Agree on unique page and master IDs and a naming convention to help team members access the right files.

- Make sure that the shared file is backed up regularly.

Feedback from stakeholders—the Discussion tab

Just a few years ago, the means to collect feedback from stakeholders about a proposed user experience were very limited, because it was rare to actually have an interactive prototype available for review on a regular basis. Axure helped revolutionize the way the user experience is expressed, by replacing static wireframe presentations with compelling interactive simulations. However, for a while, methods of collecting feedback continued to be few and somewhat limited.

Normally, you gather stakeholders in a meeting room or by video conference calls, and as you demonstrate the prototype, people respond to various aspects of the application's design. It is good practice to request the attendees to suspend their feedback until you have a chance to complete an initial walkthrough of the proposed interaction. However, it is rare that people can hold off their comments, and typically, the presentation flow is interrupted, with a risk of derailment due to tangential discussions.

Of course, experience and good facilitation skills play a major role in one's ability to drive a presentation forward in a productive way. However, regardless of the facilitation, it is objectively difficult for stakeholders to provide you with a thoughtful response, because they have a relatively brief window of opportunity to view, digest, and respond to your presentation.

The **discussion** feature is brand new to Axure 6 and is meant to address this difficulty by providing stakeholders with the means to respond to the prototype in the privacy of their office, where they can take more time to consider the screens and interactions. A new **Discussion** tab has been added to the prototype's left menu bar; this lets viewers type their comments for each page. While this new feature has a number of issues and is far from being robust it is, at the time of writing, still in *beta* form. Given Axure's record of accomplishment of listening to the user community and enhancing features, the discussion feature is likely to be an important valuable addition for users.

Discussions hosted on AxShare

AxShare has been around for over a year. It is free and in beta phase, at the time of writing. It is the foundation of an Axure cloud-based hosting service for your HTML prototypes. AxShare itself is currently hosted on the Amazon Web Services cloud platform, which is quite reliable and secure, as far as cloud environments go.

As was mentioned earlier in this chapter, in the context of using a third-party SVN hosting service for your shared repository, it is important that you get clearance to use AxShare from the relevant department in the organization you are working for. It is also a good idea to test how the corporate firewall affects access to the site, as you want to provide a hassle-free experience to stakeholders.

With AxShare, you have the following two options to facilitate a discussion with stakeholders and users:

- Host the file on AxShare. This option has several limitations, including the maximum file size that can be currently uploaded, the number of files that can be hosted, and security reservations. On the other hand, it is free and technically simple as there is no need to worry about corporate firewalls.
- Host the HTML on your own server, and still enable the discussion feature.

The first option begins by uploading your file to AxShare, as illustrated by the following screenshot:

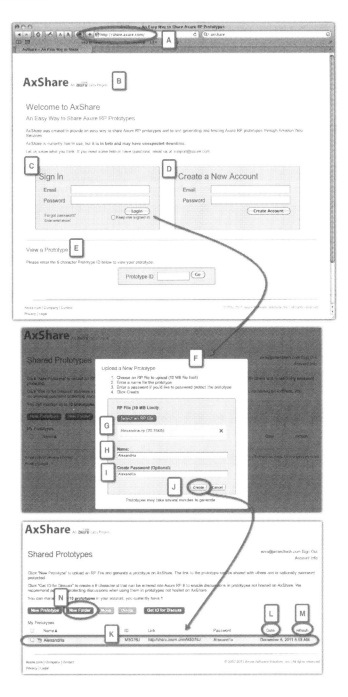

- Start by pointing your browser to `http://share.axure.com/` (A), which will link you to the AxShare website (B). As the site states—at the time of writing—AxShare is in beta, hence the association with AxureLabs.

- From this screen, you will be able to:

  ○ **Sign In** (C) to your account once you create it (D)

  ○ Link to view your uploaded prototypes (E)

- The last option is the one that stakeholders will use once you provide them with the appropriate code, password, and a link to AxShare.

- Creating an account is a breeze, as you only need to provide an e-mail address and a password you would like to use.

- Once you sign in, upload an RP file to the server (F). If you are working on a Shared Project file, export the latest version of the RP file and check the file size. The current limit on uploads is 10 MB. Use the **Choose File** button (G) to upload the RP file.

- Add the prototype's name (H) and an optional password (I). If you add a password, it will be required from everyone who will attempt to view or add feedback to your prototype. It is a good idea to set one up.

- Click on the **Create** button and the prototype will be added to a list, which will eventually have all your hosted AxShare files (K). The list can be sorted by upload date (L) and can be refreshed (M).

- You can also create folders (N), which is a convenient way to organize your uploaded files.

- Currently, you can host up to 10 files on AxShare.

You can easily manage your uploaded files, as illustrated by the following screenshot:

- Within the row of each uploaded prototype (A), click on the twisty arrow on the far right of the menu (B), for the following options for that particular project:
    ○ Renaming the prototype
    ○ Moving the prototype—as mentioned earlier, the files you upload to AxShare can be organized in folders, and this is how you move the files between folders
    ○ Viewing the discussions
    ○ Disabling the discussions
    ○ Changing the password needed to access the prototype
    ○ Deleting the prototype
    ○ Uploading a new RP file to replace the currently hosted file; if you are using the discussion feature, remember that discussions entered to pages that were deleted in the new uploaded file, will be lost

The last option is really important, because you will have a fresh iteration to present on an ongoing basis. All the comments entered by reviewers to previous versions of the file, will be preserved, as long as the pages they commented on still exist in the later version.

Discussions not hosted on AxShare

The other option to facilitate a dialog in the prototype through the **Discussion** tab is to use AxShare to generate a special code that you enter in the HTML generator configuration. The actual prototype HTML files can be placed on the server of your choice. The following screenshot illustrates this process:

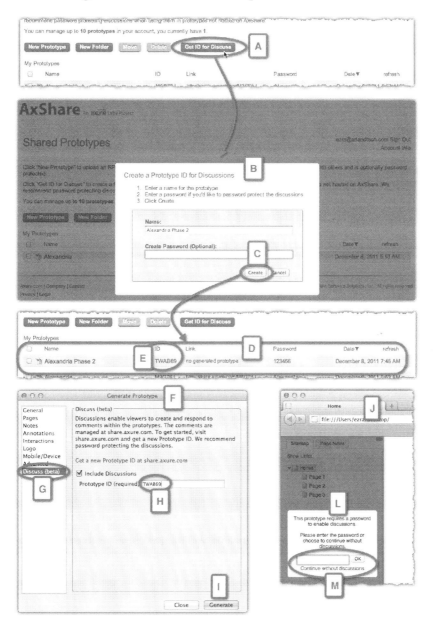

Step 1: In AxShare.com

This is a step you are responsible for.

1. After logging in, click on the **Get ID for Discuss** button (A).

2. In the **Create a Prototype ID for Discussion** pop-up (B), enter the name of the project. A password to access the **Discussion** tab is optional. Click on the **Create** button (C) to continue.

3. A new row is added to the **My Prototypes** list (D). Copy the prototype **ID** (E).

Should you protect the discussion with a password? The truth is that it is a matter of control. By not sharing the password with everyone who has access to the prototype, you are controlling who can participate in the discussion and add feedback. Consider the stakeholders that you want to get involved. If the feedback is going to be about a business strategy, perhaps it is not wise to have it exposed to say, contract developers and others who will also access the site, but from which you are not expecting feedback through the discussion option. If you are not sure, ask!

Step 2: In Axure

This too is a step you are responsible for:

1. Open the **Generate Prototype** window (F) and click on the **Discuss** option (G).

2. Type or paste the prototype ID into the field (H), and click on the **Generate** button (I) when ready.

3. Send out an e-mail to anyone you want to use the discussion and provide them with:

   ° The URL of the prototype
   ° The password to access the **Discussion** tab

Step 3: In the browser

All users who are invited will access the prototype with their browser. If a password has been enabled, the left pane will be grayed out and a panel (L) will include a field where the password should be entered (M). That is it!

In conclusion, Axure's discussion feature is promising, because it is integrated with the product. The feature is not limited to shared project files—it can also be activated on the standard RP files.

It is important to make sure, however, that stakeholders and users that are supposed to participate in the discussion can figure out a way to navigate through the prototype. Often, not all widgets have interactions assigned to them: Some features work and others don't. Let the user know in advance that, upon moving the mouse over a certain area of the screen, a guide (constructed as a hidden dynamic panel) will appear, instructing the user where to click. This layer of instructions could also include letter or number tags over certain areas on which you want feedback. These footnotes will make it easier to get a more structured feedback, as all reviewers will refer to the same elements.

Summary

Once you experience Axure's Shared Project capabilities, you may wonder how UX teams managed projects before Axure. Well obviously, you and others did, but at a premium cost of time and effort. Teams that are evaluating prototyping tools to support their work can reflect on their current workflow and methods and consider Axure's value as compared to other options in the market.

Axure's Shared Projects adds real, measurable value, by helping the UX team address three major obstacles head-on:

1. It provides a controlled environment that facilitates work on the same prototype and specifications file by multiple team members.
2. It maintains unlimited version control, which is critical for disaster recovery or reverting to a previous revision.
3. It facilitates dialog between the team and its stakeholders by proving a direct feedback in the **Discussion** pane, an Axure feature not limited just to Shared Projects, and yet complements the entire iterative process of teamwork.

These capabilities are built on top of the tool's rich, reliable, yet constantly evolving platform of UX-specific feature sets for prototyping and specifications.

Index

W

Y

Z

Thank you for buying
Axure RP 6 Prototyping Essentials

About Packt Publishing

Packt, pronounced 'packed', published its first book "*Mastering phpMyAdmin for Effective MySQL Management*" in April 2004 and subsequently continued to specialize in publishing highly focused books on specific technologies and solutions.

Our books and publications share the experiences of your fellow IT professionals in adapting and customizing today's systems, applications, and frameworks. Our solution based books give you the knowledge and power to customize the software and technologies you're using to get the job done. Packt books are more specific and less general than the IT books you have seen in the past. Our unique business model allows us to bring you more focused information, giving you more of what you need to know, and less of what you don't.

Packt is a modern, yet unique publishing company, which focuses on producing quality, cutting-edge books for communities of developers, administrators, and newbies alike. For more information, please visit our website: www.packtpub.com.

Writing for Packt

We welcome all inquiries from people who are interested in authoring. Book proposals should be sent to author@packtpub.com. If your book idea is still at an early stage and you would like to discuss it first before writing a formal book proposal, contact us; one of our commissioning editors will get in touch with you.

We're not just looking for published authors; if you have strong technical skills but no writing experience, our experienced editors can help you develop a writing career, or simply get some additional reward for your expertise.

Python Testing Cookbook

ISBN: 978-1-84951-466-8   Paperback: 364 pages

Over 70 simple but incredibly effective recipes for taking control of automated testing using powerful Python testing tools

1. Learn to write tests at every level using a variety of Python testing tools

2. The first book to include detailed screenshots and recipes for using Jenkins continuous integration server (formerly known as Hudson)

3. Explore innovative ways to introduce automated testing to legacy systems

4. Written by Greg L. Turnquist – senior software engineer and author of Spring Python 1.1

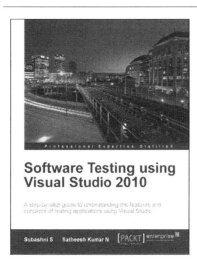

Software Testing using Visual Studio 2010

ISBN: 978-1-84968-140-7   Paperback: 400 pages

A step by step guide to understanding the features and concepts of testing applications using Microsoft Visual Studio 2010

1. Master all the new tools and techniques in Visual Studio 2010 and the Team Foundation Server for testing applications

2. Customize reports with Team foundation server

3. Get to grips with the new Test Manager tool for maintaining Test cases

4. Take full advantage of new Visual Studio features for testing an application's User Interface

Please check **www.PacktPub.com** for information on our titles

[PACKT] PUBLISHING

Liferay User Interface Development

ISBN: 978-1-84951-262-6   Paperback: 388 pages

Develop a powerful and rich user interface with Liferay Portal 6.0

1. Design usable and great-looking user interfaces for Liferay portals

2. Get familiar with major theme development tools to help you create a striking new look for your Liferay portal

3. Learn the techniques and tools to help you improve the look and feel of any Liferay portal

4. A practical guide with lots of sample code included from real Liferay Portal Projects free for use for developing your own projects

Yahoo! User Interface Library 2.x Cookbook

ISBN: 978-1-849511-62-9   Paperback: 436 pages

Over 70 simple incredibly effective recipes for taking control of Yahoo! User Interface Library like a Pro

1. Easily develop feature-rich internet applications to interact with the user using various built-in components of YUI library

2. Simple and powerful recipes explaining how to use and implement YUI 2.x components

3. Gain a thorough understanding of the YUI tools

4. Plenty of example code to help you improve your coding and productivity with the YUI Library

Please check **www.PacktPub.com** for information on our titles